Advances in Production Engineering and Management

Advances in Production Engineering and Management

Dr. R.P. Sharma

RANDOM PUBLICATIONS
NEW DELHI (INDIA)

Advances in Production Engineering and Management

ISBN 978-93-5111-658-5

Published in 2015 in India by

RANDOM PUBLICATIONS

4376-A/4B, Gali Murari Lal, Ansari Road
New Delhi-110 002
Phone : +9111-43580356, 011-23289044, 011-43142548
e-mail: sales@randompublications.com,
info@randompublications.com, randomexports@gmail.com

Type Setting by : Friends Media, Delhi-110089
Digitally Printed at : Replika Press Pvt. Ltd.

Preface

Production management, also called operations management, planning and control of industrial processes to ensure that they move smoothly at the required level. Techniques of production management are employed in service as well as in manufacturing industries. It is a responsibility similar in level and scope to other specialties such as marketing or human resource and financial management. In manufacturing operations, production management includes responsibility for product and process design, planning and control issues involving capacity and quality, and organization and supervision of the workforce.

Production engineering is a combination of manufacturing technology with management science. A production engineer typically has a wide knowledge of engineering practices and is aware of the management challenges related to production. The goal is to accomplish the production process in the smoothest, most-judicious and most-economic way.

The field of mechanical and industrial engineering embraces a broad spectrum of technical activities including mechanical design and engineering along with the classical techniques of work methods, production and facilities planning, quality control and safety. It also embraces the fields of human factors, operations research, manufacturing systems, and organisation and management systems. Product development is the process of designing, creating, and marketing an idea or product. The product can either be one that is new to the marketplace or one that is new to your particular company, or, an existing product that has been improved. In many instances a product will be labeled new and improved when substantial changes have been made.

This book is extensively illustrated to aid the students in gaining a thorough understanding of various production processes and the principles behind them.

I would like to thank my team for standing beside me throughout my career and writing this book. My special thanks go to "Random Publications" who have published the book.

– Dr. R.P. Sharma

Contents

1

Production Engineering

Production engineering is a combination of manufacturing technology with management science. A production engineer typically has a wide knowledge of engineering practices and is aware of the management challenges related to production. The goal is to accomplish the production process in the smoothest. most-judicious and most-economic way.

Fig. The Ford Motor Company's factory at Willow Run utilised Production Engineering principles to achieve record mass production of the B-24 Liberator military aircraft during World War II.

Production engineering encompasses the application of castings.machining processing. joining processes. metal cutting and tool design.metrology. machine tools. machining systems. automation. jigs and fixtures. and die and mould design and material science and design of automobile parts and machine designing and manufacturing. Production engineering also overlaps substantially with manufacturing engineering and industrial engineering. In industry. once the design is realized. production engineering concepts regarding work-study. ergonomics. operation research. manufacturing management. materials management. production planning. etc.. play important roles in efficient production processes. These deal with integrated design and efficient planning of the entire manufacturing system. which is becoming increasingly complex with the emergence of sophisticated production methods and control systems.

PRODUCTION ENGINEER

The production engineer possesses a wide set of skills. competences and attitudes based on market and scientific knowledge. These abilities are fundamental for the performance of coordinating and integrating professionals of multidisciplinary teams. The production engineer should be able to:

- Dimensional and integrate resources. Usually required to consider physical. human and financial resources at high efficiency and low cost. yet considering the possibility of continuous further improvement;
- Make proper use of math and statistics to model production systems during decision making process;
- Design. implement and refine products. services. processes and systems taking in consideration that constraints and particularities of the related communities;
- Forecast and analyse demand. Select among scientific and technological appropriate knowledge in order to design. redesign or improve product/service functionality;
- Incorporate concepts and quality techniques along all the productive system. Deploy organizational standards for control proceedings and auditing;
- Stay up-to-date with technological developments. enabling them to enterprises and society;
- Understand the relation between production systems and the environment. This relates to the use of scarce resources. production rejects and sustainability;
- Manage and optimize flow (information and production flow).

Work opportunities are available in public and private sector manufacturing organizations engaged in implementation. development and management of new production processes. information and control systems. and computer controlled inspection. assembly and handling..

The Ford Motor company's factory at Willow Run utilised Production Engineering principles to achieve record mass production of the B-24 Liberator military aircraft during World War II. Production engineering also overlaps substantially with manufacturing engineering and industrial engineering. In industry. once the design is realized. production engineering concepts regarding work-study. ergonomics. operation research. manufacturing management. materials management. production planning. etc.. play important roles in efficient production processes. These deal with integrated design and efficient planning of the entire manufacturing system. which is becoming increasingly complex with the emergence of sophisticated production methods and control systems.

Production engineer

Work opportunities are available in public and private sector manufacturing organizations engaged in implementation. development and management of new production processes. information and control systems. and computer controlled inspection. assembly and handling.

THE "FIVE M'S"

Production management's responsibilities are summarized by the "five M's": men. machines. methods. materials. and money. "Men" refers to the human element in operating systems. Since the vast majority of manufacturing personnel work in the physical production of goods. "people management" is one of the production manager's most important responsibilities.

The production manager must also choose the machines and methods of the company. first selecting the equipment and technology to be used in the manufacture of the product or service and then planning and controlling the methods and procedures for their use. The flexibility of the production process and the ability of workers to adapt to equipment and schedules are important issues in this phase of production management.

The production manager's responsibility for materials includes the management of flow processes—both physical (raw materials) and information (paperwork). The smoothness of resource movement and data flow is determined largely by the fundamental choices made in the design of the product and in the process to be used.

The manager's concern for money is explained by the importance of financing and asset utilization to most manufacturing organizations. A manager who allows excessive inventories to build up or who achieves level production and steady operation by sacrificing good customer service and timely delivery runs the risk that overinvestment or high current costs will wipe out any temporary competitive advantage that might have been obtained.

PLANNING AND CONTROL

Although the five M's capture the essence of the major tasks of production management. control summarizes its single most important issue. The production manager must plan and control the process of production so that it moves smoothly at the required level of output while meeting cost and quality objectives. Process control has two purposes: first. to ensure that operations are performed according to plan. and second. to continuously monitor and evaluate the production plan to see if modifications can be devised to better meet cost. quality. delivery. flexibility. or other objectives. For example. when demand for a product is high enough to justify continuous production. the production level might need to be adjusted from time to time to address fluctuating demand or changes in a company's market share. This is called the "production-smoothing" problem. When more than one product is involved. complex industrial engineering or operations research procedures are required to analyze the many factors that impinge on the problem. Inventory control is another important phase of production management. Inventories include raw materials. component parts. work in process. finished goods. packing and packaging materials. and general supplies. Although the effective use of financial resources is generally regarded as beyond the responsibility of production management. many manufacturing firms with large inventories (some accounting for more than 50 percent of total assets) usually hold production managers responsible for inventories. Successful inventory management. which involves the solution of the problem of which items to carry in inventory in various locations. is critical to a company's competitive success. Not carrying an item can result in delays in getting needed parts or supplies. but carrying every item at every location can tie up huge amounts of capital and result in an accumulation of obsolete. unusable stock. Managers generally rely on mathematical models and computer systems developed by industrial engineers and operations researchers to handle the problems of inventory control.

To control labour costs. managers must first measure the amount and type of work required to produce a product and then specify well-designed. efficient methods for accomplishing the necessary manufacturing tasks. The concepts of work measurement and time study introduced by Taylor and the Gilbreths. as well as incentive systems to motivate and reward high levels of worker output. are important tools in this area of management. In new operations particularly. it is important to anticipate human resource requirements and to translate them into recruiting and training Programmes so that a nucleus of appropriately skilled operators is available as production machinery and equipment are installed. Specialized groups responsible for support activities (such as equipment maintenance. plant services and production scheduling. and control activities) also need to be hired. trained. and properly equipped.

This type of careful personnel planning reduces the chance that expensive capital equipment will stand idle and that effort. time. and materials will be wasted during start-up and regular operations.

The effective use and control of materials often involves investigations of the causes of scrap and waste; this. in turn. can lead to alternative materials and handling methods to improve the production process. The effective control of machinery and equipment depends on each machine's suitability to its specific task. the degree of its utilization. the extent to which it is kept in optimum running condition. and the degree to which it can be mechanically or electronically controlled.

THE IMPORTANCE OF MODELS AND METHODS

Because of the enormous complexity of typical production operations and the almost infinite number of changes that can be made and the alternatives that can be pursued. a productive body of quantitative methods has been developed to solve production management problems. Most of these techniques have emerged from the fields of industrial engineering. operations research. and systems engineering. Specialists in these fields are increasingly using computers and information processing to solve production problems involving the masses of data associated with large numbers of workers. massive inventories. and huge quantities of work in process that characterize most of today's production operations. Indeed. many mass production operations could not run without the support of these industrial engineers and technical specialists.

PRODUCTION SYSTEM

Production system. any of the methods used in industry to create goods and services from various resources.

UNDERLYING PRINCIPLES

All production systems. when viewed at the most abstract level. might be said to be "transformation processes"—processes that transform resources into useful goods and services. The transformation process typically uses common resources such as labour. capital (for machinery and equipment. materials. etc.). and space (land. buildings. etc.) to effect a change. Economists call these resources the "factors of production" and usually refer to them as labour. capital. and land. Production managers refer to them as the "five M's": men. machines. methods. materials. and money.

When viewed as a process. a production system may be further characterized by flows (channels of movement) in the process: both the physical flow of materials. work in the intermediate stages of manufacture (work in process). and finished goods; and the flow of information and the inevitable paperwork that carry and accompany the physical flow. The physical flows are subject to the constraints of the capacity of the production system. which also limits the system's ability to meet output expectations. Similarly. the capacity of the information-handling channel of the production system may also be an important measure of a system's output.

The management of information flows. or the planning and control of the system to achieve acceptable outputs. is an important task of the production manager.

While the capacity of the system is the major factor in determining whether output expectations can be met. the additional consideration of quality must also be seen as a limiting factor. The quality of a product. measured against some objective standard. includes appearance. performance characteristics. durability. serviceability. and other physical characteristics; timeliness of delivery; cost; appropriateness of documentation and supporting materials; and so on. It is an important part of the definition of a system.

TYPES OF PRODUCTION SYSTEMS

There are three common types of basic production systems: the batch system. the continuous system. and the project system. In the batch system. general-purpose equipment and methods are used to produce small quantities of output (goods or services) with specifications that vary greatly from one batch to the next. A given quantity of a product is moved as a batch through one or more steps. and the total volume emerges simultaneously at the end of the production cycle. Examples include systems for producing specialized machine tools or heavy-duty construction equipment. specialty chemicals. and processed food products. or. in the service sector. the system for processing claims in a large insurance company. Batch production systems are often referred to as job shops.

In the continuous system. items to be processed flow through a series of steps. or operations. that are common to most other products being processed. Since large volumes of throughput are expected. specially designed equipment and methods are often used so that lower production costs can be achieved. Frequently the tasks handled by workers are divided into relatively small segments that can be quickly mastered and efficiently performed. Examples include systems for assembling automobile engines and automobiles themselves. as well as other consumer products such as televisions. washing machines. and personal computers. Continuous production systems are often referred to as assembly systems or assembly linesystems and. are common in mass production operations.

The two types of systems mentioned thus far are often found in combination. In the production of integrated circuits for electronic equipment. for example. thousands of circuits are processed as a batch on several large slices of silicon crystal through dozens. or even hundreds. of processing steps. The tiny circuits. each only a few millimetres on a side. are then separated and individually assembled with other circuit elements on a continuous line to produce the final product. The third type of production system is the project. or "one-shot" system. For a single. one-of-a-kind product. for example. a building. a ship. or the prototype of a product such as an airplane or a large computer. resources are brought together only once. Because of the singular nature of project systems. special methods of management have been developed to contain the costs of production within reasonable levels.

IMPORTANT CONSIDERATIONS

Once the general specifications of a production system have been agreed upon. including precise definitions of needed resources and output expectations. three important decisions remain. First. industrial engineers. production managers. and other specialists must choose and design the technology to be used. Their decisions must include the choice of equipment and tooling. the layout of plant space and facilities. the selection of workers and work procedures. and many other aspects of process design. These choices must be handled carefully; mistakes at this early stage can result in a business losing its competitiveness or the ability to sustain a profitable position in the market.

Next. given a choice of technology. the capacity of the system must be determined. The capacity of the system is designed to be a function of the amount of available capital. the demand forecast for the output of the facility. and many other minor factors. Again. these decisions must be made wisely. Establishing too much capacity. too soon. can burden a company with excess costs and inefficient operations. Too little capacity can make it difficult and expensive to increase output later if the market develops rapidly; this can place a company at a significant cost disadvantage if other competitors. with larger facilities. produce a product at a lower cost or with more consistent quality.

Finally. given a basic commitment to capacity. decisions must be made on the adaptability of the production volume to meet the inevitable changes in market demand that the firm will experience. Capacity in most production systems is adjusted by hiring or firing workers. by scheduling overtime or cutting back on work hours. by adding or shutting down machines or whole departments or areas of the facility. or by changing the rate of production within reasonable limits. The effectiveness of any one of these adjustment mechanisms depends largely on the technological constraints of the process itself. the economics of the industry. and the nature of the competition. In some industries. adjustment of capacity is a very difficult task. Assembly lines with specialized equipment. for example. are most efficient when run at one speed and cannot be slowed down or run intermittently without severe economic losses. In such cases. careful attention to the fundamental design of the production system is a critical factor in the overall success of the business.

2

Industrial Engineering

Industrial engineering is a branch of engineering which deals with the optimization of complex processes or systems. It is concerned with the development. improvement. implementation and evaluation of integrated systems of people. money. knowledge. information. equipment. energy. materials. analysis and synthesis. as well as the mathematical. physical and social sciences together with the principles and methods of engineering design to specify. predict. and evaluate the results to be obtained from such systems or processes. While industrial engineering is a traditional and longstanding engineering discipline subject to (and eligible for) professional engineering licensure in most jurisdictions. its underlying concepts overlap considerably with certain business-oriented disciplines such as operations management.

Depending on the subspecialties involved. industrial engineering may also be known as. or overlap with. operations management. management science. operations research.systems engineering. management engineering. manufacturing engineering. ergonomics or human factors engineering. safety engineering. or others. depending on the viewpoint or motives of the user. For example. in health care. the engineers known as health management engineers or health systems engineers are. in essence. industrial engineers by another name.

OVERVIEW

While the term originally applied to manufacturing. the use of "industrial" in "industrial engineering" can be somewhat misleading. since it has grown to encompass any methodical or quantitative approach to optimizing how a process. system. or organization operates. Some engineering universities and educational agencies around the world have changed the term "industrial" to broader terms such as "production" or "systems". leading to the typical extensions noted above. In fact. the primary U.S. professional organization for Industrial Engineers. the Institute of Industrial Engineers (IIE) has been considering changing its name to something broader (such as the Institute of Industrial and Systems Engineers). although the latest vote among membership deemed this unnecessary for the time being.

The various topics concerning industrial engineers include:

- *Accounting:* the measurement. processing and communication of financial information about economic entities
- *Operations research also known as management science:* discipline that deals with the application of advanced analytical methods to help make better decisions
- *Operations management:* an area of management concerned with overseeing. designing. and controlling the process of production and redesigning business operations in the production of goods or services.
- *Project management:* is the process and activity of planning. organizing. motivating. and controlling resources. procedures and protocols to achieve specific goals in scientific or daily problems.
- *Job design:* the specification of contents. methods and relationship of jobs in order to satisfy technological and organizational requirements as well as the social and personal requirements of the job holder.
- *Financial engineering:* the application of technical methods. especially from mathematical finance and computational finance. in the practice of finance
- *Engineering management:* a specialized form of management that is concerned with the application of engineering principles to business practice
- *Supply chain management:* the management of the flow of goods. It includes the movement and storage of raw materials. work-in-process inventory. and finished goods from point of origin to point of consumption.
- *Process engineering:* design. operation. control. and optimization of chemical. physical. and biological processes.
- *Systems engineering:* an interdisciplinary field of engineering that focuses on how to design and manage complex engineering systems over their life cycles.
- *Ergonomics:* the practice of designing products. systems or processes to take proper account of the interaction between them and the people that use them.
- *Safety engineering:* an engineering discipline which assures that engineered systems provide acceptable levels of safety.
- *Cost engineering:* practice devoted to the management of project cost. involving such activities as cost- and control- estimating. which is cost control and cost forecasting. investment appraisal. and risk analysis.
- *Value engineering:* a systematic method to improve the "value" of goods or products and services by using an examination of function.
- *Quality engineering:* a way of preventing mistakes or defects in manufactured products and avoiding problems when delivering solutions or services to customers.

- *Industrial plant configuration:* sizing of necessary infrastructure used in support and maintenance of a given facility.
- *Facility management:* an interdisciplinary field devoted to the coordination of space. infrastructure. people and organization
- Engineering design process: formulation of a plan to help an engineer build a product with a specified performance goal.
- *Logistics:* the management of the flow of goods between the point of origin and the point of consumption in order to meet some requirements. of customers or corporations.

Traditionally. a major aspect of industrial engineering was planning the layouts of factories and designing assembly lines and other manufacturing paradigms. And now. in so-called lean manufacturing systems. industrial engineers work to eliminate wastes of time. money. materials. energy. and other resources.

Examples of where industrial engineering might be used include flow process charting. process mapping. designing an assembly workstation. strategizing for various operational logistics. consulting as an efficiency expert. developing a new financial algorithm or loan system for a bank. streamlining operation and emergency room location or usage in a hospital. planning complex distribution schemes for materials or products (referred to as supply-chain management). and shortening lines (or queues) at a bank. hospital. or a theme park.Modern industrial engineers typically use predetermined motion time system. computer simulation (especially discrete event simulation). along with extensive mathematical tools for modelling. such as mathematical optimization and queue theory. and computational methods for system analysis. evaluation. and optimization.

HISTORY

Efforts to apply science to the design of processes and of production systems were made by many people in the 18th and 19th centuries. They took some time to evolve and to be synthesized into disciplines that we would label with names such as industrial engineering. production engineering. or systems engineering. For example. precursors to industrial engineering included some aspects of military science; the quest to develop manufacturing using interchangeable parts; the development of the armory system of manufacturing; the work of Henri Fayol and colleagues (which grew into a larger movement called Fayolism); and the work of Frederick Winslow Taylor and colleagues (which grew into a larger movement called scientific management). In the late 19th century. such efforts began to inform consultancy and higher education. The idea of consulting with experts about process engineering naturally evolved into the idea of teaching the concepts as curriculum.Industrial engineering courses were taught by multiple universities in Europe at the end of the 19th century. including in Germany. France. the United Kingdom. and Spain. In the United States. the first department of industrial and manufacturing engineering was established in 1909 at the Pennsylvania State University. The first doctoral degree in industrial engineering was awarded in the 1930s by Cornell University.

In general it can be said that the foundations of industrial engineering as it looks today. began to be built in the twentieth century. The first half of the century was characterized by an emphasis on increasing efficiency and reducing industrial organizations their costs. In 1909. Frederick Taylor published his theory of scientific management. which included accurate analysis of human Labour. systematic definition of methods. tools and training for employees. Taylor dealt in time using timers. set standard times and managed to increase productivity while reducing Labour costs and increasing the wages and salaries of the employees.

In 1912 Henry Laurence Gantt developed the Gantt chart which outlines actions the organization along with their relationships. This chart opens later form familiar to us today byWallace Clark.Assembly lines: moving car factory of Henry Ford (1913) accounted for a significant leap forward in the field. Ford reduced the assembly time of a car more than 700 hours to 1.5 hours. In addition. he was a pioneer of the economy of the capitalist welfare ("welfare capitalism") and the flag of providing financial incentives for employees to increase productivity.Comprehensive quality management system (TQM) developed in the forties was gaining momentum after World War II and was part of the recovery of Japan after the war.

In 1960 to 1975. with the development of decision support systems in supply such as the MRP. you can emphasize the timing issue (inventory. production. compounding. transportation. etc.) of industrial organization. Israeli scientist Dr. Jacob Rubinovitz installed the CMMS Programme developed in IAI and Control-Data (Israel) in 1976 in South Africa and worldwide.

In the seventies. with the penetration of Japanese management theories such as Kaizen and Kanban West. was transferred to highlight issues of quality. delivery time. and flexibility. In the nineties. following the global industry globalization process. the emphasis was on supply chain management. and customer-oriented business process design. Theory of constraints developed by an Israeli scientist Eliyahu M. Goldratt (1985) is also a significant milestone in the field.

SALARIES AND WORKFORCE STATISTICS

United States

The total number of engineers employed in the US in 2006 was roughly 1.5 million. Of these. 201.000 were industrial engineers (13.3%). the third most popular engineering specialty. The average starting salaries were $55.067 with a bachelor's degree. $64.759 with a master's degree. and $77.364 with a doctorate degree. This places industrial engineering at 7th of 15 among engineering bachelors degrees. 3rd of 10 among masters degrees. and 2nd of 7 among doctorate degrees in average annual salary. The median annual income of industrial engineers in the U.S. workforce is $68.620.

Norway

The average total starting salary in 2011 for Norwegian industrial engineers is NOK 5050.100 ($83.100). while the average total salary in general is NOK 1.049.054 ($172 600).

PROCESS ENGINEERING

Process engineering focuses on the design. operation. control. and optimization of chemical. physical. and biological processes. Process engineering encompasses a vast range of industries. such as chemical. petrochemical. mineral processing. advanced material. food. pharmaceutical. software development and biotechnological industries. The application of systematic computer-based methods to process engineering is process systems engineering.

SIGNIFICANT ACCOMPLISHMENTS

Several accomplishments have been made in Process Systems Engineering:

- *Process design:* synthesis of energy recovery networks. synthesis of distillation systems (azeotropic). synthesis of reactor networks. hierarchical decomposition flowsheets. superstructure optimization. design multiproduct batch plants. Design of the production reactors for the production of plutonium. design of nuclear submarines.
- *Process control:* model predictive control. controllability measures. robust control. Non-linear control. statistical process control. process monitoring. thermodynamics-based control
- *Process operations:* scheduling process networks. multiperiod planning and optimization. data reconciliation. real-time optimization. flexibility measures. fault diagnosis
- *Supporting tools:* sequential modular simulation. equation based process simulation. AI/expert systems. large-scale Non-linear programming (NLP). optimization of differential algebraic equations (DAEs). mixed-integer Non-linear programming (MINLP). global optimization

HISTORY OF PROCESS SYSTEMS ENGINEERING

Process systems engineering (PSE) is a relatively young area in chemical engineering. The first time that this term was used was in a Special Volume of the AIChE Symposium Series in 1961. However. it was not until 1982 when the first international symposium on this topic took place in Kyoto. Japan. that the term PSE started to become widely accepted.

The first textbook in the area was "Strategy of Process Engineering" by Dale F. Rudd and Charles C. Watson. Wiley. 1968. The Computing and Systems Technology (CAST) Division. Area 10 of AIChE. was founded in 1977 and currently has about 1200 members. CAST has four sections: Process Design. Process Control. Process Operations. and Applied Mathematics.

The first journal devoted to PSE was "Computers and Chemical Engineering." which appeared in 1977. The Foundations of Computer-Aided Process Design (FOCAPD) conference in 1980 in Henniker was one of the first meetings in a series on that topic in the PSE area. It is now accompanied by the successful series on Control (CPC). Operations (FOCAPO). and the world-wide series entitled Process Systems Engineering. The CACHE Corporation (Computer Aids for Chemical Engineering). which organizes these conferences. was initially launched by academics in 1970. motivated by the introduction of process simulation in the chemical engineering curriculum.Roger W.H. Sargent from Imperial College was one of the pioneers in the area. PSE is an active area of research in many other countries. particularly in the United Kingdom. Germany. Japan. Korea. and China.

SYSTEMS ENGINEERING

Systems engineering is an interdisciplinary field of engineering that focuses on how to design and manage complex engineering systems over their life cycles. Issues such as reliability. logistics. coordination of different teams (requirements management). evaluation measurements. and other disciplines become more difficult when dealing with large or complex projects. Systems engineering deals with work-processes. optimization methods. and risk management tools in such projects. It overlaps technical and human-centered disciplines such as control engineering. industrial engineering. organizational studies. and project management. Systems engineering ensures that all likely aspects of a project or system are considered. and integrated into a whole.

HISTORY

The term *systems engineering* can be traced back to Bell Telephone Laboratories in the 1940s. The need to identify and manipulate the properties of a system as a whole. which in complex engineering projects may greatly differ from the sum of the parts' properties. motivated various industries to apply the discipline.

When it was no longer possible to rely on design evolution to improve upon a system and the existing tools were not sufficient to meet growing demands. new methods began to be developed that addressed the complexity directly. The continuing evolution of systems engineering comprises the development and identification of new methods and modeling techniques. These methods aid in better comprehension of engineering systems as they grow more complex. Popular tools that are often used in the systems engineering context were developed during these times. including USL. UML. QFD. and IDEF0.

In 1990. a professional society for systems engineering. the *National Council on Systems Engineering* (NCOSE). was founded by representatives from a number of U.S. corporations and organizations. NCOSE was created to address the need for improvements in systems engineering practices and education. As a result of growing involvement from systems engineers outside of the U.S.. the name of the organization was changed to the International Council on Systems Engineering (INCOSE) in 1995. Schools in several countries offer graduate Programmes in systems engineering. and continuing education options are also available for practicing engineers.

Concept

Systems engineering signifies only an approach and. more recently. a discipline in engineering. The aim of education in systems engineering is to simply formalize the approach and in doing so. identify new methods and research opportunities similar to the way it occurs in other fields of engineering. As an approach. systems engineering is holistic and interdisciplinary in flavour.

Origins and traditional Scope

The traditional scope of engineering embraces the design. development. production and operation of physical systems. and systems engineering. as originally conceived. falls within this scope. "Systems engineering". in this sense of the term. refers to the distinctive set of concepts. methodologies. organizational structures (and so on) that have been developed to meet the challenges of engineering functional physical systems of unprecedented complexity. The Apollo Programme is a leading example of a systems engineering project.

Evolution to Broader Scope

The use of the term "systems engineer" has evolved over time to embrace a wider. more holistic concept of "systems" and of engineering processes. This evolution of the definition has been a subject of ongoing controversy. and the term continues to apply to both the narrower and broader scope.

Traditional systems engineering was seen as a branch of engineering in the classical sense. that is. as applied only to physical system. such as space craft and aircraft. More recently. systems engineering has evolved to a take on a broader meaning especially when humans were seen as an essential component of a system. Checkland. for example. captures the broader meaning of systems engineering by stating that 'engineering' "can be read in its general sense; you can engineer a meeting or a political agreement."Consistent with the broader scope of systems engineering. the Systems Engineering Body of Knowledge (SEBoK) has defined three types of systems engineering: (1) Product Systems Engineering (PSE) is the traditional systems engineering focused on the design of physical systems consisting of hardware and software. (2) Enterprise Systems Engineering (ESE) pertains to the view of enterprises. that is. organizations or combinations of organizations. as systems. (3) Service Systems Engineering (SSE) has to do with the engineering of service systems. Checkland defines a service system as a system which is conceived as serving another system. Most civil infrastructure systems are service systems.

Holistic view

Systems engineering focuses on analyzing and eliciting customer needs and required functionality early in the development cycle. documenting requirements. then proceeding with design synthesis and system validation while considering the complete problem. the system lifecycle. Oliver *et al.* claim that the systems engineering process can be decomposed into

- A *Systems Engineering Technical Process*. and
- A *Systems Engineering Management Process*.

Within Oliver's model. the goal of the Management Process is to organize the technical effort in the lifecycle. while the Technical Process includes *assessing available information*. *defining effectiveness measures*. to *create a Behaviour model*. *create a structure model*. *perform trade-off analysis*. and *create sequential build and test plan*.

Depending on their application. although there are several models that are used in the industry. all of them aim to identify the relation between the various stages mentioned above and incorporate feedback. Examples of such models include the Waterfall model and the VEE model.

Interdisciplinary field

System development often requires contribution from diverse technical disciplines. By providing a systems (holistic) view of the development effort. systems engineering helps mold all the technical contributors into a unified team effort. forming a structured development process that proceeds from concept to production to operation and. in some cases. to termination and disposal.This perspective is often replicated in educational Programmes. in that systems engineering courses are taught by faculty from other engineering departments. which helps create an interdisciplinary environment.

Managing complexity

The need for systems engineering arose with the increase in complexity of systems and projects. in turn exponentially increasing the possibility of component friction. and therefore the unreliability of the design. When speaking in this context. complexity incorporates not only engineering systems. but also the logical human organization of data. At the same time. a system can become more complex due to an increase in size as well as with an increase in the amount of data. variables. or the number of fields that are involved in the design. The International Space Station is an example of such a system.

Fig. The International Space Station is an example of a largely complex system requiring Systems Engineering.

The development of smarter control algorithms. microprocessor design. and analysis of environmental systems also come within the purview of systems engineering. Systems engineering encourages the use of tools and methods to better comprehend and manage complexity in systems. Some examples of these tools can be seen here:

- *System model. Modeling. and Simulation*.
- *System architecture*.
- *Optimization*.
- *System dynamics*.
- *Systems analysis*.
- *Statistical analysis*.
- *Reliability analysis*. and
- *Decision making*

Taking an interdisciplinary approach to engineering systems is inherently complex since the Behaviour of and interaction among system components is not always immediately well defined or understood.

Defining and characterizing such systemsand subsystems and the interactions among them is one of the goals of systems engineering. In doing so. the gap that exists between informal requirements from users. operators. marketing organizations. and technical specifications is successfully bridged.

Scope

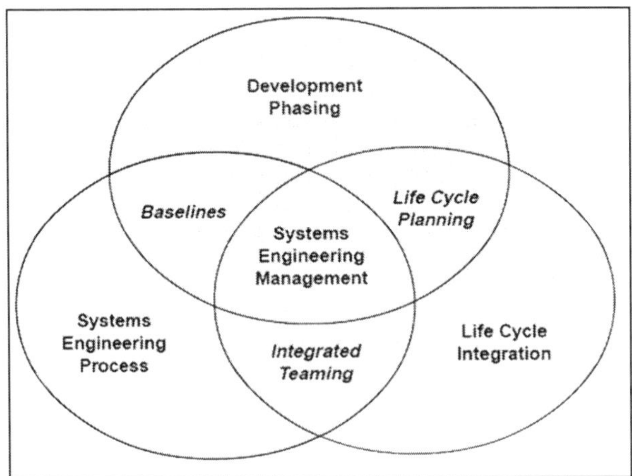

Fig. The scope of systems engineering activities

One way to understand the motivation behind systems engineering is to see it as a method. or practice. to identify and improve common rules that exist within a wide variety of systems. Keeping this in mind. the principles of systems engineering – holism. emergent Behaviour. boundary. et al. – can be applied to any system. complex or otherwise. provided systems thinking is employed at all levels. Besides Defence and aerospace. many information and technology based companies. software development firms. and industries in the field of electronics and communications require systems engineers as part of their team.

An analysis by the INCOSE Systems Engineering center of excellence (SECOE) indicates that optimal effort spent on systems engineering is about 15-20% of the total project effort. At the same time. studies have shown that systems engineering essentially leads to reduction in costs among other benefits. However. no quantitative survey at a larger scale encompassing a wide variety of industries has been conducted until recently. Such studies are underway to determine the effectiveness and quantify the benefits of systems engineering.Systems engineering encourages the use of modeling and simulation to validate assumptions or theories on systems and the interactions within them.

Use of methods that allow early detection of possible failures. in safety engineering. are integrated into the design process. At the same time. decisions made at the beginning of a project whose consequences are not clearly understood can have enormous implications later in the life of a system. and it is the task of the modern systems engineer to explore these issues and make critical decisions. No method guarantees today's decisions will still be valid when a system goes into service years or decades after first conceived. However. there are techniques that support the process of systems engineering. Examples include soft systems methodology. Jay Wright Forrester's System dynamics method. and the Unified Modeling Language (UML)—all currently being explored. evaluated. and developed to support the engineering decision process.

EDUCATION

Education in systems engineering is often seen as an extension to the regular engineering courses. reflecting the industry attitude that engineering students need a foundational background in one of the traditional engineering disciplines (*e.g.*. aerospace engineering. automotive engineering. electrical engineering. mechanical engineering.industrial engineering)—plus practical. real-world experience to be effective as systems engineers. Undergraduate university Programmes in systems engineering are rare. Typically. systems engineering is offered at the graduate level in combination with interdisciplinary study.

INCOSE maintains a continuously updated Directory of Systems Engineering Academic Programmes worldwide. As of 2009. there are about 80 institutions in United States that offer 165 undergraduate and graduate Programmes in systems engineering. Education in systems engineering can be taken as *Systems-centric* or *Domain-centric*.

- *Systems-centric* Programmes treat systems engineering as a separate discipline and most of the courses are taught focusing on systems engineering principles and practice.
- *Domain-centric* Programmes offer systems engineering as an option that can be exercised with another major field in engineering.

Both of these patterns strive to educate the systems engineer who is able to oversee interdisciplinary projects with the depth required of a core-engineer.

SYSTEMS ENGINEERING TOPICS

Systems engineering tools are strategies. procedures. and techniques that aid in performing systems engineering on a project or product. The purpose of these tools vary from database management. graphical browsing. simulation. and reasoning. to document production. neutral import/export and more.

System

There are many definitions of what a system is in the field of systems engineering. Below are a few authoritative definitions:

- ANSI/EIA-632-1999: "An aggregation of end products and enabling products to achieve a given purpose."
- DAU Systems Engineering Fundamentals: "an integrated composite of people. products. and processes that provide a capability to satisfy a stated need or objective."

- IEEE Std 1220-1998: "A set or arrangement of elements and processes that are related and whose Behaviour satisfies customer/ operational needs and provides for life cycle sustainment of the products."
- ISO/IEC 15288:2008: "A combination of interacting elements organized to achieve one or more stated purposes."
- NASA Systems Engineering Handbook: "(1) The combination of elements that function together to produce the capability to meet a need. The elements include all hardware. software. equipment. facilities. personnel. processes. and procedures needed for this purpose. (2) The end product (which performs operational functions) and enabling products (which provide life-cycle support services to the operational end products) that make up a system."
- INCOSE Systems Engineering Handbook: "homogeneous entity that exhibits predefined Behaviour in the real world and is composed of heterogeneous parts that do not individually exhibit that Behaviour and an integrated configuration of components and/or subsystems."
- INCOSE: "A system is a construct or collection of different elements that together produce results not obtainable by the elements alone. The elements. or parts. can include people. hardware. software. facilities. policies. and documents; that is. all things required to produce systems-level results. The results include system level qualities. properties. characteristics. functions. Behaviour and performance. The value added by the system as a whole. beyond that contributed independently by the parts. is primarily created by the relationship among the parts; that is. how they are interconnected."

The systems engineering process

Depending on their application. tools are used for various stages of the systems engineering process:

Using models

Models play important and diverse roles in systems engineering. A model can be defined in several ways. including:

- An abstraction of reality designed to answer specific questions about the real world
- An imitation. analogue. or representation of a real world process or structure; or
- A conceptual. mathematical. or physical tool to assist a decision maker.

Together. these definitions are broad enough to encompass physical engineering models used in the verification of a system design. as well as schematic models like afunctional flow block diagram and mathematical (*i.e.*. quantitative) models used in the trade study process. This section focuses on the last.The main reason for using mathematical models and diagrams in trade studies is to provide estimates of system effectiveness. performance or technical attributes. and cost from a set of known or estimable quantities. Typically. a collection of separate models is needed to provide all of these outcome variables.

The heart of any mathematical model is a set of meaningful quantitative relationships among its inputs and outputs. These relationships can be as simple as adding up constituent quantities to obtain a total. or as complex as a set of differential equations describing the trajectory of a spacecraft in a gravitational field. Ideally. the relationships express causality. not just correlation.

Tools for Graphic Representations

Initially. when the primary purpose of a systems engineer is to comprehend a complex problem. graphic representations of a system are used to communicate a system's functional and data requirements. Common graphical representations include:

- Functional flow block diagram (FFBD)
- Model-based design. for example Simulink. VisSim. etc.
- Data Flow Diagram (DFD)
- N2 Chart
- IDEF0 Diagram
- Use case diagram
- Sequence diagram
- USL Function Maps and Type Maps.
- Enterprise Architecture frameworks. like TOGAF. MODAF. Zachman Frameworks etc.

A graphical representation relates the various subsystems or parts of a system through functions. data. or interfaces. Any or each of the above methods are used in an industry based on its requirements. For instance. the N2 chart may be used where interfaces between systems is important. Part of the design phase is to create structural and behavioral models of the system.Once the requirements are understood. it is now the responsibility of a systems engineer to refine them. and to determine. along with other engineers. the best technology for a job.

At this point starting with a trade study. systems engineering encourages the use of weighted choices to determine the best option. A decision matrix. or Pugh method. is one way (QFD is another) to make this choice while considering all criteria that are important.

The trade study in turn informs the design. which again affects graphic representations of the system (without changing the requirements). In an SE process. this stage represents the iterative step that is carried out until a feasible solution is found. A decision matrix is often populated using techniques such as statistical analysis. reliability analysis. system dynamics (feedback control). and optimization methods.

Other Tools

Systems Modeling Language (SysML). a modeling language used for systems engineering applications. supports the specification. analysis. design. verification and validation of a broad range of complex systems.

Lifecycle Modeling Language (LML). is an open-standard modeling language designed for systems engineering that supports the full lifecycle: conceptual. utilization. support and retirement stages.

RELATED FIELDS AND SUB-FIELDS

Many related fields may be considered tightly coupled to systems engineering. These areas have contributed to the development of systems engineering as a distinct entity.

Cognitive Systems Engineering

Cognitive systems engineering (CSE) is a specific approach to the description and analysis of human-machine systems or sociotechnical systems. The three main themes of CSE are how humans cope with complexity. how work is accomplished by the use of artifacts. and how human-machine systems and socio-technical systems can be described as joint cognitive systems. CSE has since its beginning become a recognized scientific discipline. sometimes also referred to as cognitive engineering. The concept of a Joint Cognitive System (JCS) has in particular become widely used as a way of understanding how complex socio-technical systems can be described with varying degrees of resolution. The more than 20 years of experience with CSE has been described extensively.

Configuration Management

Like systems engineering. configuration management as practiced in the Defence and aerospace industry is a broad systems-level practice. The field parallels the taskings of systems engineering; where systems engineering deals with requirements development. allocation to development items and verification. configuration management deals with requirements capture. traceability to the development item. and audit of development item to ensure that it has achieved the desired functionality that systems engineering and/or Test and Verification Engineering have proven out through objective testing.

Control Engineering

Control engineering and its design and implementation of control systems.

used extensively in nearly every industry. is a large sub-field of systems engineering. The cruise control on an automobile and the guidance system for a ballistic missile are two examples. Control systems theory is an active field of applied mathematics involving the investigation of solution spaces and the development of new methods for the analysis of the control process.

Industrial Engineering

Industrial engineering is a branch of engineering that concerns the development. improvement. implementation and evaluation of integrated systems of people. money. knowledge. information. equipment. energy. material and process. Industrial engineering draws upon the principles and methods of engineering analysis and synthesis. as well as mathematical. physical and social sciences together with the principles and methods of engineering analysis and design to specify. predict. and evaluate results obtained from such systems.

Interface Design

Interface design and its specification are concerned with assuring that the pieces of a system connect and inter-operate with other parts of the system and with external systems as necessary. Interface design also includes assuring that system interfaces be able to accept new features. including mechanical. electrical and logical interfaces. including reserved wires. plug-space. command codes and bits in communication protocols. This is known as extensibility.

Human-Computer Interaction (HCI) or Human-Machine Interface (HMI) is another aspect of interface design. and is a critical aspect of modern systems engineering. Systems engineering principles are applied in thedesign of network protocols for local-area networks and wide-area networks.

Mechatronic Engineering

Mechatronic engineering. like systems engineering. is a multidisciplinary field of engineering that uses dynamical systems modeling to express tangible constructs. In that regard it is almost indistinguishable from Systems Engineering. but what sets it apart is the focus on smaller details rather than larger generalizations and relationships. As such. both fields are distinguished by the scope of their projects rather than the methodology of their practice.

Operations Research

Operations research supports systems engineering. The tools of operations research are used in systems analysis. decision making. and trade studies. Several schools teach SE courses within the operations research or industrial engineering department. highlighting the role systems engineering plays in complex projects.Operations research. briefly. is concerned with the optimization of a process under multiple constraints.

Performance Engineering

Performance engineering is the discipline of ensuring a system meets customer expectations for performance throughout its life. Performance is usually defined as the speed with which a certain operation is executed. or the capability of executing a number of such operations in a unit of time. Performance may be degraded when an operations queue to execute is throttled by limited system capacity.

For example. the performance of a packet-switched network is characterized by the end-to-end packet transit delay. or the number of packets switched in an hour. The design of high-performance systems uses analytical or simulation modeling. whereas the delivery of high-performance implementation involves thorough performance testing. Performance engineering relies heavily on statistics. queueing theory and probability theory for its tools and processes.

Programme Management and Project Management.

Programme management (or programme management) has many similarities with systems engineering. but has broader-based origins than the engineering ones of systems engineering. Project management is also closely related to both Programme management and systems engineering.

Proposal Engineering

Proposal engineering is the application of scientific and mathematical principles to design. construct. and operate a cost-effective proposal development system. Basically. proposal engineering uses the "systems engineering process" to create a cost effective proposal and increase the odds of a successful proposal.

Reliability Engineering

Reliability engineering is the discipline of ensuring a system meets customer expectations for reliability throughout its life; *i.e.*. it does not fail more frequently than expected. Reliability engineering applies to all aspects of the system.

It is closely associated with maintainability. availability (dependability or RAMS preferred by some). and logistics engineering. Reliability engineering is always a critical component of safety engineering. as in failure modes and effects analysis (FMEA) and hazard fault tree analysis. and of security engineering.

Risk Management

Risk Management. the practice of assessing and dealing with risk is one of the interdisciplinary parts of Systems Engineering. In development. acquisition.

or operational activities. the inclusion of risk in tradeoff with cost. schedule. and performance features. involves the iterative complex configuration management of traceability and evaluation to the scheduling and requirements management across domains and for the system lifecycle that requires the interdisciplinary technical approach of systems engineering.

Safety Engineering

The techniques of safety engineering may be applied by non-specialist engineers in designing complex systems to minimize the probability of safety-critical failures. The "System Safety Engineering" function helps to identify "safety hazards" in emerging designs. and may assist with techniques to "mitigate" the effects of (potentially) hazardous conditions that cannot be designed out of systems.

Scheduling

Scheduling is one of the systems engineering support tools as a practice and item in assessing interdisciplinary concerns under configuration management. In particular the direct relationship of resources. performance features. and risk to duration of a task or the dependency links among tasks and impacts across the system lifecycle are systems engineering concerns.

Security Engineering

Security engineering can be viewed as an interdisciplinary field that integrates the community of practice for control systems design. reliability. safety and systems engineering. It may involve such sub-specialties as authentication of system users. system targets and others: people. objects and processes.

Software Engineering

From its beginnings. software engineering has helped shape modern systems engineering practice. The techniques used in the handling of complexes of large software-intensive systems has had a major effect on the shaping and reshaping of the tools. methods and processes of SE.

SAFETY ENGINEERING

Safety engineering is an engineering discipline which assures that engineered systems provide acceptable levels of safety. It is strongly related to systems engineering.industrial engineering and the subset system safety engineering. Safety engineering assures that a life-critical system behaves as needed. even when components fail.

OVERVIEW

The primary goal of safety engineering is to manage risk. eliminating or reducing it to acceptable levels. Risk is the combination of the probability of a failure event. and the severity resulting from the failure. For instance. the severity of a particular failure may result in fatalities. injuries. property damage. or nothing more than annoyance. It may be a frequent. occasional. or rare occurrence. The acceptability of the failure depends on the combination of the two. Probability is often more difficult to predict than severity due to the many factors that could lead to a failure. such as mechanical failure. environmental effects. and operator error. Safety engineering attempts to reduce the frequency of failures. and ensure that when failures do occur. the consequences are not life-threatening. For example. bridges are designed to carry loads well in excess of the heaviest truck likely to use them. This reduces the likelihood of being overloaded. Most bridges are designed with redundant load paths. so that if any one structural member fails. the structure will remain standing. This reduces the severity if the bridge is overloaded.

Ideally. safety engineering starts during the early design of a system. Safety engineers consider what undesirable events can occur under what conditions. and project the related accident risk. They may then propose or require safety mitigation requirements in specifications at the start of development or changes to existing CAD designs or in-service products to make a system safer. This may done by full elimination of any type of hazards or by lowering accident risk. Far too often. rather than actually influencing the design. safety engineers are assigned to prove that an existing. completed design is safe. If the engineer discovers significant safety problems late in the development process. correcting them can be very expensive. This type of error has the potential to waste large sums of money and likely more important. human lives and environmental damage.

The exception to this conventional approach is the way some large government agencies approach safety engineering from a more proactive and proven process perspective. known as "system safety". The system safety philosophy is to be applied to complex and critical systems. such as commercial airliners. complex weapon systems. spacecraft. rail and transportation systems. air traffic control system and other complex and safety-critical industrial systems. The proven system safety methods and techniques are to prevent. eliminate and control hazards and risks through designed influences by a collaboration of key engineering disciplines and product teams. Software safety is a fast-growing field since modern systems functionality are increasingly being put under control of software. The whole concept of system safety and software safety. as a subset of systems engineering. is to influence safety-critical systems designs by conducting several types of hazard analyses to identify hazards. validate hazards and verify design. assess and if needed to specify (new) design safety features and procedures to strategically mitigate risk to acceptable levels before the system is certified.

Additionally. failure mitigation can go beyond design recommendations. particularly in the area of maintenance. There is an entire realm of safety and reliability engineeringknown as Reliability Centered Maintenance (RCM). which is a discipline that is a direct result of analyzing potential failures within a system and determining maintenance actions that can mitigate the risk of failure. This methodology is used extensively on aircraft and involves understanding the failure modes of the serviceable replaceable assemblies in addition to the means to detect or predict an impending failure. Every automobile owner is familiar with this concept when they take in their car to have the oil changed or brakes checked. Even filling up one's car with fuel is a simple example of a failure mode (failure due to fuel exhaustion). a means of detection (fuel gauge). and a maintenance action (filling the car's fuel tank). (The use of a car's odometer also to gauge fuel illustrates the concept of "redundant sensors".)

For large scale complex systems. hundreds if not thousands of maintenance actions can result from the failure analysis. These maintenance actions are based on conditions (*e.g.*. gauge reading or leaky valve). hard conditions (*e.g.*. a component is known to fail after 100 hrs of operation with 95% certainty). or require inspection to determine the maintenance action (*e.g.*. metal fatigue). The RCM concept then analyzes each individual maintenance item for its risk contribution to safety. mission. operational readiness. or cost to repair if a failure does occur. Then the sum total of all the maintenance actions are bundled into maintenance intervals so that maintenance is not occurring around the clock. but rather. at regular intervals. This bundling process introduces further complexity. as it might stretch some maintenance cycles. thereby increasing risk. but reduce others. thereby potentially reducing risk. with the end result being a comprehensive maintenance schedule. purpose built to reduce operational risk and ensure acceptable levels of operational readiness and availability.

ANALYSIS TECHNIQUES

Analysis techniques can be split into two categories: qualitative and quantitative methods. Both approaches share the goal of finding causal dependencies between a hazard on system level and failures of individual components. Qualitative approaches focus on the question "What must go wrong. such that a system hazard may occur?". while quantitative methods aim at providing estimations about probabilites. rates and/or severity of consequences.

Traditionally. safety analysis techniques rely solely on skill and expertise of the safety engineer. In the last decade model-based approaches have become prominent. In contrast to traditional methods. model-based techniques try to derive relationships between causes and consequences from some sort of model of the system.

Traditional Methods for Safety analysis

The two most common fault modeling techniques are called failure mode and effects analysis and fault tree analysis. These techniques are just ways of finding problems and of making plans to cope with failures. as in probabilistic risk assessment. One of the earliest complete studies using this technique on a commercial nuclear plant was the WASH-1400 study. also known as the Reactor Safety Study or the Rasmussen Report.

Failure modes and effects analysis

Failure Mode and Effects Analysis (FMEA) is a bottom-up. inductive analytical method which may be performed at either the functional or piece-part level. For functional FMEA. failure modes are identified for each function in a system or equipment item. usually with the help of a functional block diagram. For piece-part FMEA. failure modes are identified for each piece-part component (such as a valve. connector. resistor. or diode). The effects of the failure mode are described. and assigned a probability based on thefailure rate and failure mode ratio of the function or component. This quantiazation is difficult for software —a bug exists or not. and the failure models used for hardware components do not apply. Temperature and age and manufacturing variability affect a resistor; they do not affect software.

Failure modes with identical effects can be combined and summarized in a Failure Mode Effects Summary. When combined with criticality analysis. FMEA is known as Failure Mode. Effects. and Criticality Analysis or FMECA. pronounced "fuh-MEE-kuh".

Fault tree analysis

Fault tree analysis (FTA) is a top-down. deductive analytical method. In FTA. initiating primary events such as component failures. human errors. and external events are traced through Boolean logic gates to an undesired top event such as an aircraft crash or nuclear reactor core melt. The intent is to identify ways to make top events less probable. and verify that safety goals have been achieved.

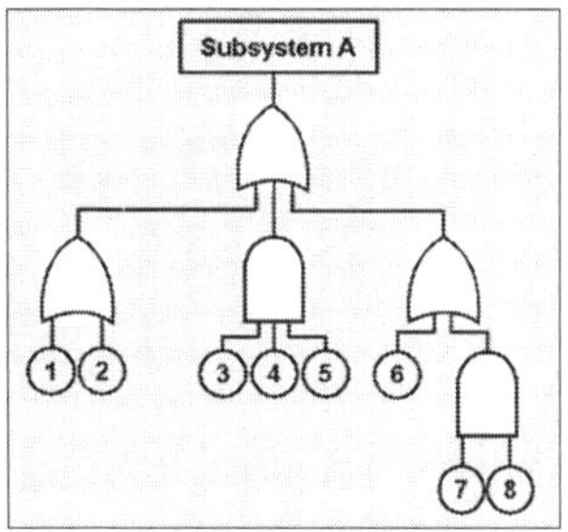

Fig. A fault tree diagram

Fault trees are a logical inverse of success trees. and may be obtained by applying de Morgan's theorem to success trees (which are directly related to reliability block diagrams).FTA may be qualitative or quantitative. When failure and event probabilites are unknown. qualitative fault trees may be analyzed for minimal cut sets. For example. if any minimal cut set contains a single base event. then the top event may be caused by a single failure. Quantitative FTA is used to compute top event probability. and usually requires computer software such as CAFTA from the Electric Power Research Institute or SAPHIRE from the Idaho National Laboratory.

Some industries use both fault trees and event trees. An event tree starts from an undesired initiator (loss of critical supply. component failure etc.) and follows possible further system events through to a series of final consequences. As each new event is considered. a new node on the tree is added with a split of probabilities of taking either branch. The probabilities of a range of "top events" arising from the initial event can then be seen.

SAFETY CERTIFICATION

Usually a failure in safety-certified systems is acceptable if. on average. less than one life per 10 hours of continuous operation is lost to failure. Most Western nuclear reactors. medical equipment. and commercial aircraft are certified to this level. The cost versus loss of lives has been considered appropriate at this level (by FAA for aircraft systems under Federal Aviation Regulations).

PREVENTING FAILURE

Once a failure mode is identified. it can usually be mitigated by adding extra or redundant equipment to the system. For example. nuclear reactors contain dangerous radiation. and nuclear reactions can cause so much heat that no substance might contain them.

Therefore reactors have emergency core cooling systems to keep the temperature down. shielding to contain the radiation. and engineered barriers (usually several. nested. surmounted by a containment building) to prevent accidental leakage. Safety-critical systems are commonly required to permit no single event or component failure to result in a catastrophic failure mode.

Most biological organisms have a certain amount of redundancy: multiple organs. multiple limbs. etc. For any given failure. a fail-over or redundancy can almost always be designed and incorporated into a system.

SAFETY AND RELIABILITY

Safety is not reliability. If a medical device fails. it should fail safely; other alternatives will be available to the surgeon. If an aircraft fly-by-wire control system fails. there is no backup. Electrical power grids are designed for both safety and reliability; telephone systems are designed for reliability. which becomes a safety issue when emergency (*e.g.* US "911") calls are placed.

Probabilistic risk assessment has created a close relationship between safety and reliability. Component reliability. generally defined in terms of component failure rate. and external event probability are both used in quantitative safety assessment methods such as FTA. Related probabilistic methods are used to determine system Mean Time Between Failure (MTBF). system availability. or probability of mission success or failure. Reliability analysis has a broader scope than safety analysis. in that non-critical failures are considered. On the other hand. higher failure rates are considered acceptable for non-critical systems.

Safety generally cannot be achieved through component reliability alone. Catastrophic failure probabilities of 10^{-9} per hour correspond to the failure rates of very simple components such as resistors or capacitors. A complex system containing hundreds or thousands of components might be able to achieve a MTBF of 10.000 to 100.000 hours. meaning it would fail at 10^{-4} or 10^{-5} per hour. If a system failure is catastrophic. usually the only practical way to achieve 10^{-9} per hour failure rate is through redundancy. Two redundant systems with independent failure modes. each having an MTBF of 100.000 hours. could achieve a failure rate on the order of 10^{-10} per hour because of the multiplication rule for independent events.

When adding equipment is impractical (usually because of expense). then the least expensive form of design is often "inherently fail-safe". That is. change the system design so its failure modes are not catastrophic. Inherent fail-safes are common in medical equipment. traffic and railway signals. communications equipment. and safety equipment.

The typical approach is to arrange the system so that ordinary single failures cause the mechanism to shut down in a safe way (for nuclear power plants. this is termed apassively safe design. although more than ordinary failures are covered). Alternately. if the system contains a hazard source such as a battery or rotor. then it may be possible to remove the hazard from the system so that its failure modes cannot be catastrophic. The U.S. Department of Defense Standard Practice for System Safety (MIL–STD–882) places the highest priority on elimination of hazards through design selection.

One of the most common fail-safe systems is the overflow tube in baths and kitchen sinks. If the valve sticks open. rather than causing an overflow and damage. the tank spills into an overflow. Another common example is that in an elevator the cable supporting the car keeps spring-loaded brakes open. If the cable breaks. the brakes grab rails. and the elevator cabin does not fall.

Some systems can never be made fail safe. as continuous availability is needed. For example. loss of engine thrust in flight is dangerous. Redundancy. fault tolerance. or recovery procedures are used for these situations (*e.g.*

multiple independent controlled and fuel fed engines). This also makes the system less sensitive for the reliability prediction errors or quality induced uncertainty for the separate items. On the other hand. failure detection and correction and avoidance of common cause failures becomes here increasingly important to ensure system level reliability.

CONTAINING FAILURE

It is common practice to plan for the failure of safety systems through containment and isolation methods. The use of isolating valves. also known as the block and bleed manifold. is very common in isolating pumps. tanks. and control valves that may fail or need routine maintenance. In addition. nearly all tanks containing oil or other hazardous chemicals are required to have containment barriers set up around them to contain 100% of the volume of the tank in the event of a catastrophic tank failure. Similarly. in a long pipeline. there are remote-closing valves at regular intervals so that a leak can be isolated. Fault isolation boundaries are similarly designed into critical electronic systems or computer software. The goal of all containment systems is to provide means of mitigating the consequences of failure. Fault isolation might also refer to the extent to which detected failures might be isolated for successful recovery. The isolation level shows the system identure level at which the failure cause can be recovered (often by replacement of a line replaceable unit).

COST ENGINEERING

"Cost engineering [is] the engineering practice devoted to the management of project cost. involving such activities as cost- and control- estimating. which is cost control and cost forecasting. investment appraisal. and risk analysis." "Cost Engineers budget. plan and monitor investment projects. They seek the optimum balance between cost. quality and time requirements."Skills and knowledge of Cost Engineers are similar to those of Quantity Surveyors.A cost engineer is "an engineer whose Judgement and experience are utilized in the application of scientific principles and techniques to problems of estimation; cost control; business planning and management science; profitability analysis; project management; and planning and scheduling."

OVERVIEW

One key objective of cost engineering is to arrive at accurate cost estimates and schedules and to avoid cost overruns and schedule slips. Cost engineering goes beyond preparing cost estimates and schedules by helping manage resources and supporting assessment and decisionmaking. "The discipline of 'cost engineering' can be considered to encompass a wide range of cost-related aspects of engineering and programme management. but in particular cost estimating.cost analysis/cost assessment. design-to-cost. schedule analysis/

planning and risk assessment." The broad array of cost engineering topics represent the intersection of the fields of project management. business management. and engineering. Most people have a limited view of what engineering encompasses. The most obvious perception is that engineering addresses technical issues such as the physical design of a structure or system. However. beyond the physical manifestation of a design of a structure or system (for example. a building). there are other dimensions to consider such as the money. time. and other resources that were invested in the creation of the building. Cost engineers refer to these investments collectively as "costs".Cost engineering then can be considered an adjunct of traditional engineering. It recognizes and focuses on the relationships between the physical and cost dimensions of whatever is being "engineered". Cost engineering is most often taught at universities as part of construction engineering. engineering management. civil engineering. and related curricula because it is most often practiced on engineering and construction capital projects. Engineering economics is a core skill and knowledge area of cost engineering.

AACE International "is dedicated to the tenets of furthering the concepts of Total Cost Management and Cost Engineering. Total Cost Management is the effective application of professional and technical expertise to plan and control resources. costs. profitability and risk. Simply stated. it is a systematic approach to managing cost throughout the life cycle of any enterprise. Programme. facility. project. product or service. This is accomplished through the application of cost engineering and cost management principles. proven methodologies and the latest technology in support of the management process.... Total Cost Management is that area of engineering practice where engineering Judgement and experience are utilized in the application of scientific principles and techniques to problems of business and Programme planning; cost estimating; economic and financial analysis; cost engineering; Programme and project management; planning and scheduling; and cost and schedule performance measurement and change control. In summary. the list of practice areas... are collectively called cost engineering; while the "process" through which these practices are applied is called total cost management or TCM.

HISTORY

Cost engineering is a field of engineering practice that began in the 1950s (AACE International was founded in 1956). The skills and knowledge areas of Cost Engineers are similar to those of Quantity Surveyors. AACE International is one of many international engineering organizations representing practitioners in these fields. The International Cost Engineering Congress (ICEC) was founded in 1976 as a Worldwide Confederation of Cost Engineering. Quantity Surveying and Project Management Societies. In 2006. AACE published the Total Cost Management (TCM) Framework which outlines an integrated process for applying the skills and knowledge of cost engineering. This has also been called the world's first process for portfolio. Programme and project management.

VALUE ENGINEERING

Value engineering (VE) is a systematic method to improve the "value" of goods or products and services by using an examination of function. Value. as defined. is the ratio of function to cost. Value can therefore be increased by either improving the function or reducing the cost. It is a primary tenet of value engineering that basic functions be preserved and not be reduced as a consequence of pursuing value improvements.

The reasoning behind value engineering is as follows: if marketers expect a product to become practically or stylistically obsolete within a specific length of time. they can design it to only last for that specific lifetime. The products could be built with higher-grade components. but with value-engineering they are not because this would impose an unnecessary cost on the manufacturer. and to a limited extend also an increased cost on the purchaser. Value engineering will reduce these costs. A company will typically use the least expensive components that satisfy the product's lifetime projections.

Due to the very short life spans however which is often a result of this "value engineering technique" planned obsolescence has become associated with product deterioration and inferior quality. Vance Packard once claimed this practice gave engineering as a whole a bad name. as it directed creative engineering energies Towards short-term market ends. Philosophers such as Herbert Marcuse and Jacque Fresco have also criticized the economic and societal implications of this model.

ORIGINS

Value engineering began at General Electric Co. during World War II. Because of the war. there were shortages of skilled labour. raw materials. and component parts. Lawrence Miles. Jerry Leftow. and Harry Erlicher at G.E. looked for acceptable substitutes. They noticed that these substitutions often reduced costs. improved the product. or both. What started out as an accident of necessity was turned into a systematic process. They called their technique "value analysis".

LEGAL TERMINOLOGY OF VALUE ENGINEERING IN THE USA

In the United States. value engineering is specifically spelled out in Public Law 104-106. which states. "Each executive agency shall establish and maintain cost-effective value engineering procedures and processes."

Value engineering is sometimes taught within the project management or industrial engineering body of knowledge as a technique in which the value of a system's outputs isoptimized by crafting a mix of performance (function) and costs. In most cases this practice identifies and removes unnecessary expenditures. thereby increasing the value for the manufacturer and/or their customers.VE follows a structured thought process that is based exclusively on "function". *i.e.* what something "does" not what it is. For example a screw driver that is being used to stir a can of paint has a "function" of mixing the contents of a paint can and not the original connotation of securing a screw into a screw-hole. In value engineering "functions" are always described in a two word abridgement consisting of an active verb and measurable noun (what is being done - the verb - and what it is being done to - the noun) and to do so in the most non-prescriptive way possible. In the screw driver and can of paint example. the most basic function would be "blend liquid" which is less prescriptive than "stir paint" which can be seen to limit the action (by stirring) and to limit the application (only considers paint). This is the basis of what value engineering refers to as "function analysis".Value engineering uses rational logic (a unique "how" - "why" questioning technique) and the analysis of function to identify relationships that increase value. It is considered a quantitative method similar to the scientific method. which focuses on hypothesis-conclusion approaches to test relationships. and operations research. which uses model building to identify predictive relationships.

Value engineering is also referred to as "value management" or "value methodology" (VM). and "value analysis" (VA). VE is above all a structured problem solving process based on function analysis—understanding something with such clarity that it can be described in two words. the active verb and measurable noun abridgement. For example. the function of a pencil is to "make marks". This then facilitates considering what else can make marks. From a spray can. lipstick. a diamond on glass to a stick in the sand. one can then clearly decide upon which alternative solution is most appropriate.

THE JOB PLAN

Value engineering is often done by systematically following a multi-stage job plan. Larry Miles' original system was a six-step procedure which he called the "value analysis job plan." Others have varied the job plan to fit their constraints. Depending on the application. there may be four. five. six. or more stages. One modern version has the following eight steps:

1. Preparation
2. Information
3. Analysis
4. Creation
5. Evaluation
6. Development
7. Presentation
8. Follow-up

Four basic steps in the job plan are:

- Information gathering - This asks what the requirements are for the object. Function analysis. an important technique in value engineering. is usually done in this initial stage. It tries to determine what functions or performance characteristics are important. It asks questions like; What does the object do? What must it do? What should it do? What could it do? What must it not do?
- Alternative generation (creation) - In this stage value engineers ask; What are the various alternative ways of meeting requirements? What else will perform the desired function?
- Evaluation - In this stage all the alternatives are assessed by evaluating how well they meet the required functions and how great the cost savings will be.
- Presentation - In the final stage. the best alternative will be chosen and presented to the client for final decision.

ENGINEERING DESIGN PROCESS

The engineering design process is a methodical series of steps that engineers use in creating functional products and processes.

The steps tend to get articulated. subdivided. and/or illustrated in a variety of different ways. but regardless. they generally reflect certain core principles regarding the underlying concepts and their respective sequence and interrelationship. Also. the process is highly iterative - *i.e.* parts of the process often need to be repeated many times before production of a product can begin - though the part(s) that get iterated and the number of such cycles in any given project can be highly variable.

...It is a decision making process (often iterative) in which the basic sciences. mathematics. and engineering sciences are applied to convert resources optimally to meet a stated objective. Among the fundamental elements of the design process are the establishment of objectives and criteria. synthesis. analysis. construction. testing and evaluation

—ABET

One framing of the engineering design process focuses on the following general aspects: research. conceptualization. feasibility assessment. establishing design requirements. preliminary design. detailed design. production planning and tool design. and production. Whether and in what sense each of these things - or approximate synonyms of such - may be deemed a “step” or substep per se in the engineering design process (or anyone’s preferred formulation of it). many of these concepts often tend to be involved.

RESEARCH

A significant amount of time is spent on research. or locating information.

Consideration should be given to the existing applicable literature. problems and successes associated with existing solutions. costs. and marketplace needs.The source of information should be relevant. including existing solutions. Reverse engineering can be an effective technique if other solutions are available on the market.

Other sources of information include the Internet. local libraries. available government documents. personal organizations. trade journals. vendor catalogs and individual expertsavailable.

FEASIBILITY

At first. a feasibility study is carried out after which schedules. resource plans and. estimates for the next phase are developed. The feasibility study is an evaluation and analysis of the potential of a proposed project which is based on extensive investigation and research to support the process of decision making. It outlines and analyses several alternatives or methods of achieving desired outcome.

The feasibility study helps to narrow the scope of the project to identify the best scenario. A Feasibility Report is generated following which Post Feasibility Review is performed.

The purpose of a feasibility assessment is to determine whether the engineer's project can proceed into the design phase. This is based on two criteria: the project needs to be based on an achievable idea. and it needs to be within cost constraints. It is important to have an engineer with experience and good Judgement to be involved in this portion of the feasibility study.

CONCEPTUALIZATION

Following Feasibility. a Concept Study (Conceptualization. Conceptual Engineering) is performed. A Concept Study is the phase of project planning that includes producing ideas and taking into account the pros and cons of implementing those ideas.

This stage of a project is done to minimize the likelihood of error. manage costs. assess risks. and evaluate the potential success of the intended project.

Conceptual engineering and design is performed on a wide range of facilities and related infrastructure. including floating and fixed platform topsides. compliant piled towers. subsea developments. pipelines. compressor stations. refineries and petrochemical plants. FPSO topsides. heavy oil production facilities. floating LNG vessels. LNG plants. gas processing and other industrial facilities

Methods of Conceptualization

Once an engineering issue is defined. solutions must be identified. These solutions can be found by using ideation. or the mental process by which ideas are generated. The following are the most widely used techniques:

- Trigger word - a word or phrase associated with the issue at hand is stated. and subsequent words and phrases are evoked. For example. to *move* something from one place to another may evoke *run. swim. roll.* etc.
- morphological chart - independent design characteristics are listed in a chart. and different engineering solutions are proposed for each solution. Normally. a preliminary sketch and short report accompany the morphological chart.
- synectics - the engineer imagines him or herself as the item and asks. "What would I do if I were the system?" This unconventional method of thinking may find a solution to the problem at hand.the vital aspects of the conceptualization step is synthesis. Synthesis is the process of taking the element of the concept and arranging them in the proper way. Synthesis creative process is present in every design.
- brainstorming - this popular method involves thinking of different ideas. typically as part of a small group. and adopting these ideas in some form as a solution to the problem

ESTABLISHING THE DESIGN REQUIREMENTS

Establishing design requirements is one of the most important elements in the design process. and this task is normally performed at the same time as and the feasibility analysis.

The design requirements control the design of the project throughout the engineering design process. Some design requirements include hardware and software parameters. maintainability. availability. and testability.

PRELIMINARY DESIGN

The preliminary design. or high-level design (also called FEED). bridges the gap between the design concept and the detailed design phase. In this task. the overall system configuration is defined. and schematics. diagrams. and layouts of the project will provide early project configuration. During detailed design and optimization. the parameters of the part being created will change. but the preliminary design focuses on creating the general framework to build the project on.

DETAILED DESIGN

The next phase of engineering following FEED is the Detailed Design (Detailed Engineering) phase which may consist of procurement as well. This phase builds on the already developed FEED. aiming to further elaborate each aspect of the project by complete description through solid modeling. drawings as well as specifications.

Some of the said specifications include:

- Operating parameters
- Operating and Non-operating environmental stimuli
- Test requirements
- External dimensions
- Maintenance and testability provisions
- Materials requirements
- Reliability requirements
- External surface treatment
- Design life
- Packaging requirements
- External marking
- input machine

The advancement of computer-aided design. or CAD. Programmes have made the detailed design phase more efficient. This is because a CAD Programme can provide optimization. where it can reduce volume without hindering the part's quality.

It can also calculate stress and displacement using the finite element method to determine stresses throughout the part. It is the engineer's responsibility to determine whether these stresses and displacements are allowable. so the part is safe.

PRODUCTION PLANNING AND TOOL DESIGN

The production planning and tool design is nothing more than planning how to mass-produce the project and which tools should be used in the manufacturing of the part. Tasks to complete in this step include selecting the material. selection of the production processes. determination of the sequence of operations. and selection of tools. such as jigs. fixtures. and tooling. This task also involves testing a working prototype to ensure the created part meets qualification standards.

PRODUCTION

With the completion of qualification testing and prototype testing. the engineering design process is finalized. The part must now be manufactured. and the machines must be inspected regularly to make sure that they do not break down and slow production.

PRODUCT DESIGN

Product design is the process of creating a new product to be sold by a business to its customers. A very broad concept. it is essentially the efficient and effective generation and development of ideas through a process that leads to new products.

In a systematic approach. product designers conceptualize and evaluate ideas. turning them into tangible inventions and products. The product designer's role is to combine art. science. and technology to create new products that people can use. Their evolving role has been facilitated by digital tools that now allow designers to communicate. visualize. analyze and actually produce tangible ideas in a way that would have taken greater manpower in the past.

Product design is sometimes confused with (and certainly overlaps with) industrial design. and has recently become a broad term inclusive of service. software. and physical product design. Industrial design is concerned with bringing artistic form and usability. usually associated with craft design and ergonomics. together in order to mass-produce goods. Other aspects of product design include engineering design. particularly when matters of functionality or utility (*e.g.* problem-solving) are at issue. though such boundaries are not always clear.

PRODUCT DESIGN PROCESS

There are various product design processes and many focus on different aspects. The process shown below. for example. is "The Seven Universal Stages of Creative Problem-Solving." outlined by Don Koberg and Jim Bagnell. It helps designers formulate their product from ideas. This process is usually completed by a group of people. *i.e.* industrial designers. field experts (*e.g.* prospective users). engineers. etc. depending upon the products involved. The process focuses on figuring out what is required. brainstorming possible ideas. creating mock prototypes. and then generating the product. However. that is not the end of the process.

At this point. product designers would still need to execute the idea. making it into an actual product and then evaluate its success by seeing if any improvements are necessary.The product design process has experienced huge leaps in evolution over the last few years with the rise and adoption of 3D printing. New consumer-friendly 3D printers can produce dimensional objects and print upwards with a plastic like substance opposed to traditional printers that spread ink across a page.

The design process follows a guideline involving three main sections:

- Analysis
- Concept
- Synthesis

The latter two sections are often revisited. depending on how often the design needs touch-ups. to improve or to better fit the criteria. This is a continuous loop. where feedback is the main component. To break it down even more. the seven stages specify how the process works. Analysis consists of two stages. concept is only one stage. and synthesis encompasses the other four.

Analysis

- Accept Situation: Here. the designers decide on committing to the project and finding a solution to the problem. They pool their resources into figuring out how to solve the task most efficiently.
- Analyze: In this stage. everyone in the team begins research. They gather general and specific materials which will help to figure out how their problem might be solved. This can range from statistics. questionnaires. and articles. among many other sources.

Concept

- Define: This is where the key issue of the matter is defined. The conditions of the problem become objectives. and restraints on the situation become the parameters within which the new design must be constructed.

Synthesis

- Ideate: The designers here brainstorm different ideas. solutions for their design problem. The ideal brainstorming session does not involve any bias or Judgement. but instead builds on original ideas.
- Select: By now. the designers have narrowed down their ideas to a select few. which can be guaranteed successes and from there they can outline their plan to make the product.
- Implement: This is where the prototypes are built. the plan outlined in the previous step is realized and the product starts to become an actual object.
- Evaluate: In the last stage. the product is tested. and from there. improvements are made. Although this is the last stage. it does not mean that the process is over. The finished prototype may not work as well as hoped so new ideas need to be brainstormed.

DEMAND-PULL INNOVATION AND INVENTION-PUSH INNOVATION

Most product designs fall under one of two categories: demand-pull innovation or invention-push innovation.Demand-pull happens when there is an opportunity in the market to be explored by the design of a product. This product design attempts to solve a design problem. The design solution may be the development of a new product or developing a product that's already on the market. such as developing an existing invention for another purpose.Invention-push innovation happens when there is an advancement in intelligence.

This can occur through research or it can occur when the product designer comes up with a new product design idea.

PRODUCT DESIGN EXPRESSION

Design expression comes from the combined effect of all elements in a product. Colour tone. shape and size should direct a person's thoughts towards buying the product.Therefore it is in the product designer's best interest to consider the audiences who are most likely to be the product's end consumers. Keeping in mind how consumers will perceive the product during the design process will direct towards the product's success in the market. However. even within a specific audience. it is challenging to cater to each possible personality within that group.

The solution to that is to create a product that. in its designed appearance and function. expresses a personality or tells a story. Products that carry such attributes are more likely to give off a stronger expression that will attract more consumers. On that note it is important to keep in mind that design expression does not only concern the appearance of a product. but also its function. For example. as humans our appearance as well as our actions are subject to people's Judgement when they are making a first impression of us. People usually do not appreciate a rude person even if they are good looking. Similarly. a product can have an attractive appearance but if its function does not follow through it will most likely drop in regards to consumer interest. In this sense. designers are like communicators. they use the language of different elements in the product to express something.

PRODUCT DESIGN CONSIDERATIONS

Product design is not an easy task. The stakeholders involved all demand something different from the product designer and from the design process.

- The manufacturer is concerned with production cost; in the end. the manufacturer wants an economically produced product.
- The purchaser looks at price. appearance. and prestige value.
- The end user is concerned with usability and functionality of the final product.
- The maintenance and repair department focuses on how well the final product can be maintained: is the product easily reassembled. disassembled. diagnosed. and serviced?

Stakeholders' needs vary from one another and it is the product designer's job to incorporate those needs into their design.

TRENDS IN PRODUCT DESIGN

Product designers need to consider all of the details: the ways people use and abuse objects. faulty products. errors made in the design process. and the desirable ways in which people wish they could use objects. Many new designs will fail and many won't even make it to market. Some designs eventually become obsolete. The design process itself can be quite frustrating usually taking 5 or 6 tries to get the product design right. A product that fails in the marketplace the first time may be re-introduced to the market 2 more times. If it continues to fail. the product is then considered to be dead because the market believes it to be a failure. Most new products fail. even if it's a great idea. All types of product design are clearly linked to the economic health of manufacturing sectors.

Innovation provides much of the competitive impetus for the development of new products. with new technology often requiring a new design interpretation.

INDUSTRIAL DESIGN

Fig. An iPod. an industrially designed product.

It only takes one manufacturer to create a new product paradigm to force the rest of the industry to catch up - fueling further innovation. Products designed to benefit people of all ages and abilities—without penalty to any group—accommodate our swelling aging population by extending independence and supporting the changing physical and sensory needs we all encounter as we grow older.

Fig. KitchenAid 5 qt. Stand Mixer. designed in 1937 by Egmont Arens. remains very successful today

Fig. Western Electric Model 302 telephone. found throughout the United States from 1937 until the introduction of touch-tone dialing.

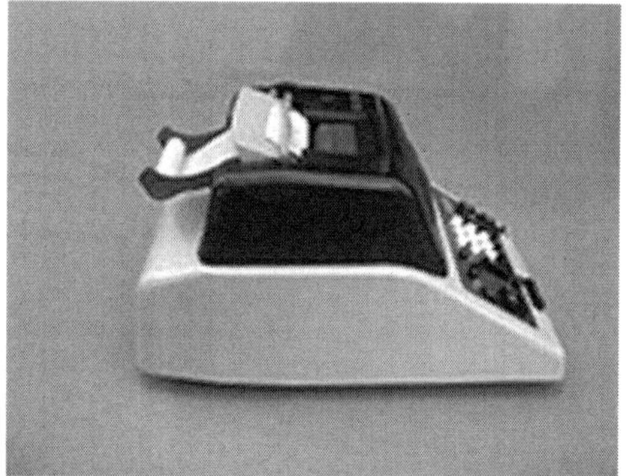

Fig. Calculator Olivetti Divisumma 24 designed in 1956 by Marcello Nizzoli

Industrial design is the use of both applied art and applied science to improve the aesthetics. design. ergonomics. functionality. and/or usability of a product. and it may also be used to improve the product's marketability and even production. The role of an industrial designer is to create and execute design solutions for problems of form. usability. physical ergonomics. marketing. brand development. and sales.

Industrial design can overlap significantly with engineering design. and in different countries the boundaries of the two concepts can vary. but in general engineering focuses principally on functionality or Utility of Products whereas industrial design focuses principally on*aesthetic and user-interface* aspects of products.

In many jurisdictions this distinction is effectively defined by credentials and/or licensurerequired to engage in the practice of engineering. "Industrial design" as such does not overlap much with the engineering sub-discipline of industrial engineering. except for the latter's sub-specialty of ergonomics.

HISTORY

The first use of the term "industrial design" is often attributed to the industrial designer Joseph Claude Sinel in 1919 (although he himself denied this in interviews). but the discipline predates 1919 by at least a decade. Christopher Dresser is considered the world's first industrial designer. Industrial design's origins lie in the industrialization of consumer products. For instance the Deutscher Werkbund. founded in 1907 and a precursor to the Bauhaus. was a state-sponsored effort to integrate traditional crafts and industrial mass-production techniques. to put Germany on a competitive footing with England and the United States.

The earliest use of the term may have been in *The Art Union*. A monthly Journal of the Fine Arts. 1839:

"Dyce's report to the Board of Trade on foreign schools of Design for Manufactures. Mr Dyces official visit to France. Prussia and Bavaria for the purpose of examining the state of schools of design in those countries will be fresh in the recollection of our readers. His report on this subject was ordered to be printed some few months since. on the motion of Mr Hume."

"The school of St Peter. at Lyons was founded about 1750 for the instruction of draftsmen employed in preparing patterns for the silk manufacture. It has been much more successful than the Paris school and having been disorganized by the revolution. was restored by Napoleon and differently constituted. being then erected into an Academy of Fine Art: to which the study of design for silk manufacture was merely attached as a subordinate branch. It appears that all the students who entered the school commence as if they were intended for artists in the higher sense of the word and are not expected to decide as to whether they will devote themselves to the Fine Arts or to Industrial Design. until they have completed their exercises in drawing and painting of the figure from the antique and from the living model. It is for this reason. and from the fact that artists for industrial purposes are both well paid and highly considered (as being well instructed men) that so many individuals in France engage themselves in *both* pursuits."

The practical draughtsman's book of industrial design by Jacques-Eugène Armengaud was printed in 1853.

Robert Lepper helped to establish one of the country's first industrial design degree Programmes at Carnegie Institute of Technology.

EDUCATION

Product design and industrial design overlap into the fields of user interface design. information design. and interaction design. Various schools of industrial design and design engineering specialize in one of these aspects. ranging from pure art colleges (product styling) through mixed Programmes of engineering and design. related disciplines such as exhibit design and interior design—to schools that almost completely subordinated aesthetic design to concerns of usage and ergonomics(the so-called *functionalist* school).

University and Institutions

Degrees in industrial design are offered at universities worldwide and typically take four to five years of study. The study results in a Bachelor of Industrial Design (B.I.D.) orBachelor of Science (B.Sc). Afterwards. the bachelor programme can be extended to postgraduate degrees such as Master of Design. Master of Fine Arts and others to aMaster of Arts or Master of Science.

DEFINITION OF INDUSTRIAL DESIGN

Industrial design studies function and form—and the connection between product. user. and environment. Generally. industrial design professionals work in small scale design. rather than overall design of complex systems such as buildings or ships. Industrial designers don't usually design motors. electrical circuits. or gearing that make machines move. but they may affect technical aspects through usability design and form relationships. Usually. they work with other professionals such as marketers to identify and fulfill customer needs and expectations.

DESIGN PROCESS

Fig. A Fender Stratocaster with sunburst finish. one of the most widely recognized electric guitars in the world.

Design. itself. is often difficult to describe to non-designers and engineers. because the meaning accepted by the design community is not made of words. Instead. the definition is created as a result of acquiring a critical framework for the analysis and creation of artifacts. One of the many accepted (but intentionally unspecific) definitions of design originates from Carnegie Mellon's School of Design. "Design is the process of taking something from its existing state and moving it to a preferred state." This applies to new artifacts. whose existing state is undefined. and previously created artifacts. whose state stands to be improved.

Although the process of design may be considered 'creative.' many analytical processes also take place. In fact. many industrial designers often use various design methodologies in their creative process. Some of the processes that are commonly used are user research. sketching. comparative product research. model making. prototyping and testing. These processes are best defined by the industrial designers and/or other team members. Industrial designers often utilize 3D software. computer-aided industrial design and CAD Programmes to move from concept to production. They may also build a prototype first and then use industrial CT scanning to test for interior defects and generate a CAD model. From this the manufacturing process may be modified to improve the product.

Product characteristics specified by industrial designers may include the overall form of the object. the location of details with respect to one another. colors. texture. form. and aspects concerning the use of the product. Additionally they may specify aspects concerning the production process. choice of materials and the way the product is presented to the consumer at the point of sale. The inclusion of industrial designers in a product development process may lead to added value by improving usability. lowering production costs and developing more appealing products.

Industrial design may also focus on technical concepts. products. and processes. In addition to aesthetics. usability. and ergonomics. it can also encompass engineering. usefulness. market placement. and other concerns—such as psychology. desire. and the emotional attachment of the user. These values and accompanying aspects that form the basis of industrial design can vary—between different schools of thought. and among practicing designers.

INDUSTRIAL DESIGN RIGHTS

Industrial design rights are intellectual property rights that make exclusive the visual design of objects that are not purely utilitarian. A design patent would also be considered under this category. An industrial design consists of the creation of a shape. configuration or composition of pattern or Colour. or combination of pattern and Colour in three-dimensional form containing aesthetic value. An industrial design can be a two- or three-dimensional pattern used to produce a product. industrial commodity or handicraft. Under the Hague Agreement Concerning the International Deposit of Industrial Designs. a WIPO-administered treaty. a procedure for an international registration exists. An applicant can file for a single international deposit with WIPO or with the national office in a country party to the treaty. The design will then be protected in as many member countries of the treaty as desired.

SALES PROCESS ENGINEERING

Sales process engineering is the engineering of better sales processes. It is thus the quest to design better ways of selling. making salespeople's efforts more productive. It has been described as "the systematic application of scientific and mathematical principles to achieve the practical goals of a particular sales process". Selden pointed outthat in this context. sales referred to the output of a process involving a variety of functions across an organization. and not that of a "sales department" alone. Primary areas of application span functions including sales. marketing. and customer service.

HISTORY

As early as 1900–1915. advocates of scientific management. such as Frederick Winslow Taylor and Harlow Stafford Person. recognized that their ideas could be applied not only to manual labour and skilled trades but also to management. professions. and sales. Person promoted an early form of sales process engineering. At the time. our postwar senses of the terms *sales process engineering* and *sales engineering* did not yet exist; Person called his efforts "sales engineering".

The evolution of modern corporate life in the 1920s through 1960s. exemplified by professional management monographs of the time. further sought to apply analysis and synthesis to improve the methods of salespeople as well as the rest of the office workforce.

Management trends of the 1980s and 1990s. such as business process reengineering. influenced sales process engineering as much as many other business processes. The upturn in interest in applying a more systematic approach to these areas was spurred by a number of factors. Todd Youngblood (2004) emphasized "three core principles" that typify such efforts. His principles were continuous improvement of the sales process; metrics to quantitatively judge the rate and degree of improvement; and a well-defined sales process.

In the 2000s and 2010s. the evolution of customer relationship management (CRM) and salesforce automation. especially the development of powerful new web-based software to automate and augment them (CRM systems. sales force management systems. marketing information systems). has been the forefront of increasing the productivity of sales and marketing people.

FUTURE DIRECTIONS]

As in other areas of applied science. future directions for sales process engineering include broadening the available pool of underlying observational data (the standard refrain of "more research is needed"); publishing further application of the principles; and advancing educational efforts to teach and disseminate the relevant body of knowledge.

3

Engineering Management

INTRODUCTION

Engineering Management is a specialized form of management that is concerned with the application of engineeringprinciples to business practice. Engineering management is a career that brings together the technological problem-solving savvy of engineering and the organizational. administrative. and planning abilities of management in order to oversee complex enterprises from conception to completion.

Example areas of engineering are product development. manufacturing. construction. design engineering. industrial engineering. technology. production. or any other field that employs personnel who perform an engineering function.

Successful engineering managers typically require training and experience in business and engineering. Technically inept managers tend to be deprived of support by their technical team. and non-commercial managers tend to lack commercial acumen to deliver in a market economy. Largely. engineering managers manage engineers who are driven by non-entrepreneurial thinking. and thus require the necessary people skills to coach. mentor and motivate technical professionals. Engineering professionals joining manufacturing companies sometimes become engineering managers by default after a period of time. They are required to learn how to manage once they are on the job. though this is usually an ineffective way to develop managerial abilities.

HISTORY

Stevens Institute of Technology is believed to have the oldest Engineering management department. established as the School of Business Engineering in 1908. This was later called the Bachelor of Engineering in Engineering Management (BEEM) Programme and moved into the School of Systems and Enterprises. Drexel University's Engineering Management Programme was established in 1959. In 1967 the first university department titled "Engineering Management" was founded at the Missouri University of Science and Technology (Missouri S&T. formerly the University of Missouri-Rolla).Outside the USA. in Germany the first department concentrating on Engineering Management was established 1927 in Berlin. In Turkey the Istanbul Technical University has aManagement Engineering Department established in 1982. offering a number of graduate and undergraduate Programmes in Management Engineering.

In UK the University of Warwick has a specialised department WMG (previously known as Warwick Manufacturing Group) established in 1980. which offers a graduate programme in MSc Engineering Business Management.

More recently in the United Kingdom. Teesside University's School of Science and Engineering introduced an MSc Engineering Management alongside its engineering-focussed MSc Project Management.

Michigan Technological University began an Engineering Management Programme in the School of Business and Economics in the Fall of 2012.

In Canada. Memorial University of Newfoundland has started a complete Master Degree Programme in Engineering Management Master of Engineering Management. It is a unique and one of a kind of Programme started in Canada for the very first time.

AREAS

Operations research and supply chain management

Operations research deals with quantitative models of complex operations and uses these models to support decision-making in any sector of industry or public services. Supply chain management is the process of planning. implementing and managing the flow of goods. services and related information from the point of origin to the point of consumption.

Information technologies

The "information technologies" theme focuses on how technology is designed and managed to support effective decision-making. Topics deal with technical applications insoftware design and development. data mining and telecommunication as well as the organizational and social issues associated with the use of information technologies.

Decision engineering

Decision engineering seeks to use engineering principles in the creation of a decision. which it views as an engineering artifact in its own right.

From this point of view. the creation of a decision includes agreeing to objectives. developing a detailed specification. and then creating a decision model. which captures the key cause-and-effect elements of the decision environment (a systems thinking approach) with a focus on the particular decision. instead of the entire system (which can be otherwise intractable). Like other engineered artifacts. a decision model can be subject to Quality assurance review. and-since it is documented-is amenable to Process improvement over time. Decision engineering models draw from the information technologies for data supporting the decision. but are distinguished from IT in that they model the decision. not just the data supporting it.

Management Of Technology

The Management of Technology (MOT) theme builds on the foundation of management topics in accounting. finance. economics. organizational Behaviour and organizational design. Courses in this theme deal with operational and organizational issues related to managing innovation and technological change.

EDUCATION

Engineering Management Programmes typically include instruction in accounting. economics. finance. project management. systems engineering. mathematical modeling and optimization. management information systems. quality control and six sigma. operations research. human resources management. industrial psychology. safety and health.

There are many options for entering into engineering management. albeit that the foundation requirement is an engineering degree (or other computer science. mathematics orscience degree) and a business degree.

Undergraduate Degrees

Although most engineering management Programmes are geared for graduate studies. there are a few elite institutions that teach EM at the undergraduate level. Some of the ones that are accredited and/or recognized by ASEM include:

West Point (United States Military Academy). Norwich University. New York Institute of Technology. Stevens Institute of Technology. Rensselaer Polytechnic Institute. George Washington University. Arizona State University. Graduates of these Programmes regularly command nearly $65.000 their first year out of school.

Outside the USA. Istanbul Technical University Management Engineering Department offers an elite undergraduate degree in Management Engineering. attracting top students.

The University of Waterloo offers a 4-year undergraduate degree (5 years including co-op education) in the field of Management Engineering. This is the first Programme of its kind in Canada. In Peru. Pacifico University offers a 5-year undergraduate degree in this field. the first Programme in this country.

Graduate Degrees

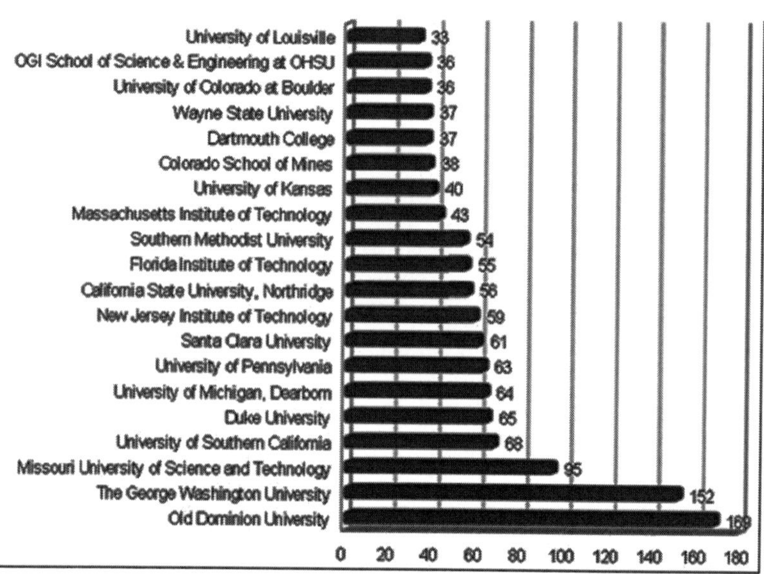

Missouri S&T is credited with awarding the first Ph.D. in Engineering Management in 1984. The National Institute of Industrial Engineering based in Mumbai has been awarding degrees in the field of Post Graduate Diploma in Industrial Engineering since 1973 and the Fellowship (Doctoral) degrees have been awarded since 2008. Massachusetts Institute of Technology offers a Master in System Design and Management. which is a member of the Consortium of Engineering Management.

Students in the University of Kansas' Engineering Management Programme are practicing professionals employed by over 100 businesses. manufacturing. government or consulting firms. There are over 200 actively enrolled students in the Programme and approximately 500 alumni.

Istanbul Technical University Management Engineering Department offers a graduate degree. and a Ph.D. degree in Management Engineering.

According to the American Society for Engineering Education (ASEE) PRISM Magazine (March 2008) the largest Master's of Engineering Management (MEM) Programmes (in terms of degrees awarded for 2005 -2006) are shown in the following chart.

CONSULTING

As engineering firms are usually small partnerships. they cannot afford in-house management. therefore giving rise to the need for engineering management consultancy. It involves providing management consulting advice that is specific to engineering. Indifferent from the traditional focus of the. A T Kearney.Boston Consulting Group andMcKinsey. science and engineering requires a particularly holistic approach involving art and science. There are many branches of engineering management consultancy (commerce). including law. accounting. human resources. marketing. politics. economics. finance. public affairs. and communication. Commonly. engineering management consultants are also used when firms require special technical knowledge. though many prefer to use engineering educational consultants for such a task. to upgrade organizational knowledge and in able to keep the intellectual property confidential. Though many firms opt to use traditional management consulting firms. many lack the know-how to tailor the traditional theories to accommodate technical workers.

Engineering management consulting is concerned with the development. improvement. implementation and evaluation of integrated systems of people. money. knowledge. information. equipment. energy. materials and/or processes. Consultants strive to improve upon existing processes. products or systems. Engineering management consulting draws upon the principles and methods of engineering analysis and synthesis. as well as the mathematical. physical and social sciences together with the principles and methods of engineering design to specify. predict. and evaluate the results to be obtained from such systems or processes. Engineering management consulting puts a focus on the social impact of the product. process or system that is being analyzed.

Examples of where engineering management consulting might be used include designing an assembly workstation. strategizing for various operational logistics. consulting as an efficiency expert. developing a new financial algorithm or loan system for a bank. streamlining operation and emergency room location or usage in a hospital. planning complex distribution schemes for materials or products (referred to as Supply Chain Management). and shortening lines (or queues) at a bank. hospital. or a theme park. Management engineering consultants typically use computer simulation (especially discrete event simulation). along with extensive mathematical tools and modeling and computational methods for system analysis. evaluation. and optimization.

PROFESSIONAL ORGANIZATIONS

There are a number of societies and organizations dedicated to the field of engineering management. One of the largest societies is a division of IEEE. the Engineering Management Society. which regularly publishes a trade magazine. Another prominent professional organization in the field is the American Society of Engineering Management (ASEM). which was founded in 1979 by a group of 20 engineering managers from industry. ASEM currently certifies engineering managers (two levels) via the Associate Engineering Manager (AEM) or Professional Engineering Manager (PEM) certification exam. The Master of Engineering Management Programmes Consortium is a newly formed consortium of prominent universities intended to raise the value and visibility of the MEM degree. Also. engineering management university Programmes have the possibility of being accredited by ABET or ATMAE. In Canada. the Canadian Society for Engineering Management (CSEM) is a constituent society of the Engineering Institute of Canada (EIC). Canada's oldest learned engineering society.

MANUFACTURING

Manufacturing is the production of merchandise for use or sale using Labour and machines. tools. chemical and biological processing. or formulation. The term may refer to a range of human activity. from handicraft to high tech. but is most commonly applied to industrial production. in which raw materials are transformed into finished goods on a large scale. Such finished goods may be used for manufacturing other. more complex products. such as aircraft. household appliances or automobiles. or sold towholesalers. who in turn sell them to retailers. who then sell them to end users – the "consumers".

Manufacturing takes turns under all types of economic systems. In a free market economy. manufacturing is usually directed Towards the mass production of products for sale to consumers at a profit. In a collectivist economy. manufacturing is more frequently directed by the state to supply a centrally planned economy. In mixed market economies. manufacturing occurs under some degree of government regulation.

Modern manufacturing includes all intermediate processes required for the production and integration of a product's components. Some industries. such as semiconductor and steel manufacturers use the term *fabrication* instead.

The manufacturing sector is closely connected with engineering and industrial design. Examples of major manufacturers in North America include

General Motors Corporation. General Electric. Procter and Gamble. General Dynamics. Boeing. Pfizer. and Precision Castparts. Examples in Europe include Volkswagen Group. Siemens. and Michelin. Examples in Asia include Toyota. Samsung. and Bridgestone.

HISTORY AND DEVELOPMENT

- In its earliest form. manufacturing was usually carried out by a single skilled artisan with assistants. Training was by apprenticeship. In much of the pre-industrial world. theguild system protected the privileges and trade secrets of urban artisans.
- Before the Industrial Revolution. most manufacturing occurred in rural areas. where household-based manufacturing served as a supplemental subsistence strategy toagriculture (and continues to do so in places). Entrepreneurs organized a number of manufacturing households into a single enterprise through the putting-out system.
- Toll manufacturing is an arrangement whereby a first firm with specialized equipment processes raw materials or semi-finished goods for a second firm.

Fig. Assembly of Section 41 of a Boeing 787 Dreamliner

INDUSTRIAL POLICY

Economics of manufacturing

According to some economists. manufacturing is a wealth-producing sector of an economy. whereas a service sector tends to be wealth-consuming. Emerging technologieshave provided some new growth in advanced manufacturing employment opportunities in the Manufacturing Belt in the United States. Manufacturing provides important material support for national infrastructure and for national Defence.

On the other hand. most manufacturing may involve significant social and environmental costs. The clean-up costs of hazardous waste. for example. may outweigh the benefits of a product that creates it. Hazardous materials may expose workers to health risks. These costs are now well known and there is effort to address them by improvingefficiency. reducing waste. using industrial symbiosis. and eliminating harmful chemicals. The increased use of technologies such as 3D printing also offer the potential to reduce the environmental impact of producing finished goods through distributed manufacturing.

The negative costs of manufacturing can also be addressed legally. Developed countries regulate manufacturing activity with Labour laws and environmental laws.

Across the globe. manufacturers can be subject to regulations and pollution taxes to offset the environmental costs of manufacturing activities. Labour unions and craft guilds have played a historic role in the negotiation of worker rights and wages. Environment laws and Labour protections that are available in developed nations may not be available in the third world.Tort law and product liability impose additional costs on manufacturing. These are significant dynamics in the on-going process. occurring over the last few decades. of manufacture-based industries relocating operations to "developing-world" economies where the costs of production are significantly lower than in "developed-world" economies.

Manufacturing and investment

Surveys and analyses of trends and issues in manufacturing and investment around the world focus on such things as:

- The nature and sources of the considerable variations that occur cross-nationally in levels of manufacturing and wider industrial-economic growth;
- Competitiveness; and
- Attractiveness to foreign direct.

In addition to general overviews. researchers have examined the features and factors affecting particular key aspects of manufacturing development. They have compared production and investment in a range of Western and non-Western countries and presented case studies of growth and performance in important individual industries and market-economic sectors.

On June 26. 2009. Jeff Immelt. the CEO of General Electric. called for the United States to increase its manufacturing base employment to 20% of the workforce. commenting that the U.S. has outsourced too much in some areas and can no longer rely on the financial sector and consumer spending to drive demand. Further. while U.S. manufacturing performs well compared to the rest of the U.S. economy. research shows that it performs poorly compared to manufacturing in other high-wage countries. A total of 3.2 million – one in six U.S. manufacturing jobs – have disappeared between 2000 and 2007. In the UK. EEF the manufacturers organisation has led calls for the UK economy to be rebalanced to rely less on financial services and has actively promoted the manufacturing agenda.

MANUFACTURING PROCESS MANAGEMENT

Manufacturing process management (MPM) is a collection of technologies and methods used to define how products are to be manufactured. MPM differs from ERP/MRPwhich is used to plan the ordering of materials and other resources. set manufacturing schedules. and compile cost data.

A cornerstone of MPM is the central repository for the integration of all these tools and activities aids in the exploration of alternative production line scenarios; making assembly lines more efficient with the aim of reduced lead time to product launch. shorter product times and reduced work in progress (WIP) inventories as well as allowing rapid response to product or product changes.

DESIGN ENGINEER

Design Engineer is a general term that covers multiple engineering disciplines including electrical. mechanical. chemical engineer. aeronautical engineer. civil. and structural/building/architectural engineers. The uniting concept is a focus on applying the 'engineering design process. *in which engineers develop new products or processes with a primary emphasis on functional utility.*

While industrial designers may be responsible for the conceptual aesthetic and ergonomic aspects of a design. the design engineer usually works with a team of engineers and other designers to develop conceptual and detailed designs. They may work with industrial designers and marketers to develop the product concept and specifications. and may direct the design effort. In many engineering areas. a distinction is made between the design engineer and the planning engineer in design; Analysis is important for planning engineers. while synthesis is more paramount for design engineers. Test engineers are also sometimes contrasted from design engineers. as test engineers tend to focus more on the evaluation and analysis of prototypes (rather than their conception).

When the design involves public safety. the design engineer is usually required to be licensed. for example a Professional Engineer in the U.S and Canada. There is usually an 'industrial exemption' for design engineers working on project internal to companies and not delivering professional services directly to the public.

DESIGN ENGINEER TASKS

They may work in a team along with industrial designers to create the drawings necessary for prototyping and production. or in the case of buildings. for construction. However. with the advent of CAD and solid modeling software (PTC Creo. SolidWorks. SpaceClaim. Solid Edge. KeyCreator Autodesk Inventor. boss. NX. CATIA. etc.. for example) the design engineers may create the drawings themselves.

The next responsibility of many design engineers is prototyping. A model of the product is created and reviewed. Prototypes are either functional or non-functional. Functional "alpha" prototypes are used for testing and the non-functional are used for form and fit checking. Virtual prototyping software like Ansys or Comsol may also be used. This stage is where design flaws are found and corrected. and tooling. manufacturing fixtures. and packaging are developed.

Once the "alpha" prototype is finalized. after many iterations. the next step is the "beta" pre-production prototype. The design engineer. working with a industrial engineer andmanufacturing engineer and a quality engineer reviews an initial run of components and assemblies for design compliance and fabrication/manufacturing methods analysis. This is often determined through statistical process control. Variations in the product are correlated to aspects of the process and eliminated. The most common metric used is theprocess capability index C_{pk}. A C_{pk} of 1.0 is considered the baseline acceptance for full production go-ahead.

The design engineer may follow the product and make requested changes and corrections throughout the life of the product. This is referred to as "cradle to grave" engineering.The design process is an information intensive one and design engineers have been found to spend 56% of their time engaged in various information behaviours. including 14% actively searching for information. Furthermore. in addition to design engineers' core technical competence. research has also demonstrated the critical nature of their personal attributes. project management skills. and cognitive abilities to succeed in the role.

Amongst other more detailed findings. a recent work sampling study found that design engineers spend 62.92% of their time engaged in technical work. 40.37% in social work. and 49.66% in computer-based work. Furthermore. there was considerable overlap between these different types of work. with engineers spending 24.96% of their time engaged in technical and social work. 37.97% in technical and non-social. 15.42% in non-technical and social. and 21.66% in non-technical and non-social.

DECISION ENGINEERING

Decision engineering (more recently called Decision Intelligence by The Decision Intelligence Institute International and companies like Quantellia) is a framework that unifies a number of best practices for organizational decision making. It is based on the recognition that. in many organizations. decision making could be improved if a more structured approach were used. Decision engineering seeks to overcome a decision making "complexity ceiling". which is characterized by a mismatch between the sophistication of organizational decision making practices and the complexity of situations in which those decisions must be made. As such. it seeks to solve some of the issues identified around complexity theory and organizations. In this sense. decision engineering represents a practical application of the field of complex systems. which helps organizations to navigate the complex systems in which they find themselves. Decision engineering can also be thought of as a framework that brings advanced analytics techniques to the desktop of the non-expert decision maker. as well as incorporating. and then extending. inductive reasoning and machine learning techniques to overcome the problems articulated inBlack swan theory.Decision engineering proponents believe that many organizations continue to make poor decisions. In response. decision engineering seeks to unify a number of decision making best practices.

Decision engineering builds on the insight that it is possible to *design* the decision itself. using principles previously used for designing more tangible objects like bridges and buildings.The use of a *visual* design language representing decisions is an important element of decision engineering. since it provides an intuitive common language readily understood by all decision participants. A visual metaphor improves the ability to reason about complex systems as well as to enhance collaboration.In addition to visual decision design. there are other two aspects of engineering disciplines that aid mass adoption. These are: 1) the creation of a shared language of design elements and 2) the use of a common methodology or process.

MOTIVATION

The need for a unified methodology of decision making is driven by a number of factors that organizations face as they make difficult decisions in a complex internal and external environment.Recognition of the broad-based inability of current methods to solve decision making issues in practice comes from several sources. including government sources and industries such as telecommunications. media. the automotive industry. and pharmaceuticals.

Examples:

- The *outcomes* of decisions are becoming more complex. going well beyond next quarter's revenues or other tangible outcomes to multiple goals that must be satisfied together. some of which are often intangible:

The car is becoming an expression of identity. values. and personal control in ways that move far beyond traditional segmentation and branding. For example. fuel efficiency will be only one consideration for a socially responsible vehicle (SRV). What percent of the parts are recyclable? What is the vehicle's total carbon footprint? Are there child Labour inputs? Toxic paints. glues. or plastics? How transparent is the supply chain? Is the seller accountable for recycling? What methods are used? Are fair Labour practices employed?

— Shoshana Zuboff. *The GM Solution: Life Boats. Not Life Support. Business Week. November 18. 2008*

- Global increase in complexity:

We live in a dynamic world in which the pace. scope. and complexity of change are increasing. The continued march of globalization. the growing number of independent actors. and advancing technology have increased global connectivity. interdependence and complexity. creating greater uncertainties. systemic risk and a less predictable future. These changes have led to reduced warning times and compressed decision cycles.

— Director of National Intelligence. *Vision 2015: A Globally Networked and Integrated Intelligence Enterprise*

TRANSFERRING ENGINEERING PRINCIPLES

Unlike other decision making tools and methodologies. decision engineering seeks to bring to bear a number of engineering practices to the process of creating a decision. These include requirements analysis. specification. scenario planning. quality assurance. security. and the use of design principles. During the decision execution phase. outputs produced during the design phase can be used in a number of ways; monitoring approaches like business dashboards and assumption based planningare used to track the outcome of a decision and to trigger replanning as appropriate. One view of how some of these elements combine is shown in the diagram at the start of this article.

Decision engineering has the potential to improve the quality of decisions made. the ability to make them more quickly. the ability to align organizational resources more effectively around a change in decisions. and lowers the risks associated with decisions. Furthermore. a designed decision can be reused and modified as new information is obtained.

BRINGING NUMERICAL METHODS TO THE DESKTOP

Although many elements of decision engineering. such as Sensitivity analysis and analytics are mature disciplines. they are not in wide use by decision makers. Decision engineering seeks to create a visual language that serves to facilitate communication between them and quantitative experts. allowing broader utilization of these and other numerical and technical approaches. In particular. dependency links in a decision model represent cause-and-effect (as in a causal loop diagram). data flow (as in a data flow diagram). or other relationships. As an example. one link might represent the connection between "mean time to repair a problem with telephone service" and "customer satisfaction". where a short repair time would presumably raise customer satisfaction. The functional form of these dependencies can be determined by a number of approaches. Numerical approaches. which analyze data to determine these functions. include machine learning and analytics algorithms (including artificial neural networks). as well as more traditional regression analysis. Results fromoperations research and many other quantitative approaches have a similar role to play.

When data is not available (or is too noisy. uncertain. or incomplete). these dependency links can take on the form of rules as might be found in an expert system or rule-based system. and so can be obtained through knowledge engineering. In this way. a decision model represents a mechanism for combining multiple relationships. as well as symbolic and subsymbolic reasoning. into a complete solution to determining the outcome of a practical decision.

ORIGINS

It is interesting to note that. despite decades of development of decision support system and methodologies (like decision analysis). these are still less popular thanspreadsheets as primary tools for decision making. Decision engineering seeks to bridge this gap. creating a critical mass of users of a common methodology and language for the core entities included in a decision. such as assumptions. external values. facts. data. and conclusions. If a pattern from previous industries holds. such a methodology will also facilitate technology adoption. by clarifying common maturity models and road maps that can be shared from one organization to another.

The decision engineering approach is multidisciplinary. unifying findings on cognitive bias and decision making. situational awareness. critical and creative thinking. collaboration and organizational design. with engineering technologies.

Decision engineering is considered an improvement upon current organizational decision making practices. which include the use of spreadsheets. text (sequential in nature. so is not a good fit for how information flows through a decision structure). and verbal argument. The movement from these largely informal structures to one in which a decision is documented in a well understood. visual language. echoes the creation of common blueprint methodologies in construction. with promise of similar benefits.

Decision engineering is both a very new and also a very old discipline. Many of its elements—such as the language of assessing assumptions. using logic to support an argument. the necessity of critical thinking to evaluate a decision. and understanding the impacts of bias—are ancient. Yet the realization that these elements can form a coherent whole that provides significant benefits to organizations by focusing on a common methodology is relatively new.

VISUAL DECISION DESIGN

Because it makes visible the otherwise invisible reasoning structures used in complex decisions. the design aspect of decision engineering draws from other conceptual representation technologies like mind mapping. conceptual graphs. and semantic networks.The basic idea is that a visual metaphor enhances intuitive thinking. inductive reasoning. and pattern recognition—important cognitive skills usually less accessible in a verbal or text discussion. A business decision map can be seen as one approach to a formal decision language to support decision engineering.

MANAGEMENT CONSULTING

Management consulting. the practice of helping organizations to improve their performance. operates primarily through the analysis of existing organizational problems and the development of plans for improvement. Organizations may draw upon the services of management consultants for a number of reasons. including gaining external (and presumably objective) advice and access to the consultants' specialized expertise.

As a result of their exposure to and relationships with numerous organizations. consulting firms are also said to be aware of industry "best practices". although the specific nature of situations under consideration may limit the transferability of such practices from one organization to another.

Consultancies may also provide organizational change management assistance. development of coaching skills. process analysis. technology implementation. strategydevelopment. or operational improvement services. Management consultants often bring their own proprietary methodologies or frameworks to guide the identification of problems and to serve as the basis for recommendations for more effective or efficient ways of performing work tasks.

HISTORY

Management consulting grew with the rise of management as a unique field of study. The first management consulting firm was Arthur D. Little Inc.. founded in 1886 as a partnership. and later incorporated in 1909. Though Arthur D. Little later became a general management consultancy. it originally specialised in technical research.

As Arthur D. Little focused on technical research for the first few years. probably the first real management consulting organization was that started by Frederick Winslow Taylor. who in 1893 opened an independent consulting practice in Philadelphia. His business card read "Consulting Engineer - Systematizing Shop Management and Manufacturing Costs a Specialty". By inventing Scientific Management. also known as Taylor's method. Frederick Winslow Taylor invented the first method of organizing work. spawning the careers of many more management consultants. One of Taylor's early collaborators. Morris Llewellyn Cooke. for example. opened his own management consultancy in 1905. Taylor's method was used worldwide until industry switched to a method invented by W. Edwards Deming.

Booz Allen Hamilton was founded by Edwin G. Booz. a graduate of the Kellogg School of Management at Northwestern University. in 1914 as a management consultancy and the first to serve both industry and government clients. In 1926. James O. McKinsey. professor of Managerial Accounting at the University of Chicago Booth School of Business. founded McKinsey.

The initial period of growth in the consulting industry was triggered by the Glass-Steagall Banking Act in the 1930s. and was driven by demand for advice on finance. strategy. and organization. From the 1950s onwards consultancies not only expanded their activities considerably in the United States but also opened offices in Europe and later in Asia and South America. After World War II. a number of new management consulting firms formed. bringing a rigorous analytical approach to the study of management and strategy. Work carried out at McKinsey. Boston Consulting Group. AT Kearney. Booz Allen Hamilton. and the Harvard Business School during the 1960s and 1970s developed the tools and approaches that would define the new field of strategic management. setting the groundwork for many consulting firms to follow. In 1983. Harvard Business School's influence on the industry continued with the founding of the now defunct Monitor Group by six professors.

The industry experienced significant growth in the 1980s and 1990s. gaining considerable importance in relation to national gross domestic product. In 1980 there were only five consulting firms with more than 1.000 consultants worldwide. whereas by the 1990s there were more than thirty firms of this size. An earlier wave of growth in the early 1980s was driven by demand for strategy and organization consultancies. The wave of growth in the 1990s was driven by both strategy and information technology advice. In the second half of the 1980s the big accounting firms entered the IT consulting segment. The then Big Eight. now Big Four. accounting firms (PricewaterhouseCoopers; KPMG; Ernst and Young; Deloitte Touche Tohmatsu) had always offered advice in addition to their traditional services. but from the late 1980s onwards these activities became increasingly important in relation to the maturing market of accounting and auditing. By the mid-1990s these firms had outgrown those service providers focusing on corporate strategy and organization. While three of the Big Four legally divided the different service lines after the Enron scandals and the ensuing breakdown of Arthur Andersen. they are now back in the consulting business.

The industry stagnated in 2001 before recovering after 2003. with a current trend towards a clearer segmentation of management consulting firms. In recent years. management consulting firms actively recruit top graduates from Ivy League universities. Rhodes Scholars. and students from top MBA Programmes.

FUNCTION

The functions of consulting services are commonly broken down into eight task categories. Consultants can function as bridges for information and knowledge. and that external consultants can provide these bridging services more economically than client firms themselves. Marvin Bower. McKinsey's long-term director. has mentioned the benefits of a consultant's externality. that they have varied experience outside the client company.

Consultants have specialised skills on tasks that would involve high internal coordination costs for clients. such as organization-wide changes or the implementation of information technology. In addition. because of economies of scale. their focus and experience in gathering information worldwide and across industries renders their information search less costly than for clients.

APPROACHES

In general. various approaches to consulting can be thought of as lying somewhere along a continuum. with an 'expert' or prescriptive approach at one end. and a facilitative approach at the other. In the expert approach. the consultant takes the role of expert. and provides expert advice or assistance to the client. with. compared to the facilitative approach. less input from. and fewer collaborations with the client(s). With a facilitative approach. the consultant focuses less on specific or technical expert knowledge. and more on the *process* of consultation itself. Because of this focus on process. a facilitative approach is also often referred to as 'process consulting.' with Edgar Schein being considered the best-known practitioner.

Many consulting firms are organized in a structured matrix. where one 'axis' describes a business function or type of consulting: for example. strategy. operations. technology. executive leadership. process improvement. talent management. sales. etc. The second axis is an industry focus: for example. oil and gas. retail. automotive. Together. these form a matrix. with consultants occupying one or more 'cells' in the matrix. For example. one consultant may specialize in operations for the retail industry. and another may focus on process improvement in the downstream oil and gas industry.

Specialization

Management consulting refers generally to the provision of business services. but there are numerous specialties. such as information technology consulting. human resource consulting. virtual management consulting and others. many of which overlap. and most of which are offered by the larger diversified consultancies. So-called "boutique" consultancies. however. are smaller organizations focusing upon a few of such specialties.

The 1990s saw an increase in what has been termed a 'future-based' approach. This emphasised language and alignment of people within an organization to a common vision of the future of the organization. as set out in the book "Three Laws of Performance". The essential concept here was that the way people perform is seen to correlate to the way that world occurs for them. and that future-based language could alter the way the future actually occurs for them. These principles were increasingly employed in organizations that had experienced a market transition or a merger requiring the blending of two corporate cultures. However. towards the end of the 1990s the approach declined due to a perception that the concept outlined in this book did not in practice offer added value to organizations.

CURRENT STATE OF THE INDUSTRY

Management consulting has grown quickly. with growth rates of the industry exceeding 20% in the 1980s and 1990s. As a business service. consulting remains highly cyclical and linked to overall economic conditions. The consulting industry shrank during the 2001-2003 period. but grew steadily until the recent economic downturn in 2009. Since then the market has stabilised.Currently. there are three main types of consulting firms. Large. diversified organizations. Medium-sized management consultancies and boutique firms that have focused areas of consulting expertise in specific industries. functional areas. technologies. or regions of the world.

Revenue Model

Traditionally. the consulting industry charged on a time and materials basis. billing for staff consultants based upon the hours worked plus out-of-pocket expenses such as travel costs. During the late 1990s and early 2000s. there was a shift to more results-based pricing. either with fixed bids for defined deliverables or some form of results-based pricing in which the firm would be paid a fraction of the value delivered. The current trend seems to Favour a hybrid with components of fixed pricing and risk-sharing by both the consulting firm and client.

TRENDS

The use of management consultancy is becoming more prevalent in non-business fields including the public sector; as the need for professional and specialist support grows. other industries such as government. quasi-government and not-for-profit agencies are turning to the same managerial principles which have helped the private sector for years.An industry structural trend which arose in the early part of the 21st century was the spin-off or separation of the consulting and accounting units of the large diversified professional advisory firms most notably Deloitte.

Ernst and Young. PwC and KPMG. For these firms. which began operation as accounting and audit firms. management consulting was a new extension to their organization. But after a number of highly publicised scandals over accounting practices. such as the Enron scandal. these firms began divestiture of their management-consulting units. to more easily comply with the tighter regulatory scrutiny that followed. In some parts of the world. this trend is now being reversed where the firms are rapidly rebuilding their management consulting arms. as their corporate websites clearly demonstrate.

Rise of Internal Corporate Consulting Groups

Added to these approaches are corporations that set up their own internal consulting groups. hiring *internal management consultants* either from within the corporation or from external firms' employees. Many corporations have internal groups of as many as 25 to 30 full-time consultants.

Internal consulting groups are often formed around a number of practice areas. commonly including: organizational development. process management. information technology. design services. training. and development.

Advantages

There are several potential benefits to employing internal consultants:

- If properly managed and empowered. internal consulting groups evaluate engagement on projects in light of the corporation's strategic and tactical objectives.
- Often. the internal consultant requires less ramp up time on a project due to familiarity with the corporation. and is able to guide a project through to implementation — a step that would often be too costly if an external consultant were used.
- Internal relationship provides opportunities to keep certain corporate information private.
- It is likely that the time and materials cost of internal consultants is significantly less than external consultants operating in the same capacity.
- Internal consulting positions can be used to recruit and develop potential senior managers of the organization.

Note: Corporations need to be conscious of and consistent with how internal consultant costs are accounted for on both a project and organizational level to evaluate cost effectiveness.

- Internal consultants may be specifically suited to either:

1. Lead external consulting project teams. or
2. Act as organizational subject matter experts 'embedded' with external consulting teams under the direction of organizational management.

A group of internal consultants can closely monitor and work with external consulting firms. This would ensure better delivery. quality. and overall operating relationships. External firms providing consulting services have a dichotomy in priority. The health of the external firm is in aggregate more important than that of their client (though of course the health of their client can have a direct impact on their own health).

Disadvantages

- The internal consultant may not bring the objectivity to the consulting relationship that an external firm can.
- An internal consultant also may not bring to the table best practices from other corporations. A way to mitigate this issue is to recruit experience into the group and/or proactively provide diverse training to internal consultants.
- Internal consultants may face corporate politics just as any group in an organization.
- Where the consulting industry is strong and consulting compensation high. it can be difficult to recruit candidates.
- It is often difficult to accurately measure the true costs and benefits of an internal consulting group.
- When financial times get tough. internal consulting groups that have not effectively demonstrated economic value (costs vs. benefits) are likely to face size reductions or reassignment.
- Internal consultants are employees themselves. thus do not question their own job

GOVERNMENT CONSULTANTS

The use of management consulting in governments is widespread in many countries but can be subject to misunderstandings and resultant controversy.

United States

In the US. Computer Sciences Corporation's Federal Consulting Practice. Accenture. Booz Allen Hamilton. and Deloitte Consulting LLP. amongst others. have established a profile for consulting within government organizations and functions.

United Kingdom

In the UK. the use of external management consultants within government has sometimes been contentious due to perceptions of variable value for money. From 1997 to 2006. for instance. the UK government reportedly spent £20 billion on management consultants. raising questions in the House of Commons as to the returns upon such investment

The UK has also experimented with providing longer-term use of management consultancy techniques provided internally. particularly to the high-demand consultancy arenas of local government and the National Health Service; the Local Government Association's Improvement and Development Agency and the public health National Support Teams; both generated positive feedback at cost levels considered a fraction of what external commercial consultancy input would have incurred.

India

In India. NABARD Consultancy Services (NABCONS) provides consultancy services in the field of agriculture. rural development and management. It is the wholly owned subsidiary of National Bank for Agriculture and Rural Development (NABARD)which is the apex bank of the country with regard to agriculture and rural development. NABARD is owned by Government of India and Reserve Bank of India. Agriculture Finance Corporation Limited provides consultancy mainly to governments and related institutions.

Europe

European Standard EN 16114:2011 "Management consultancy services"

New Zealand

In New Zealand the Government's role in providing some infrastructure and services is greater than in some countries because of insufficient scale in the private sector. smaller capital markets and historic political support for government service provision. New Zealand governments do. however. hire in expertise to complement the advice of professional public servants. While management consultants contribute to policy and strategy development the Government tends to use management consultants for strategic review and for strategy execution. There is a distinction between management consultants (who generally provide advice and fixed deliverables. often for a fixed fee) and professional contractors (who work for an hourly or daily rate providing specialist services). Official figures from 2007 to 2009 show annual expenditure of about NZ$150 -NZ$180 Million by the NZ Government on consultants but this is understated. While multinational consultancy firms provide advice on major projects and in specialist areas the majority of management consultants providing advice to the New Zealand government are sole practitioners or members of small consultancy practices. The range of services provided is large covering change management. strategic review. project and programme management. procurement. organizational design. etc.

CRITICISM

Despite consistently growing revenues. management consultancy also consistently attracts a significant amount of criticism. both from clients as well as from management scholars.

Management consultants are sometimes criticized for overuse of buzzwords. reliance on and propagation of management fads. and a failure to develop plans that are executable by the client. A number of critical books about management consulting argue that the mismatch between management consulting advice and the ability of executives to actually create the change suggested results in substantial damages to existing businesses. In his book

Flawed Advice and the Management Trap. Chris Argyris believes that much of the advice given today has real merit. However. a close examination shows that most advice given today contains gaps and inconsistencies that may prevent positive outcomes in the future.

More disreputable consulting firms are sometimes accused of delivering empty promises. despite high fees. and charged with "stating the obvious" or lacking the experience upon which to base their advice. These consultants bring few innovations. instead offering generic and "prepackaged" strategies and plans that are irrelevant to the client's particular issue. They may fail to prioritise their responsibilities. placing their own firm's interests before those of the clients.

Another concern is the promise of consulting firms to deliver on the sustainability of results. At the end of an engagement between the client and consulting firms. there is often an expectation that the consultants will audit the project results for a period of time to ensure that their efforts are sustainable. Although sustainability is promoted by some consulting firms. it is difficult to implement because of the disconnect between the client and consulting firms after the project closes.

Further criticisms include: disassembly of the business (by firing employees) in a drive to cut costs. only providing analysis reports. junior consultants charging senior rates. reselling similar reports to multiple clients as "custom work". lack of innovation. overbilling for days not worked. speed at the cost of quality. unresponsive large firms and lack of (small) client focus. lack of clarity of deliverables in contracts. not customizing specific research report criteria and secrecy.

4

Manufacturing Engineering

INTRODUCTION

Manufacturing engineering is a discipline of engineering dealing with different manufacturing practices and includes the research. design and development of systems. processes. machines. tools and equipment. The manufacturing engineer's primary focus is to turn raw materials into a new or updated product in the most economic. efficient and effective way possible.

OVERVIEW

Manufacturing engineers develop and create physical artifacts. production processes. and technology. It is a very broad area which includes the design and development of products. The manufacturing engineering discipline has very strong overlaps with mechanical engineering. industrial engineering. electrical engineering. electronic engineering. computer science. materials management. andoperations management. Manufacturing engineers' success or failure directly impacts the advancement of technology and the spread of innovation. This field of manufacturing engineering emerged from tool and die discipline in the early 20th century. It expanded greatly from the 1960s when industrialized countries introduced factories with:

1. Numerical control machine tools and automated systems of production.
2. Advanced statistical methods of quality control: These factories were pioneered by the American electrical engineer William Edwards Deming. who was initially ignored by his home country. The same methods of quality control later turned Japanese factories into world leaders in cost-effectiveness and production quality.
3. Industrial robots on the factory floor. introduced in the late 1970s: These computer-controlled welding arms and grippers could perform simple tasks such as attaching a car door quickly and flawlessly 24 hours a day. This cut costs and improved production speed.

HISTORY

The history of manufacturing engineering can be traced to factories in the mid 19th century USA and 18th century UK. Although large home production sites and workshops were established in ancient China. ancient Rome and the Middle East. the Venice Arsenal provides one of the first examples of a factory in the modern sense of the word. Founded in 1104 in the Republic of Venice several hundred years before the Industrial Revolution. this factory mass-produced ships on assembly lines using manufactured parts. The Venice Arsenal apparently produced nearly one ship every day and. at its height. employed 16.000 people.

Many historians regard Matthew Boulton's Soho Manufactory (established in 1761 in Birmingham) as the first modern factory. Similar claims can be made for John Lombe's silk mill in Derby (1721). or Richard Arkwright's Cromford Mill (1771). The Cromford Mill was purpose-built to accommodate the equipment it held and to take the material through the various manufacturing processes.

One historian. Murno Gladst. contends that the first factory was in Potosí. The Potosi factory took advantage of the abundant silver that was mined nearby and processed silver ingot slugs into coins.

British colonies in the 19th century built factories simply as buildings where a large number of workers gathered to perform hand Labour. usually in textile production. This proved more efficient for the administration and distribution of materials to individual workers than earlier methods of manufacturing. such as cottage industries or the putting-out system.

Cotton mills used inventions such as the steam engine and the power loom to pioneer the industrial factories of the 19th century. where precision machine tools and replaceable parts allowed greater efficiency and less waste. This experience formed the basis for the later studies of manufacturing engineering. Between 1820 and 1850. non-mechanized factories supplanted traditional artisan shops as the predominant form of manufacturing institution.

Henry Ford further revolutionized the factory concept and thus manufacturing engineering in the early 20th century with the innovation of mass production. Highly specialized workers situated alongside a series of rolling ramps would build up a product such as (in Ford's case) an automobile. This concept dramatically decreased production costs for virtually all manufactured goods and brought about the age of consumerism.

Modern developments

Modern manufacturing engineering studies include all intermediate processes required for thc production and integration of a product's components. Some industries. such as semiconductor and steel manufacturers use the term "fabrication" for these processes.

Fig. KUKA industrial robots being used at a bakery for food production

Automation is used in different processes of manufacturing such as machining and welding. Automated manufacturing refers to the application of automation to produce goods in a factory.

The main advantages of automated manufacturing for the manufacturing process are realized with effective implementation of automation and include: higher consistency and quality. reduction of lead times. simplification of production. reduced handling. improved work flow. and improved worker morale.

Robotics is the application of mechatronics and automation to create robots. which are often used in manufacturing to perform tasks that are dangerous. unpleasant. or repetitive.

These robots may be of any shape and size. but all are preprogrammed and interact physically with the world. To create a robot. an engineer typically employs kinematics (to determine the robot's range of motion) and mechanics (to determine the stresses within the robot). Robots are used extensively in manufacturing engineering.

Robots allow businesses to save money on Labour. perform tasks that are either too dangerous or too precise for humans to perform economically. and to ensure better quality.

Many companies employ assembly lines of robots. and some factories are so robotized that they can run by themselves.

Outside the factory. robots have been employed in bomb disposal. space exploration. and many other fields. Robots are also sold for various residential applications.

EDUCATION

Certification Programmes in Manufacturing Engineering

Manufacturing engineers possess a bachelor's degree in engineering with a major in manufacturing engineering. The length of study for such a degree is usually four to five years followed by five more years of professional practice to qualify as a professional engineer.

Working as a manufacturing engineering technologist involves a more applications-oriented qualification path. Academic degrees for manufacturing engineers are usually the Bachelor of Engineering. [BE] or [BEng]. and the Bachelor of Science. [BS] or [BSc]. For manufacturing technologists the required degrees are Bachelor of Technology [B.TECH] or Bachelor of Applied Science [BASc] in Manufacturing. depending upon the university. Masters degrees in engineering manufacturing include Master of Engineering [ME] or [MEng] in Manufacturing.

Master of Science [M.Sc] in Manufacturing Management. Master of Science [M.Sc] in Industrial and Production Management. and Master of Science [M.Sc] as well as Master of Engineering [ME] in Design. which is a subdiscipline of manufacturing. Doctoral [PhD] or [DEng] level courses in manufacturing are also available depending on the university.

The undergraduate degree curriculum generally includes courses in physics. mathematics. computer science. project management. and specific topics in mechanical and manufacturing engineering. Initially such topics cover most. if not all. of the subdisciplines of manufacturing engineering. Students then choose to specialize in one or more subdisciplines towards the end of their degree work.

Syllabus

The foundational curriculum for a bachelor's degree in manufacturing engineering is very similar to that for mechanical engineering. and includes:

- Statics and dynamics
- Strength of materials and solid mechanics
- Instrumentation and measurement
- Applied thermodynamics. heat transfer. energy conversion. and HVAC
- Fluid mechanics and fluid dynamics
- Mechanism design (including kinematics and dynamics)
- Manufacturing technology or processes
- Hydraulics and pneumatics
- Mathematics - in particular. calculus. differential equations. statistics. and linear algebra.
- Engineering design and graphics
- Circuit Analysis
- Lean manufacturing
- Mechatronics and control theory
- Automation and reverse engineering
- Quality assurance and control

- Material science
- Drafting. CAD (including solid modeling). and CAM. etc.

A bachelor's degree in these two areas will typically differ only by a few specialized classes. although the mechanical engineering degree requires more mathematics expertise.

MANUFACTURING ENGINEERING CERTIFICATION

Certification and licensure:

In some countries. "professional engineer" is the term for registered or licensed engineers who are permitted to offer their professional services directly to the public.Professional Engineer. abbreviatied (PE - USA) or (PEng - Canada). is the designation for licensure in North America.

In order to qualify for this license. a candidate needs a bachelor's degree from an ABET recognized university in the USA. a passing score on a state examination. and four years of work experience usually gained via a structured internship. In the USA. more recent graduates have the option of dividing this licensure process into two segments.

The Fundamentals of Engineering (FE) exam is often taken immediately after graduation and the Principles and Practice of Engineering exam is taken after four years of working in a chosen engineering field.Society of Manufacturing Engineers (SME) certifications (USA):The SME administers qualifications specifically for the manufacturing industry.

These are not degree level qualifications and are not recognized at the professional engineering level. Qualified candidates for the Certified Manufacturing Technologist Certificate (CMfgT) must pass a three-hour. 130-question multiple-choice exam.

The exam covers math. manufacturing processes. manufacturing management. automation. and related subjects. Additionally. a candidate must have at least four years of combined education and manufacturing-related work experience.Certified Manufacturing Engineer (CMfgE) is an engineering qualification administered by the Society of Manufacturing Engineers. Dearborn. Michigan. USA.

Candidates qualifying for a Certified Manufacturing Engineer credential must pass a four-hour. 180 question multiple-choice exam which covers more in-depth topics than does the CMfgT exam. CMfgE candidates must also have eight years of combined education and manufacturing-related work experience. with a minimum of four years of work experience.

Certified Engineering Manager (CEM). The Certified Engineering Manager Certificate is also designed for engineers with eight years of combined education and manufacturing experience. The test is four hours long and has 160 multiple-choice questions. The CEM certification exam covers business processes. teamwork. responsibility. and other management-related categories.

MODERN TOOLS

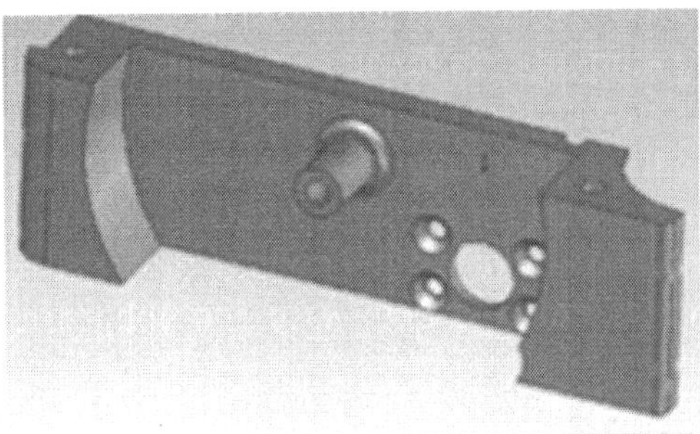

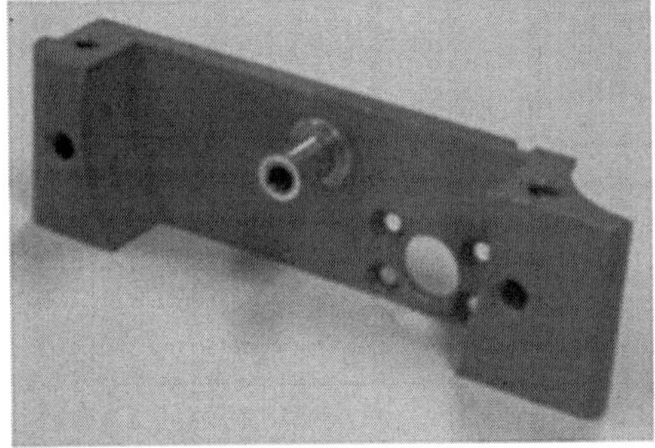

Fig. CAD model and CNC machined part

Many manufacturing companies. especially those in industrialized nations. have begun to incorporate computer-aided engineering (CAE) Programmes into their existing design and analysis processes. including 2D and 3D solid modeling computer-aided design (CAD).

This method has many benefits. including easier and more exhaustive visualization of products. the ability to create virtual assemblies of parts. and ease of use in designing mating interfaces and tolerances. Other CAE Programmes commonly used by product manufacturers include product life cycle management (PLM) tools and analysis tools used to perform complex simulations. Analysis tools may be used to predict product response to expected loads. including fatigue life and manufacturability.

These tools include finite element analysis (FEA). computational fluid dynamics (CFD). and computer-aided manufacturing (CAM).

Using CAE Programmes. a mechanical design team can quickly and cheaply iterate the design process to develop a product that better meets cost. performance. and other constraints. No physical prototype need be created until the design nears completion. allowing hundreds or thousands of designs to be evaluated. instead of relatively few.

In addition. CAE analysis Programmes can model complicated physical phenomena which cannot be solved by hand. such as viscoelasticity. complex contact between mating parts. or non-Newtonian flows.Just as manufacturing engineering is linked with other disciplines. such as mechatronics. multidisciplinary design optimization (MDO) is also being used with other CAE Programmes to automate and improve the iterative design process. MDO tools wrap around existing CAE processes. allowing product evaluation to continue even after the analyst goes home for the day.

They also utilize sophisticated optimization algorithms to more intelligently explore possible designs. often finding better. innovative solutions to difficult multidisciplinary design problems.

SUBDISCIPLINES

Mechanics

Mechanics. in the most general sense. is the study of forces and their effects on matter. Typically. engineering mechanics is used to analyze and predict the acceleration and deformation (both elastic and plastic) of objects under known forces (also called loads) or stresses. Subdisciplines of mechanics include:

- Statics. the study of non-moving bodies under known loads
- Dynamics (or kinetics). the study of how forces affect moving bodies
- Mechanics of materials. the study of how different materials deform under various types of stress
- Fluid mechanics. the study of how fluids react to forces
- Continuum mechanics. a method of applying mechanics that assumes that objects are continuous (rather than discrete)

If the engineering project were to design a vehicle. statics might be employed to design the frame of the vehicle in order to evaluate where the stresses will be most intense.

Dynamics might be used when designing the car's engine to evaluate the forces in the pistons and cams as the engine cycles. Mechanics of materials might be used to choose appropriate materials for the manufacture of the frame and engine. Fluid mechanics might be used to design a ventilation system for the vehicle or to design the intake system for the engine.

Kinematics

Kinematics is the study of the motion of bodies (objects) and systems (groups of objects). while ignoring the forces that cause the motion. The movement of a crane and the oscillations of a piston in an engine are both simple kinematic systems. The crane is a type of open kinematic chain. while the piston is part of a closed four-bar linkage. Engineers typically use kinematics in the design and analysis of mechanisms. Kinematics can be used to find the possible range of motion for a given mechanism. or. working in reverse. can be used to design a mechanism that has a desired range of motion.

Drafting

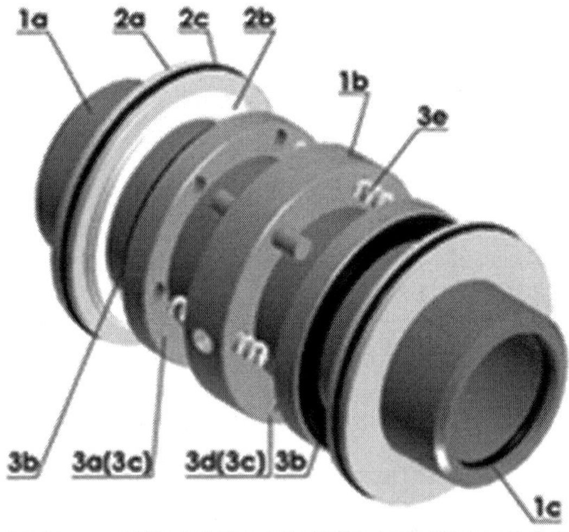

Fig. A CAD model of a mechanical double seal

Drafting or technical drawing is the means by which manufacturers create instructions for manufacturing parts. A technical drawing can be a computer model or hand-drawn schematic showing all the dimensions necessary to manufacture a part. as well as assembly notes. a list of required materials. and other pertinent information.

A U.S engineer or skilled worker who creates technical drawings may be referred to as a drafter or draftsman. Drafting has historically been a two-dimensional process. but computer-aided design (CAD) Programmes now allow the designer to create in three dimensions.

Instructions for manufacturing a part must be fed to the necessary machinery. either manually. through programmed instructions. or through the use of a computer-aided manufacturing (CAM) or combined CAD/CAM Programme.

Optionally. an engineer may also manually manufacture a part using the technical drawings. but this is becoming an increasing rarity with the advent of computer numerically controlled (CNC) manufacturing. Engineers primarily manufacture parts manually in the areas of applied spray coatings. finishes. and other processes that cannot economically or practically be done by a machine.

Drafting is used in nearly every subdiscipline of mechanical and manufacturing engineering. and by many other branches of engineering and architecture. Three-dimensional models created using CAD software are also commonly used in finite element analysis (FEA) andcomputational fluid dynamics (CFD).

Mechatronics

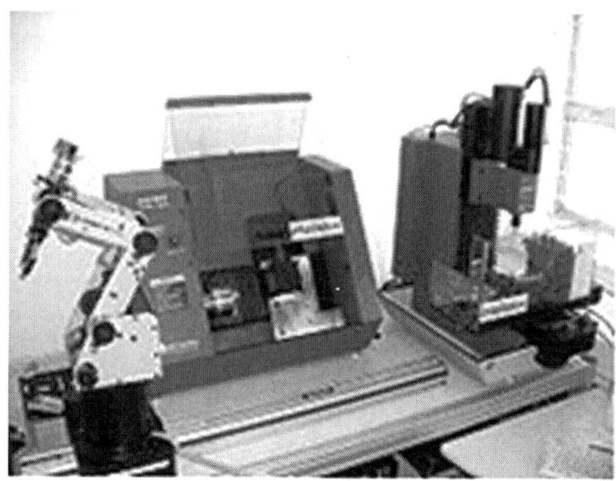

Fig. Training FMS with learning robotSCORBOT-ER 4u. workbench CNC mill and CNC lathe

Mechatronics is an engineering discipline that deals with the convergence of electrical. mechanical and manufacturing systems. Such combined systems are known as electromechanical systems and are widespread.

Examples include automated manufacturing systems. heating. ventilation and air-conditioning systems. and various aircraft and automobile subsystems.

The term mechatronics is typically used to refer to macroscopic systems. but futurists have predicted the emergence of very small electromechanical devices. Already such small devices. known as Microelectromechanical systems (MEMS). are used in automobiles to initiate the deployment of airbags. in digital projectors to create sharper images. and in inkjet printers to create nozzles for high-definition printing.

In the future it is hoped that such devices will be used in tiny implantable medical devices and to improve optical communication.

Textile engineering

Textile engineering courses deal with the application of scientific and engineering principles to the design and control of all aspects of Fibre. textile. and apparel processes. products. and machinery.

These include natural and man-made materials. interaction of materials with machines. safety and health. energy conservation. and waste and pollution control. Additionally. students are given experience in plant design and layout. machine and wet process design and improvement. and designing and creating textile products. Throughout the textile engineering curriculum. students take classes from other engineering and disciplines including: mechanical. chemical. materials and industrial engineering.

EMPLOYMENT

Manufacturing engineering is just one facet of the engineering industry. Manufacturing engineers enjoy improving the production process from start to finish. They have the ability to keep the whole production process in mind as they focus on a particular portion of the process. Successful students in manufacturing engineering degree Programmes are inspired by the notion of starting with a natural resource. such as a block of wood. and ending with a usable. valuable product. such as a desk. produced efficiently and economically. Manufacturing engineers are closely connected with engineering and industrial design efforts. Examples of major companies that employ manufacturing engineers in the United States include General Motors Corporation. Ford Motor Company. Chrysler. Boeing. Gates Corporation and Pfizer. Examples in Europe include Airbus. Daimler. BMW. Fiat.Navistar International. and Michelin Tyre.

FRONTIERS OF RESEARCH

Flexible manufacturing systems

Fig. A typical FMS system

A flexible manufacturing system (FMS) is a manufacturing system in which there is some amount of flexibility that allows the system to react to changes. whether predicted or unpredicted. This flexibility is generally considered to fall into two categories. both of which have numerous subcategories. The first category. machine flexibility. covers the system's ability to be changed to produce new product types and the ability to change the order of operations executed on a part. The second category. called routing flexibility. consists of the ability to use multiple machines to perform the same operation on a part. as well as the system's ability to absorb large-scale changes. such as in volume. capacity. or capability.

Most FMS systems comprise three main systems. The work machines. which are often automated CNC machines. are connected by a material handling system to optimize parts flow. and to a central control computer. which controls material movements and machine flow. The main advantages of an FMS is its high flexibility in managing manufacturing resources like time and effort in order to manufacture a new product. The best application of an FMS is found in the production of small sets of products from a mass production.

Computer integrated manufacturing

Computer-integrated manufacturing (CIM) in engineering is a method of manufacturing in which the entire production process is controlled by computer. Traditionally separated process methods are joined through a computer by CIM. This integration allows the processes to exchange information and to initiate actions. Through this integration. manufacturing can be faster and less error-prone. although the main advantage is the ability to create automated manufacturing processes. Typically CIM relies on closed-loop control processes based on real-time input from sensors. It is also known as flexible design and manufacturing.

Friction stir welding

Fig. Close-up view of a friction stir weld tack tool

Friction stir welding was discovered in 1991 by The Welding Institute (TWI). This innovative steady state (non-fusion) welding technique joins previously un-weldable materials. including several aluminum alloys. It may play an important role in the future construction of airplanes. potentially replacing rivets. Current uses of this technology to date include: welding the seams of the aluminum main space shuttle external tank. the Orion Crew Vehicle test article. Boeing Delta II and Delta IV Expendable Launch Vehicles and the SpaceX Falcon 1 rocket; armor plating for amphibious assault ships; and welding the wings and fuselage panels of the new Eclipse 500 aircraft from Eclipse Aviation. among an increasingly growing range of uses.

Other areas of research are Product Design. MEMS (Micro-Electro-Mechanical Systems). Lean Manufacturing. Intelligent Manufacturing Systems. Green Manufacturing. Precision Engineering. Smart Materials. etc.

COMPUTER-INTEGRATED MANUFACTURING

Fig. Manufacturing Systems Integration Programme. NIST 2008.

Computer-integrated manufacturing (CIM) is the manufacturing approach of using computers to control the entire productionprocess. This integration allows individual processes to exchange information with each other and initiate actions. Through the integration of computers. manufacturing can be faster and less error-prone. although the main advantage is the ability to create automated manufacturing processes. Typically CIM relies on closed-loop control processes. based on real-time input from sensors. It is also known as *flexible design and manufacturing*.

OVERVIEW

The term "computer-integrated manufacturing" is both a method of manufacturing and the name of a computer-automated system in which individual engineering. production. marketing. and support functions of a manufacturing enterprise are organized. In a CIM system functional areas such as design. analysis. planning. purchasing. cost accounting. inventory control. and distribution are linked through the computer with factory floor functions such as materials handling and management. providing direct control and monitoring of all the operations.As a method of manufacturing. three components distinguish CIM from other manufacturing methodologies:

- Means for data storage. retrieval. manipulation and presentation;
- Mechanisms for sensing state and modifying processes;
- Algorithms for uniting the data processing component with the sensor/ modification component.

CIM is an example of the implementation of information and communication technologies (ICTs) in manufacturing.CIM implies that there are at least two computers exchanging information. *e.g.* the controller of an arm robot and a micro-controller of a CNC machine.Some factors involved when considering a CIM implementation are the production volume. the experience of the company or personnel to make the integration. the level of the integration into the product itself and the integration of the production processes. CIM is most useful where a high level of ICT is used in the company or facility. such as CAD/CAM systems. the availability of process planning and its data.

HISTORY

The idea of "digital manufacturing" was prominent the 1980s. when computer-integrated manufacturing was developed and promoted by machine tool manufacturers and theComputer and Automated Systems Association and Society of Manufacturing Engineers (CASA/SME).

"CIM is the integration of total manufacturing enterprise by using integrated systems and data communication coupled with new managerial philosophies that improve organizational and personnel efficiency." ERHUM

vComputer-integrated manufacturing topics

Key challenges

There are three major challenges to development of a smoothly operating computer-integrated manufacturing system:

- Integration of components from different suppliers: When different machines. such as CNC. conveyors and robots. are using different communications protocols (In the case of AGVs. even differing lengths of time for charging the batteries) may cause problems.
- Data integrity: The higher the degree of automation. the more critical is the integrity of the data used to control the machines. While the CIM system saves on Labour of operating the machines. it requires extra human Labour in ensuring that there are proper safeguards for the data signals that are used to control the machines.
- Process control: Computers may be used to *assist* the human operators of the manufacturing facility. but there must always be a competent engineer on hand to handle circumstances which could not be foreseen by the designers of the control software.

Subsystems in computer-integrated manufacturing

A computer-integrated manufacturing system is not the same as a *"lights-out" factory*. which would run completely independent of human intervention. although it is a big step in that direction. Part of the system involves flexible manufacturing. where the factory can be quickly modified to produce different products. or where the volume of products can be changed quickly with the aid of computers. Some or all of the following subsystems may be found in a CIM operation:

Computer-aided techniques:

- CAD (computer-aided design)
- CAE (computer-aided engineering)
- CAM (computer-aided manufacturing)
- CAPP (computer-aided process planning)
- CAQ (computer-aided quality assurance)
- PPC (production planning and control)
- ERP (enterprise resource planning)
- A business system integrated by a common database.

Devices and equipment required:

- CNC. Computer numerical controlled machine tools
- DNC. Direct numerical control machine tools
- PLCs. Programmable logic controllers
- Robotics
- Computers
- Software
- Controllers
- Networks
- Interfacing
- Monitoring equipment

Technologies:

- FMS. (flexible manufacturing system)
- ASRS. automated storage and retrieval system
- AGV. automated guided vehicle
- Robotics
- Automated conveyance systems

Others:

- Lean manufacturing

Cimosa

CIMOSA (Computer Integrated Manufacturing Open System Architecture). is a 1990s European proposal for an open system architecture for CIM developed by the AMICE Consortium as a series of ESPRIT projects. The goal of CIMOSA was "to help companies to manage change and integrate their facilities and operations to face world wide competition. It provides a consistent architectural framework for both enterprise modeling and enterprise integration as required in CIM environments".CIMOSA provides a solution for business integration with four types of products:

- The CIMOSA Enterprise Modeling Framework. which provides a reference architecture for enterprise architecture

- CIMOSA IIS. a standard for physical and application integration.
- CIMOSA Systems Life Cycle. is a life cycle model for CIM development and deployment.
- Inputs to standardization. basics for international standard development.

CIMOSA according to Vernadat (1996). coined the term business process and introduced the process-based approach for integrated enterprise modeling based on a cross-boundaries approach. which opposed to traditional function or activity-based approaches. With CIMOSA also the concept of an "Open System Architecture" (OSA) for CIM was introduced. which was designed to be vendor-independent. and constructed with standardised CIM modules. Here to the OSA is "described in terms of their function. information. resource. and organizational aspects. This should be designed with structured engineering methods and made operational in a modular and evolutionary architecture for operational use".

FLEXIBLE MANUFACTURING SYSTEM

Fig. A typical FMS.

A flexible manufacturing system (FMS) is a manufacturing system in which there is some amount of flexibility that allows the system to react in case of changes. whether predicted or unpredicted. This flexibility is generally considered to fall into two categories. which both contain numerous subcategories.

The first category. *machine flexibility*. covers the system's ability to be changed to produce new product types. and ability to change the order of operations executed on a part. The second category is called *routing flexibility*. which consists of the ability to use multiplemachines to perform the same operation on a part. as well as the system's ability to absorb large-scale changes. such as in volume. capacity. or capability.

Most FMS consist of three main systems. The work machines which are often automated CNC machines are connected by a material handling system to optimize parts flow and the central control computer which controls material movements and machine flow.The main advantages of an FMS is its high flexibility in managing manufacturing resources like time and effort in order to manufacture a new product. The best application of an FMS is found in the production of small sets of products like those from a mass production.

Advantages

- Reduced manufacturing cost
- Lower cost per unit produced.
- Greater labour productivity.
- Greater machine efficiency.
- Improved quality.
- Increased system reliability.
- Reduced parts inventories.
- Adaptability to CAD/CAM operations.
- Shorter lead times

Disadvantages

- Cost to implement.
- Substantial pre-planning
- Requirement of skilled labour
- Complicated system

Industrial FMS Communication

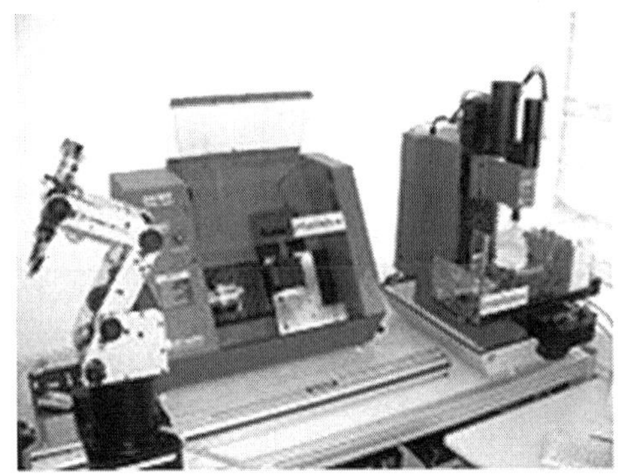

Fig. Training FMS with learning robotSCORBOT-ER 4u. workbench CNC Mill and CNC Lathe

An Industrial Flexible Manufacturing System (FMS) consists of robots. Computer-controlled Machines. Numerical controlled machines (CNC). instrumentation devices. computers. sensors. and other stand alone systems such as inspection machines. The use of robots in the production segment of manufacturing industries promises a variety of benefits ranging from high utilization to high volume of productivity. Each Robotic cell or node will be located along a material handling system such as a conveyor or automatic guided vehicle. The production of each part or work-piece will require a different combination of manufacturing nodes. The movement of parts from one node to another is done through the material handling system. At the end of part processing. the finished parts will be routed to an automatic inspection node. and subsequently unloaded from the Flexible Manufacturing System.

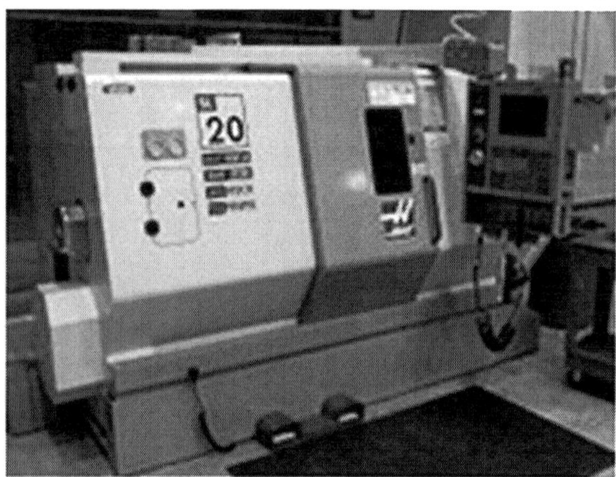

Fig. CNC machine

The FMS data traffic consists of large files and short messages. and mostly come from nodes. devices and instruments. The message size ranges between a few bytes to several hundreds of bytes. Executive software and other data. for example. are files with a large size. while messages for machining data. instrument to instrument communications. status monitoring. and data reporting are transmitted in small size.

There is also some variation on response time. Large Programme files from a main computer usually take about 60 seconds to be down loaded into each instrument or node at the beginning of FMS operation. Messages for instrument data need to be sent in a periodic time with deterministic time delay. Other types of messages used for emergency reporting are quite short in size and must be transmitted and received with an almost instantaneous response. The demands for reliable FMS protocol that support all the FMS data characteristics are now urgent. The existing IEEE standard protocols do not fully satisfy the real time communication requirements in this environment. The delay of CSMA/CD is unbounded as the number of nodes increases due to the message collisions. Token Bus has a deterministic message delay. but it does not support prioritized access scheme which is needed in FMS communications. Token Ring provides prioritized access and has a low message delay. however. its data transmission is unreliable. A single node failure which may occur quite often in FMS causes transmission errors of passing message in that node. In addition. the topology of Token Ring results in high wiring installation and cost.

A design of FMS communication protocol that supports a real time communication with bounded message delay and reacts promptly to any emergency signal is needed. Because of machine failure and malfunction due to heat. dust. and electromagnetic interference is common. a prioritized mechanism and immediate transmission of emergency messages are needed so that a suitable recovery procedure can be applied. A modification of standard Token Bus to implement a prioritized access scheme was proposed to allow transmission of short and periodic messages with a low delay compared to the one for long messages.

FLEXIBILITY

Flexibility in manufacturing means the ability to deal with slightly or greatly mixed parts. to allow variation in parts assembly and variations in process sequence. change the production volume and change the design of certain product being manufactured.

3D PRINTING

Fig. An ORDbot Quantum 3D printer

Fig. Timelapse video of a hyperboloidobject (designed by George W. Hart) made of PLA using a RepRap "Prusa Mendel" 3D printer for molten polymer deposition

3D printing or additive manufacturing (AM) refers to any of the various processes for printing a three-dimensional object. Primarily*additive processes* are used. in which successive layers of material are laid down under computer control. These objects can be of almost any shape or geometry. and are produced from a 3D model or other electronic data source. A 3D printer is a type of industrial robot.

HISTORY

Terminology and methods

Fig. CAD Model used for 3D Printing

Early AM equipment and materials were developed in the 1980s. In 1984. Chuck Hull of 3D Systems Corporation.invented a process known as stereolithography. in which layers are added by curing photopolymers with UV lasers. Hull defined the process as a "system for generating three-dimensional objects by creating a cross-sectional pattern of the object to be formed." He also developed the STL (STereoLithography) file format widely accepted by 3D printing software as well as the digital slicing and infill strategies common to many processes today. The term *3D printing* originally referred to a process employing standard and custom inkjet print heads. The technology used by most 3D printers to date—especially hobbyist and consumer-oriented models—is fused deposition modeling. a special application of plastic extrusion.AM processes for metal sintering or melting (such as selective laser sintering. direct metal laser sintering. and selective laser melting) usually went by their own individual names in the 1980s and 1990s.

Nearly all metalworking production at the time was by casting. fabrication. stamping. and machining; even though plenty of automation was applied to those technologies (such as by robot welding and CNC). the idea of a tool or head moving through a 3D work envelope transforming a mass of raw material into a desired shape layer by layer was associated by most people only with processes that removed metal (rather than adding it). such as CNC milling. CNC EDM. and many others.

The umbrella term *additive manufacturing* gained wider currency in the decade of the 2000s as the various additive processes matured and it became clear that soon metal removal would no longer be the sole occupant of the aforementioned paradigm.

It was during this decade that the term *subtractive manufacturing* appeared as a retronym for the large family of machining processes with metal removal as their common theme. However. at the time. the term *3D printing* still referred only to the polymer technologies in most minds. and the term *AM* was likelier to be used in metalworking contexts than among polymer/inkjet/stereolithography enthusiasts. By the early 2010s. the terms *3D printing* and *additive manufacturing* developed senses in which they were synonymous umbrella terms for all AM technologies.

Although this was a departure from their earlier technically narrower senses. it reflects the simple fact that the technologies all share the common theme of sequential-layer material addition/joining throughout a 3D work envelope under automated control. (Other terms that have appeared. which are usually used as AM synonyms (although sometimes ashypernyms). have been *desktop manufacturing*. *rapid manufacturing* [as the logical production-level successor to *rapid prototyping*]. and *on-demand manufacturing* [which echoes *on-demand printing* in the 2D sense of *printing*].)

The 2010s were the first decade in which metal parts such as engine brackets and large nuts would be grown (either before or instead of machining) in job production rather than obligately being machined from bar stock or plate. The term *subtractive* has not replaced the term*machining*. instead complementing it when a term that covers any removal method is needed.

Applications

Fig. Model of a turbine showing the benefits of 3d printing in industry

AM technologies found applications starting in the 1980s in product development. data visualization. rapid prototyping. and specialized manufacturing. Their expansion into production (job production. mass production. and distributed manufacturing) has been under development in the decades since. Industrial production roles within the metalworking industries achieved significant scale for the first time in the early 2010s. Since the start of the 21st century there has been a large growth in the sales of AM machines. and their price has dropped substantially. According to Wohlers Associates. a consultancy. the market for 3D printers and services was worth $2.2 billion worldwide in 2012. up 29% from 2011. There are many applications for AM technologies. including architecture. construction (AEC). industrial design. automotive. aerospace. military.engineering. dental and medical industries. biotech (human tissue replacement). fashion. footwear. jewelry. eyewear. education. geographic information systems. food. and many other fields.

In 2005. a rapidly expanding hobbyist and home-use market was established with the inauguration of the open-sourceRepRap and Fab@Home projects. Virtually all home-use 3D printers released to-date have their technical roots in the on-going RepRap Project and associated open-source software initiatives. In distributed manufacturing. one study has found that 3D printing could become a mass market product enabling consumers to save money associated with purchasing common household objects. For example. instead of going to a store to buy an object made in a factory byinjection molding (such as a measuring cup or a funnel). a person might instead print it at home from a downloaded 3D model.

GENERAL PRINCIPLES

Modeling

Main article: 3D modeling3D printable models may be created with a computer aided design package or via 3D scanner. The manual modeling process of preparing geometric data for 3D computer graphics is similar to plastic arts such as sculpting. 3D scanning is a process of analysing and collecting digital data on the shape and appearance of a real object. Based on this data. three-dimensional models of the scanned object can then be produced.

Both manual and automatic creation of 3D printable models is difficult for average consumers. This is why several 3D printing marketplaces have emerged over the last years. Among the most popular are Shapeways. Thingiverse. MyMiniFactory andThreeding

Printing

Before printing a 3D model from an STL file. it must first be processed by a piece of software called a "slicer" which converts the model into a series of thin layers and produces a G-code file containing instructions tailored to a specific printer. Several open source slicer Programmes exist. including Skeinforge. Slic3r. KISSlicer. and Cura.The 3D printer follows the G-code instructions to lay down successive layers of liquid. powder. paper or sheet material to build the model from a series of cross sections. These layers. which correspond to the virtual cross sections from the CAD model. are joined or automatically fused to create the final shape. The primary advantage of this technique is its ability to create almost any shape or geometric feature.

Printer resolution describes layer thickness and X-Y resolution in dots per inch (dpi) or micrometres (μm). Typical layer thickness is around 100 μm (250 DPI). although some machines such as the *Objet Connex* series and 3D Systems' *ProJet* series can print layers as thin as 16 μm (1.600 DPI). X-Y resolution is comparable to that of laser printers. The particles (3D dots) are around 50 to 100 μm (510 to 250 DPI) in diameter. Construction of a model with contemporary methods can take anywhere from several hours to several days. depending on the method used and the size and complexity of the model. Additive systems can typically reduce this time to a few hours. although it varies widely depending on the type of machine used and the size and number of models being produced simultaneously.

Traditional techniques like injection moulding can be less expensive for manufacturing polymer products in high quantities. but additive manufacturing can be faster. more flexible and less expensive when producing relatively small quantities of parts. 3D printers give designers and concept development teams the ability to produce parts and concept models using a desktop size printer.

Finishing

Though the printer-produced resolution is sufficient for many applications. printing a slightly oversized version of the desired object in standard resolution and then removing material with a higher-resolution subtractive process can achieve greater precision. As with the LUMEX Avance-25 [3] and other machines slated for IMTS 2014 IMTS Press Release | International Manufacturing Technology Show

PROCESSES

Fig. The Audi RSQ was made with rapid prototyping industrial KUKA robots

Some additive manufacturing techniques are capable of using multiple materials in the course of constructing parts. Some are able to print in multiple colours and Colour combinations simultaneously. Some also utilise supports when building. Supports are removable or dissolvable upon completion of the print. and are used to support overhanging features during construction.

Several different 3D printing processes have been invented since the late 1970s. The printers were originally large. expensive. and highly limited in what they could produce.

A large number of additive processes are now available. The main differences between processes are in the way layers are deposited to create parts and in the materials that are used. Some methods melt or soften material to produce the layers. *e.g.* selective laser melting(SLM) or direct metal laser sintering (DMLS). selective laser sintering (SLS). fused deposition modeling (FDM). while others cure liquid materials using different sophisticated technologies. *e.g.* stereolithography (SLA). With laminated object manufacturing (LOM). thin layers are cut to shape and joined together (*e.g.* paper. polymer. metal).

Each method has its own advantages and drawbacks. which is why some companies consequently offer a choice between powder and polymer for the material used to build the object. Other companies sometimes use standard. off-the-shelf business paper as the build material to produce a durable prototype. The main considerations in choosing a machine are generally speed. cost of the 3D printer. cost of the printed prototype. cost and choice of materials. and Colour capabilities.

SEMICONDUCTOR DEVICE FABRICATION

Semiconductor device fabrication is the process used to create the integrated circuits that are present in everyday electrical and electronic devices. It is a multiple-step sequence of photolithographic and chemical processing steps during which electronic circuits are gradually created on a wafer made of pure semiconducting material. Silicon is almost always used. but various compound semiconductors are used for specialized applications.

The entire manufacturing process. from start to packaged chips ready for shipment. takes six to eight weeks and is performed in highly specialized facilities referred to as fabs.

HISTORY

When feature widths were far greater than about 10 micrometres. purity was not the issue that it is today in device manufacturing. As devices became more integrated. cleanrooms became even cleaner. Today. the fabs are pressurized with filtered air to remove even the smallest particles. which could come to rest on the wafers and contribute to defects. The workers in a semiconductor fabrication facility are required to wear cleanroom suits to protect the devices from human contamination.

Semiconductor device manufacturing has spread from Texas and California in the 1960s to the rest of the world. includingEurope. the Middle East. and Asia. It is a global business today.

The leading semiconductor manufacturers typically have facilities all over the world. Intel. the world's largest manufacturer. has facilities in Europe and Asia as well as the U.S. Other top manufacturers include Taiwan Semiconductor Manufacturing Company (Taiwan).

United Microelectronics Corporation (Taiwan).STMicroelectronics (Europe). Analog Devices (US). Integrated Device Technology (US). Atmel (US/ Europe). Freescale Semiconductor(US). Samsung (Korea). Texas Instruments (US). IBM (US). GlobalFoundries (Germany. Singapore. US). Toshiba (Japan). NEC Electronics (Japan). Infineon (Europe. US. Asia). Renesas (Japan). Fujitsu (Japan/US). NXP Semiconductors (Europe and US). Micron Technology (US). Hynix (Korea). and SMIC (China).

WAFERS

A typical wafer is made out of extremely pure silicon that is grown into mono-crystalline cylindrical ingots (boules) up to 300 mm (slightly less than 12 inches) in diameter using the Czochralski process. These ingots are then sliced into wafers about 0.75 mm thick and polished to obtain a very regular and flat surface.

PROCESSING

In semiconductor device fabrication. the various processing steps fall into four general categories: deposition. removal. patterning. and modification of electrical properties.

- *Deposition* is any process that grows. coats. or otherwise transfers a material onto the wafer. Available technologies include physical vapor deposition (PVD). chemical vapor deposition (CVD). electrochemical deposition (ECD). molecular beam epitaxy (MBE) and more recently. atomic layer deposition (ALD) among others.
- *Removal* is any process that removes material from the wafer; examples include etch processes (either wet or dry) and chemical-mechanical planarization (CMP).
- *Patterning* is the shaping or altering of deposited materials. and is generally referred to as lithography. For example. in conventional lithography. the wafer is coated with a chemical called a *photoresist*; then. a machine called a *stepper* focuses. aligns. and moves a mask. exposing select portions of the wafer below to short wavelength light; the exposed regions are washed away by a developer solution. After etching or other processing. the remaining photoresist is removed by plasma ashing.

- *Modification of electrical properties* has historically entailed doping transistor *sources* and *drains* (originally by diffusion furnaces and later by ion implantation). These doping processes are followed by furnace annealing or. in advanced devices. by rapid thermal annealing (RTA); annealing serves to activate the implanted dopants. Modification of electrical properties now also extends to the reduction of a material's dielectric constant in low-k insulators via exposure to ultraviolet light in UV processing (UVP).

Modern chips have up to eleven metal levels produced in over 300 sequenced processing steps.

Front-end-of-line (FEOL) processing

FEOL processing refers to the formation of the transistors directly in the silicon. The raw wafer is engineered by the growth of an ultrapure. virtually defect-free silicon layer through epitaxy. In the most advanced logic devices. *prior* to the silicon epitaxy step. tricks are performed to improve the performance of the transistors to be built.

One method involves introducing a *straining step* wherein a silicon variant such as silicon-germanium (SiGe) is deposited. Once the epitaxial silicon is deposited. the crystal lattice becomes stretched somewhat. resulting in improved electronic mobility.

Another method. called *silicon on insulator* technology involves the insertion of an insulating layer between the raw silicon wafer and the thin layer of subsequent silicon epitaxy. This method results in the creation of transistors with reduced parasitic effects.

Gate oxide and implants

Front-end surface engineering is followed by growth of the gate dielectric (traditionally silicon dioxide). patterning of the gate. patterning of the source and drain regions. and subsequent implantation or diffusion of dopants to obtain the desired complementary electrical properties.

In dynamic random access memory (DRAM) devices. storagecapacitors are also fabricated at this time. typically stacked above the access transistor (the now defunct DRAM manufacturer Qimonda implemented these capacitors with trenches etched deep into the silicon surface).

Back-end-of-line (BEOL) processing

Metal layers

Once the various semiconductor devices have been created. they must be interconnected to form the desired electrical circuits. This occurs in a series of wafer processing steps collectively referred to as BEOL (not to be confused with *back end* of chip fabrication. which refers to the packaging and testing stages). BEOL processing involves creating metal interconnecting wires that are isolated by dielectric layers.

The insulating material has traditionally been a form of SiO_2 or a silicate glass. but recently new low dielectric constant materials are being used (such as silicon oxycarbide). typically providing dielectric constants around 2.7 (compared to 3.9 for SiO_2). although materials with constants as low as 2.2 are being offered to chipmakers.

Interconnect

Fig. Synthetic detail of a standard cell through four layers of planarized copper interconnect. down to the polysilicon (pink). wells (greyish) and substrate (green).

Historically. the metal wires have been composed of aluminium. In this approach to wiring (often called *subtractive aluminium*). blanket films of aluminium are deposited first. patterned. and then etched. leaving isolated wires. Dielectric material is then deposited over the exposed wires. The various metal layers are interconnected by etching holes (called *"vias")* in the insulating material and then depositing tungsten in them with a CVD technique; this approach is still used in the fabrication of many memory chips such as dynamic random access memory (DRAM). because the number of interconnect levels is small (currently no more than four).

More recently. as the number of interconnect levels for logic has substantially increased due to the large number of transistors that are now interconnected in a modern microprocessor. the timing delay in the wiring has become so significant as to prompt a change in wiring material (from aluminium to copper layer) and a change in dielectric material (from silicon dioxides to newer low-K insulators). This performance enhancement also comes at a reduced cost via damascene processing. which eliminates processing steps. As the number of interconnect levels increases. planarization of the previous layers is required to ensure a flat surface prior to subsequent lithography. Without it. the levels would become increasingly crooked. extending outside the depth of focus of available lithography. and thus interfering with the ability to pattern. CMP (chemical-mechanical planarization) is the primary processing method to achieve such planarization. although dry *etch back* is still sometimes employed when the number of interconnect levels is no more than three.

WAFER TEST

The highly serialized nature of wafer processing has increased the demand for metrology in between the various processing steps. For example. thin film metrology based onellipsometry or reflectometry. is used to tightly control the thickness of gate oxide. as well as the thickness. refractive index and extinction coefficient of photoresist and other coatings. Wafer test metrology equipment is used to verify that the wafers haven't been damaged by previous processing steps up until testing; if too many dies on one wafer have failed. the entire wafer is scrapped to avoid the costs of further processing.

DEVICE TEST

Once the front-end process has been completed. the semiconductor devices are subjected to a variety of electrical tests to determine if they function properly. The proportion of devices on the wafer found to perform properly is referred to as the yield. Manufacturers are typically secretive about their yields. but it can be as low as 30%. The fab tests the chips on the wafer with an electronic tester that presses tiny probes against the chip. The machine marks each bad chip with a drop of dye. Currently. electronic dye marking is possible if wafer test data is logged into a central computer database and chips are "binned" (*i.e.* sorted into virtual bins) according to predetermined test limits. The resulting binning data can be graphed. or logged. on a wafer map to trace manufacturing defects and mark bad chips. This map can also be used during wafer assembly and packaging.Chips are also tested again after packaging. as the bond wires may be missing. or analog performance may be altered by the package. This is referred to as the "final test".

Usually. the fab charges for testing time. with prices in the order of cents per second. Testing times vary from a few milliseconds to a couple of seconds. and the test software is optimized for reduced testing time. Multiple chip (multi-site) testing is also possible. because many testers have the resources to perform most or all of the tests in parallel.Chips are often designed with "testability features" such as scan chains or a "built-in self-test" to speed testing. and reduce testing costs. In certain designs that use specialized analog fab processes. wafers are also laser-trimmed during the testing. in order to achieve tightly-distributed resistance values as specified by the design.Good designs try to test and statistically manage *corners* (extremes of silicon Behaviour caused by a high operating temperature combined with the extremes of fab processing steps). Most designs cope with at least 64 corners.

DIE PREPARATION

Once tested. a wafer is typically reduced in thickness before the wafer is scored and then broken into individual dies. a process known as wafer dicing. Only the good. unmarked chips are packaged.

PACKAGING

Plastic or ceramic packaging involves mounting the die. connecting the die pads to the pins on the package. and sealing the die. Tiny wires are used to connect the pads to the pins. In the old days. wires were attached by hand. but now specialized machines perform the task. Traditionally. these wires have been composed of gold. leading to a lead frame (pronounced "leed frame") of solder-plated copper; lead is poisonous. so lead-free "lead frames" are now mandated by RoHS.Chip scale package (CSP) is another packaging technology. A plastic dual in-line package. like most packages. is many times larger than the actual die hidden inside. whereas CSP chips are nearly the size of the die; a CSP can be constructed for each die *before* the wafer is diced.The packaged chips are retested to ensure that they were not damaged during packaging and that the die-to-pin interconnect operation was performed correctly. A laser then etches the chip's name and numbers on the package.

ROBOTICS

Fig. The Shadow robot hand system

Robotics is the branch of mechanical engineering. electrical engineering and computer science that deals with the design. construction. operation. and application of robots. as well as computer systems for their control. sensory feedback. and information processing.

These technologies deal with automated machines that can take the place of humans in dangerous environments or manufacturing processes. or resemble humans in appearance. Behaviour. and/or cognition. Many of today's robots are inspired by nature contributing to the field of bio-inspired robotics.

The concept of creating machines that can operate autonomously dates back to classical times. but research into the functionality and potential uses of robots did not grow substantially until the 20th century.

Throughout history. robotics has been often seen to mimic human Behaviour. and often manage tasks in a similar fashion. Today. robotics is a rapidly growing field. as technological advances continue. research. design. and building new robots serve various practical purposes. whether domestically. commercially. or militarily. Many robots do jobs that are hazardous to people such as defusing bombs. mines and exploring shipwrecks.

To view robotics as an application of the principles of motions together with motors to provide motion and sensors to provide location and velocity may miss the inherent complexity of the discipline.

A real robot does face potential for errors due to a number of reasons. including: incorrect parameter (for example: mass. direction. distance) values. frictional forces and terrain estimations. play at the link joints. calibration errors in sensors. errors in the values read from the sensors. The resulting errors in robot actions need corrections; preferably. without any explicit human help.

These corrections cannot be precomputed by using the laws of physics and must be generated. as they are detected. by the robot as it executes the operation to enhance their ability to avoid immobilization. accommodate degraded performance and even self-recover.

The needed correction differs from one repetition of an operation to the next due to unpredictability of many of the influences.

ETYMOLOGY

The word *robotics* was derived from the word *robot*. which was introduced to the public by Czech writer Karel Èapek in his play *R.U.R. (Rossum's Universal Robots)*. which was published in 1920. The word *robot* comes from the Slavic word *robota*. which means labour.

The play begins in a factory that makes artificial people called *robots*. creatures who can be mistaken for humans similar to the modern ideas of androids. Karel Èapek himself did not coin the word. He wrote a short letter in reference to an etymology in the*Oxford English Dictionary* in which he named his brother Josef Èapek as its actual originator.

According to the *Oxford English Dictionary*. the word *robotics* was first used in print by Isaac Asimov. in his science fiction short story "Liar". published in May 1941 in *Astounding Science Fiction*.

Asimov was unaware that he was coining the term; since the science and technology of electrical devices is *electronics*. he assumed *robotics* already referred to the science and technology of robots.

In some of Asimov's other works. he states that the first use of the word *robotics* was in his short story *Runaround* (Astounding Science Fiction.

March 1942). However. the original publication of "Liar!" predates that of "Runaround" by ten months. so the former is generally cited as the word's origin.

HISTORY OF ROBOTICS

In 1927 the *Maschinenmensch* ("machine-human") gynoid humanoid robot (also called "Parody". "Futura". "Robotrix". or the "Maria impersonator"). the first depiction of a robot ever to appear on film. was played by German actress Brigitte Helm in Fritz Lang's film Metropolis.

Date	**Significance**	**Robot Name**	**Inventor**
Third century B.C. and earlier	One of the earliest descriptions of automata appears in the *Lie Zi* text. on a much earlier encounter between King Mu of Zhou (1023–957 BC) and a mechanical engineer known as Yan Shi. an 'artificer'. The latter allegedly presented the king with a life-size, human-shaped figure of his mechanical handiwork.		Yan Shi
First century A.D. and earlier	Descriptions of more than 100 machines and automata, including a fire engine. a wind organ. a coin-operated machine. and a steam-powered engine. in *Pneumatica* and *Automata* by Heron of Alexandria		Ctesibius, Philo of Byzantium, Heron of Alexandria. and others
c. 420 B.C.E	A wooden. steam propelled bird. which was able to fly		Archytas of Tarentum
1206	Created early humanoid automata. programmable automaton band	Robot band. hand-washing automaton,automated moving peacocks	Al-Jazari
1495	Designs for a humanoid robot	Mechanical knight	Leonardo da Vinci
1738	Mechanical duck that was able to eat, flap its wings. and excrete	Digesting Duck	Jacques de Vaucanson
1898	Nikola Tesla demonstrates first radio-controlled vessel.	Teleautomaton	Nikola Tesla
1921	First fictional automatons called "robots" appear in the play *R.U.R.*	Rossum's Universal Robots	Karel Čapek
1930s	Humanoid robot exhibited at the 1939 and 1940 World's Fairs	Elektro	Westinghouse Electric Corporation

In 1942 the science fiction writer Isaac Asimov formulated his Three Laws of Robotics.In 1948 Norbert Wiener formulated the principles of cybernetics. the basis of practical robotics. Fully autonomous robots only appeared in the second half of the 20th century. The first digitally operated and programmable robot. the Unimate. was installed in 1961 to lift hot pieces of metal from a die casting machine and stack them. Commercial and industrial robots are widespread today and used to perform jobs more cheaply. or more accurately and reliably. than humans.

They are also employed in jobs which are too dirty. dangerous. or dull to be suitable for humans. Robots are widely used in manufacturing. assembly. packing and packaging. transport. earth and space exploration. surgery. weaponry. laboratory research. safety. and the mass production of consumer and industrial goods.

ROBOTIC ASPECTS

Fig. Robotic Construction

Fig. Electrical Aspect

There are many types of robots; they are used in many different environments and for many different uses. although being very diverse in application and form they all share three basic similarities when it comes to their construction:

1. Robots all have some kind of mechanical construction. a frame. form or shape that usually is the solution/result for a set task or problem. For example. if you want a robot to travel across heavy dirt or mud.

you might think to use tracker treads. so the form of your robot might be a box with tracker treads. The treads being the mechanical construction for traveling across the problem of heavy mud or dirt. This mechanical aspect usually deals with a real world application of an object or of itself. example lifting. moving. carrying. flying. swimming. running. walking...etc. The mechanical aspect is mostly the creator's solution to completing the assigned task and dealing with the physics of the environment around it. example: gravity. friction. resistance...etc. Form follows function.

2. Robots have an electrical aspect to them in them. in the form of wires. sensors. circuits. batteries ...etc. Example: the tracker tread robot that was mentioned earlier will need some kind of power to actually move the tracker treads. That power comes in the form of electricity. which will have to travel through a wire and originate from a battery. a basic electrical circuit. Even gas poweredmachines that get their power mainly from gas still require an electrical current to start the gas using process which is why most gas powered machines like cars. have batteries. The electrical aspect of robots is used for movement: as in the control of motorswhich are used mostly were motion is needed. Sensing: electrical signals are used to determine things like heat. sound. position. and energy status. Operation: robots need some level of electrical energy supplied to their motors and/or sensors in order to be turned on. and do basic operations.
3. All robots contain some level of computer programming (code). A Programme is how a robot decides when or how to do something. For example: what if the tractor tread robot (from our previous examples) needs to move across a muddy road. even though it has the correct mechanical construction. and it receives the correct amount of power from its battery. it does not go anywhere. Why? What actually tells the robot to move? A Programme. Even if you had a remote control and you pushed a button telling it to move forward it will still need a Programme relating the button you pushed to the action of moving forward. Programmes are the core essence of a robot. it could have excellent mechanical/electrical construction. but if its Programme is poorly constructed its performance will be very poor or it may not perform at all. There are three different types of robotic Programmes: RC. AI hybrid. RC stands for radio control. a robot with this type of Programme has a Pre-existing set of commands that it will only do if and when it receives a signal from a control source. most of the time the control source is a human being with a remote control.

It is perhaps more appropriate to view devices controlled primarily by human commands as falling in the discipline of automation rather than robotics. AI stand for artificial intelligence. robots with this kind of programming interact with their environment on their own without a control source. Robots with AI create solutions to objects/problems they encounter by using their Pre-existing programming to decide. understand. learn and/or create. Hybrid is a form of Programme that incorporates both AI and RC functions. For example: your robot may work completely on its own. encounter a problem. come up with two solutions like an AI system. and then rely completely on you to decide what to do like a RC system. Robots have three aspect of construction mechanical. electrical and programming.

MECHATRONICS

Mechatronics is a design process that includes a combination of mechanical engineering. electrical engineering. telecommunications engineering. control engineering andcomputer engineering. Mechatronics is a multidisciplinary field of engineering. that is to say. it rejects splitting engineering into separate disciplines. Originally. mechatronics just included the combination of mechanics and electronics. hence the word is a combination of mechanics and electronics; however. as technical systems have become more and more complex the word has been broadened to include more technical areas.

The word “mechatronics” originated in Japanese-English and was created by Tetsuro Mori. an engineer of Yaskawa Electric Corporation. The word “mechatronics” was registered as trademark by the company in Japan with the registration number of “46-32714” in 1971. However. Afterwards the company released the right of using the word to public. and the word “mechatronics” spread to the rest of the world. Nowadays. the word is translated in each language and the word is considered as an essential term for industry.French standard NF E 01-010 gives the following definition: “approach aiming at the synergistic integration of mechanics. electronics. control theory. and computer science within product design and manufacturing. in order to improve and/or optimize its functionality”.Many people treat “mechatronics” as a modern buzzword synonymous with “electromechanical engineering”. However. other people draw a distinction between an “electromechanical component”—does not include a computer; an electro-mechanical computer (such as the Z4)—does not include an electronic computer; vs. a “mechatronic system”—a computer-controlled mechanical system. including both an electronic computer and electromechanical components.

DESCRIPTION

A mechatronics engineer unites the principles of mechanics. electronics.

and computing to generate a simpler. more economical and reliable system. The term "mechatronics" was coined by Tetsuro Mori. the senior engineer of the Japanese company Yaskawa in 1969. An industrial robot is a prime example of a mechatronics system; it includes aspects of electronics. mechanics. and computing to do its day-to-day jobs.

Engineering cybernetics deals with the question of control engineering of mechatronic systems. It is used to control or regulate such a system. Through collaboration. the mechatronic modules perform the production goals and inherit flexible and agile manufacturing properties in the production scheme. Modern production equipment consists of mechatronic modules that are integrated according to a control architecture.

The most known architectures involve hierarchy. polyarchy. heterarchy. and hybrid. The methods for achieving a technical effect are described by control algorithms. which might or might not utilize formal methods in their design. Hybrid systems important to mechatronics include production systems. synergy drives. planetary exploration rovers. automotive subsystems such as anti-lock braking systems and spin-assist. and everyday equipment such as autofocus cameras. video. hard disks. and CD players.

FRICTION STIR WELDING

Fig. The bulkhead and nosecone of theOrion spacecraft are joined using friction stir welding.

Friction-stir welding (FSW) is a solid-state joining process (the metal is not melted) that uses a third body tool to join two facing surfaces. Heat is generated between the tool and material which leads to a very soft region near the FSW tool. It then mechanically intermixes the two pieces of metal at the place of the joint. then the softened metal (due to the elevated temperature) can be joined using mechanical pressure (which is applied by the tool). much like joining clay. or dough. It is primarily used on aluminium. and most often on extruded aluminum (non-heat treatable alloys). and on structures which need superior weld strength without a post weld heat treatment.It was invented and experimentally proven at The Welding Institute UK in December 1991. TWI holds patents on the process. the first being the most descriptive.

PRINCIPLE OF OPERATION

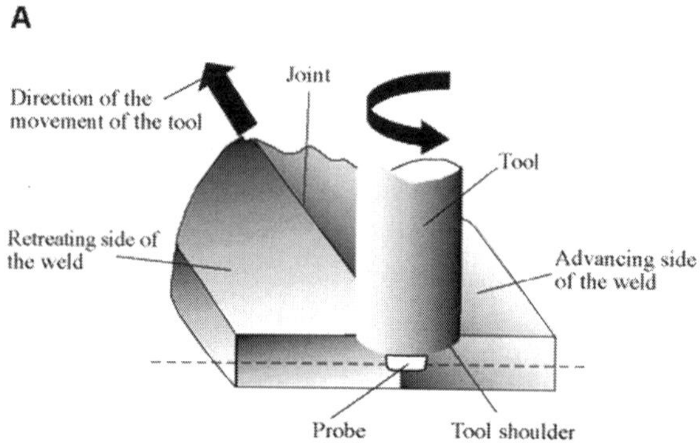

Fig. Schematic diagram of the FSW process: (A) Two discrete metal workpieces butted together. along with the tool (with a probe).

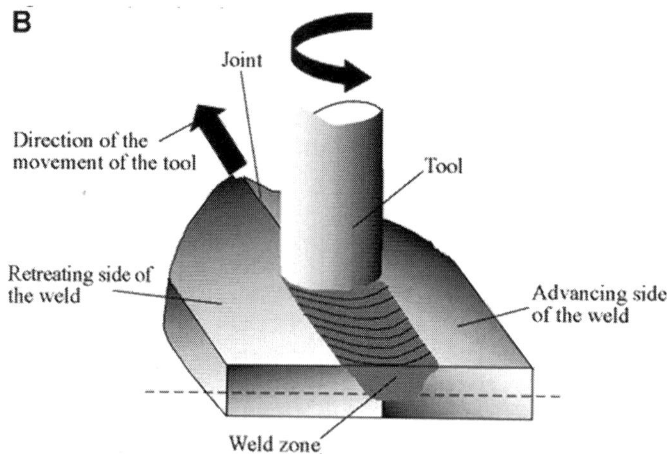

Fig. (B) The progress of the tool through the joint. also showing the weld zone and the region affected by the tool shoulder.

A constantly rotated non consumable cylindrical-shouldered tool with a profiled probe is transversely fed at a constant rate into a butt joint between two clamped pieces of butted material. The probe is slightly shorter than the weld depth required. with the tool shoulder riding atop the work surface.Frictional heat is generated between the wear-resistant welding components and the work pieces. This heat. along with that generated by the mechanical mixing process and the adiabatic heat within the material. cause the stirred materials to soften without melting. As the pin is moved forward. a special profile on its leading face forces plasticised material to the rear where clamping force assists in a forged consolidation of the weld.

This process of the tool traversing along the weld line in a plasticised tubular shaft of metal results in severe solid statedeformation involving dynamic recrystallization of the base material.

MICROSTRUCTURAL FEATURES

The solid-state nature of the FSW process. combined with its unusual tool and asymmetric nature. results in a highly characteristic microstructure. The microstructure can be broken up into the following zones:

- The *stir zone* (also nugget. dynamically recrystallised zone) is a region of heavily deformed material that roughly corresponds to the location of the pin during welding. The grains within the stir zone are roughly equiaxed and often an order of magnitude smaller than the grains in the parent material. A unique feature of the stir zone is the common occurrence of several concentric rings which has been referred to as an "onion-ring" structure. The precise origin of these rings has not been firmly established. although variations in particle number density. grain size and texture have all been suggested.
- The *flow arm zone* is on the upper surface of the weld and consists of material that is dragged by the shoulder from the retreating side of the weld. around the rear of the tool. and deposited on the advancing side.
- The *thermo-mechanically affected zone* (TMAZ) occurs on either side of the stir zone. In this region the strain and temperature are lower and the effect of welding on the microstructure is correspondingly smaller. Unlike the stir zone the microstructure is recognizably that of the parent material. albeit significantly deformed and rotated. Although the term TMAZ technically refers to the entire deformed region it is often used to describe any region not already covered by the terms stir zone and flow arm.
- The *heat-affected zone* (HAZ) is common to all welding processes. As indicated by the name. this region is subjected to a thermal cycle but is not deformed during welding. The temperatures are lower than those in the TMAZ but may still have a significant effect if the microstructure is thermally unstable. In fact. in age-hardened aluminium alloys this region commonly exhibits the poorest mechanical properties.

ADVANTAGES AND LIMITATIONS

The solid-state nature of FSW leads to several advantages over fusion welding methods as problems associated with cooling from the liquid phase are avoided. Issues such asporosity. solute redistribution. solidification cracking and liquation cracking do not arise during FSW. In general. FSW has been found to produce a low concentration of defects and is very tolerant of variations in parameters and materials.

Nevertheless. FSW is associated with a number of unique defects. Insufficient weld temperatures. due to low rotational speeds or high traverse speeds. for example. mean that the weld material is unable to accommodate the extensive deformation during welding. This may result in long. tunnel-like defects running along the weld which may occur on the surface or subsurface. Low temperatures may also limit the forging action of the tool and so reduce the continuity of the bond between the material from each side of the weld. The light contact between the material has given rise to the name "kissing-bond". This defect is particularly worrying since it is very difficult to detect using Non-destructive methods such as X-ray or ultrasonic testing. If the pin is not long enough or the tool rises out of the plate then the interface at the bottom of the weld may not be disrupted and forged by the tool. resulting in a lack-of-penetration defect. This is essentially a notch in the material which can be a potential source of fatigue cracks.

A number of potential advantages of FSW over conventional fusion-welding processes have been identified:

- Good mechanical properties in the as-welded condition
- Improved safety due to the absence of toxic fumes or the spatter of molten material.
- No consumables — A threaded pin made of conventional tool steel. *e.g.*. hardened H13. can weld over 1 km (0.62 mi) of aluminium. and no filler or gas shield is required for aluminium.
- Easily automated on simple milling machines — lower setup costs and less training.
- Can operate in all positions (horizontal. vertical. etc.). as there is no weld pool.
- Generally good weld appearance and minimal thickness under/over-matching. thus reducing the need for expensive machining after welding.
- Low environmental impact.

However. some disadvantages of the process have been identified:

- Exit hole left when tool is withdrawn.
- Large down forces required with heavy-duty clamping necessary to hold the plates together.
- Less flexible than manual and arc processes (difficulties with thickness variations and non-linear welds).
- Often slower traverse rate than some fusion welding techniques. although this may be offset if fewer welding passes are required.

IMPORTANT WELDING PARAMETERS

Tool rotation and Traverse Speeds

There are two tool speeds to be considered in friction-stir welding; how fast the tool rotates and how quickly it traverses the interface. These two parameters have considerable importance and must be chosen with care to ensure a successful and efficient welding cycle. The relationship between the welding speeds and the heat input during welding is complex but. in general. it can be said that increasing the rotation speed or decreasing the traverse speed will result in a hotter weld. In order to produce a successful weld it is necessary that the material surrounding the tool is hot enough to enable the extensive plastic flow required and minimize the forces acting on the tool. If the material is too cold then voids or other flaws may be present in the stir zone and in extreme cases the tool may break.Excessively high heat input. on the other hand may be detrimental to the final properties of the weld. Theoretically. this could even result in defects due to the liquation of low-melting-point phases (similar to liquation cracking in fusion welds). These competing demands lead onto the concept of a "processing window": the range of processing parameters *viz.* tool rotation and traverse speed. that will produce a good quality weld. Within this window the resulting weld will have a sufficiently high heat input to ensure adequate material plasticity but not so high that the weld properties are excessively deteriorated.

Tool tilt and Plunge Depth

The plunge depth is defined as the depth of the lowest point of the shoulder below the surface of the welded plate and has been found to be a critical parameter for ensuring weld quality. Plunging the shoulder below the plate surface increases the pressure below the tool and helps ensure adequate forging of the material at the rear of the tool. Tilting the tool by 2–4 degrees. such that the rear of the tool is lower than the front. has been found to assist this forging process.

The plunge depth needs to be correctly set. both to ensure the necessary downward pressure is achieved and to ensure that the tool fully penetrates the weld. Given the high loads required. the welding machine may deflect and so reduce the plunge depth compared to the nominal setting. which may result in flaws in the weld. On the other hand. an excessive plunge depth may result in the pin rubbing on the backing plate surface or a significant undermatch of the weld thickness compared to the base material. Variable load welders have been developed to automatically compensate for changes in the tool displacement while TWI have demonstrated a roller system that maintains the tool position above the weld plate.

Tool design

Fig. FSW of two USIBOR 1500 high-strength steel sheets

The design of the tool is a critical factor as a good tool can improve both the quality of the weld and the maximum possible welding speed.

It is desirable that the tool material is sufficiently strong. tough. and hard wearing at the welding temperature. Further it should have a good oxidation resistance and a lowthermal conductivity to minimise heat loss and thermal damage to the machinery further up the drive train. Hot-worked tool steel such as AISI H13 has proven perfectly acceptable for welding aluminium alloys within thickness ranges of 0.5 – 50 mm but more advanced tool materials are necessary for more demanding applications such as highly abrasive metal matrix composites or higher melting point materials such as steel or titanium.

Improvements in tool design have been shown to cause substantial improvements in productivity and quality. TWI has developed tools specifically designed to increase the penetration depth and thus increasing the plate thicknesses that can be successfully welded. An example is the "whorl" design that uses a tapered pin with re-entrant features or a variable pitch thread to improve the downwards flow of material. Additional designs include the Triflute and Trivex series. The Triflute design has a complex system of three tapering. threaded re-entrant flutes that appear to increase material movement around the tool. The Trivex tools use a simpler. non-cylindrical. pin and have been found to reduce the forces acting on the tool during welding.

The majority of tools have a concave shoulder profile which acts as an escape volume for the material displaced by the pin. prevents material from extruding out of the sides of the shoulder and maintains downwards pressure and hence good forging of the material behind the tool. The Triflute tool uses an alternative system with a series of concentric grooves machined into the surface which are intended to produce additional movement of material in the upper layers of the weld.

Widespread commercial applications of friction stir welding process for steels and other hard alloys such as titanium alloys will require the development of cost-effective and durable tools. Material selection. design and cost are important considerations in the search for commercially useful tools for the welding of hard materials. Work is continuing to better understand the effects of tool material's composition. structure. properties and geometry on their performance. durability and cost.

WELDING FORCES

During welding a number of forces will act on the tool:

- A downwards force is necessary to maintain the position of the tool at or below the material surface. Some friction-stir welding machines operate under load control but in many cases the vertical position of the tool is preset and so the load will vary during welding.
- The traverse force acts parallel to the tool motion and is positive in the traverse direction. Since this force arises as a result of the resistance of the material to the motion of the tool it might be expected that this force will decrease as the temperature of the material around the tool is increased.
- The lateral force may act perpendicular to the tool traverse direction and is defined here as positive towards the advancing side of the weld.
- Torque is required to rotate the tool. the amount of which will depend on the down force and friction coefficient (sliding friction) and/or the flow strength of the material in the surrounding region (stiction).

In order to prevent tool fracture and to minimize excessive wear and tear on the tool and associated machinery. the welding cycle is modified so that the forces acting on the tool are as low as possible. and abrupt changes are avoided. In order to find the best combination of welding parameters. it is likely that a compromise must be reached. since the conditions that favour low forces (*e.g.* high heat input. low travel speeds) may be undesirable from the point of view of productivity and weld properties.

FLOW OF MATERIAL

Early work on the mode of material flow around the tool used inserts of a different alloy. which had a different contrast to the normal material when viewed through a microscope. in an effort to determine where material was moved as the tool passed. The data was interpreted as representing a form of in-situ extrusion where the tool. backing plate and cold base material form the "extrusion chamber" through which the hot. plasticised material is forced. In this model the rotation of the tool draws little or no material around the front of the pin instead the material parts in front of the pin and passes down either side. After the material has passed the pin the side pressure exerted by the "die" forces the material back together and consolidation of the join occurs as the rear of the tool shoulder passes overhead and the large down force forges the material.More recently. an alternative theory has been advanced that advocates considerable material movement in certain locations. This theory holds that some material does rotate around the pin. for at least one rotation. and it is this material movement that produces the "onion-ring" structure in the stir zone. The researchers used a combination of thin copper strip inserts and a "frozen pin" technique. where the tool is rapidly stopped in place. They suggested that material motion occurs by two processes:

1. Material on the advancing front side of a weld enters into a zone that rotates and advances with the pin. This material was very highly deformed and sloughs off behind the pin to form arc-shaped features when viewed from above (*i.e.* down the tool axis). It was noted that the copper entered the rotational zone around the pin. where it was broken up into fragments. These fragments were only found in the arc shaped features of material behind the tool.
2. The lighter material came from the retreating front side of the pin and was dragged around to the rear of the tool and filled in the gaps between the arcs of advancing side material. This material did not rotate around the pin and the lower level of deformation resulted in a larger grain size.

The primary advantage of this explanation is that it provides a plausible explanation for the production of the onion-ring structure.

The marker technique for friction stir welding provides data on the initial and final positions of the marker in the welded material. The flow of material is then reconstructed from these positions. Detailed material flow field during friction stir welding can also be calculated from theoretical considerations based on fundamental scientific principles. Material flow calculations are routinely used in numerous engineering applications. Calculation of material flow fields in friction stir welding can be undertaken both using comprehensive numerical simulations or simple but insightful analytical equations. The comprehensive models for the calculation of material flow fields also provide important information such as geometry of the stir zone and the torque on the tool. The numerical simulations have shown the ability to correctly predict the results from marker experiments and the stir zone geometry observed in friction stir welding experiments.

GENERATION AND FLOW OF HEAT

For any welding process it is. in general. desirable to increase the travel speed and minimise the heat input as this will increase productivity and possibly reduce the impact of welding on the mechanical properties of the weld. At the same time it is necessary to ensure that the temperature around the tool is sufficiently high to permit adequate material flow and prevent flaws or tool damage.

When the traverse speed is increased. for a given heat input. there is less time for heat to conduct ahead of the tool and the thermal gradients are larger. At some point the speed will be so high that the material ahead of the tool will be too cold. and the flow stress too high. to permit adequate material movement. resulting in flaws or tool fracture. If the "hot zone" is too large then there is scope to increase the traverse speed and hence productivity.

The welding cycle can be split into several stages during which the heat flow and thermal profile will be different:

- *Dwell.* The material is preheated by a stationary. rotating tool to achieve a sufficient temperature ahead of the tool to allow the traverse. This period may also include the plunge of the tool into the workpiece.
- *Transient heating.* When the tool begins to move there will be a transient period where the heat production and temperature around the tool will alter in a complex manner until an essentially steady-state is reached.
- *Pseudo steady-state.* Although fluctuations in heat generation will occur the thermal field around the tool remains effectively constant. at least on the macroscopic scale.
- *Post steady-state.* Near the end of the weld heat may "reflect" from the end of the plate leading to additional heating around the tool.

Heat generation during friction-stir welding arises from two main sources: friction at the surface of the tool and the deformation of the material around the tool. The heat generation is often assumed to occur predominantly under the shoulder. due to its greater surface area. and to be equal to the power required to overcome the contact forces between the tool and the workpiece. The contact condition under the shoulder can be described by sliding friction. using a friction coefficient ì and interfacial pressure P. or sticking friction. based on the interfacial shear strength at an appropriate temperature and strain rate. Mathematical approximations for the total heat generated by the tool shoulder Q_{total} have been developed using both sliding and sticking friction models:

$$Q_{total} = \frac{2}{3}\pi P\mu\omega\left(R^3_{shoulder} - R^3_{pin}\right) \text{ (Sliding)}$$

$$Q_{total} = \frac{2}{3}\pi\tau\omega\left(R^3_{shoulder} - R^3_{pin}\right) \text{ (Sticking)}$$

where ù is the angular velocity of the tool. $R_{shoulder}$ is the radius of the tool shoulder and R_{pin} that of the pin. Several other equations have been proposed to account for factors such as the pin but the general approach remains the same. A major difficulty in applying these equations is determining suitable values for the friction coefficient or the interfacial shear stress. The conditions under the tool are both extreme and very difficult to measure. To date. these parameters have been used as "fitting parameters" where the model works back from measured thermal data to obtain a reasonable simulated thermal field. While this approach is useful for creating process models to predict. for example. residual stresses it is less useful for providing insights into the process itself.

APPLICATIONS

The FSW process is currently patented by TWI in most industrialised countries and licensed for over 183 users. Friction stir welding and its variants friction stir spot welding andfriction stir processing are used for the following industrial applications: shipbuilding and offshore. aerospace. automotive. rolling stock for railways. general fabrication. robotics. and computers.

Shipbuilding and Offshore

Two Scandinavian aluminium extrusion companies were the first to apply FSW commercially to the manufacture of fish freezer panels atSapa in 1996. as well as deck panels and helicopter landing platforms at Marine Aluminium Aanensen. Marine Aluminium Aanensen subsequently merged with Hydro Aluminium Maritime to become Hydro Marine Aluminium. Some of these freezer panels are now produced by Riftec and Bayards. In 1997 two-dimensional friction stir welds in the hydrodynamically flared bow section of the hull of the ocean viewer vessel *The Boss* were produced at Research Foundation Institute with the first portable FSW machine. The *Super Liner Ogasawara* at Mitsui Engineering and Shipbuilding is the largest friction stir welded ship so far. The *Sea Fighter* of Nichols Bros and the*Freedom* class Littoral Combat Ships contain prefabricated panels by the FSW fabricators Advanced Technology and Friction Stir Link. Inc. respectively. The *Houbei* class missile boat has friction stir welded rocket launch containers of China Friction Stir Centre. HMNZS*Rotoiti* in New Zealand has FSW panels made by Donovans in a converted milling machine. Various companies apply FSW toarmor plating for amphibious assault ships

Aerospace

Fig. Longitudinal and circumferential friction stir welds are used for theFalcon 9 rocket booster tank at the SpaceX factory

Boeing applies FSW to the Delta II and Delta IV expendable launch vehicles. and the first of these with a friction stir welded Interstage module was launched in 1999. The process is also used for the Space Shuttle external tank. for Ares I and for the Orion Crew Vehicletest article at NASA as well as Falcon 1 and Falcon 9 rockets at SpaceX. The toe nails for ramp of Boeing C-17 Globemaster IIIcargo aircraft by Advanced Joining Technologies and the cargo barrier beams for the Boeing 747 Large Cargo Freighter were the first commercially produced aircraft parts. FAA approved wings and fuselage panels of the Eclipse 500 aircraft were made at Eclipse Aviation. and this company delivered 259 friction stir welded business jets. before they were forced. Floor panels for Airbus A400M military aircraft are now made by Pfalz Flugzeugwerke and Embraer used FSW for the Legacy 450 and 500 Jets Friction stir welding also is employed for fuselage panels on the Airbus A380. BRÖTJE-Automation GmbH uses friction stir welding – through the DeltaN FS® system – for gantry production machines developed for the aerospace sector as well as other industrial applications.

Automotive

Fig. The centre tunnel of the Ford GT is made from two aluminium extrusions friction stir welded to a bent aluminium sheet and houses the fuel tank

Aluminium engine cradles and suspension struts for stretched Lincoln Town Car were the first automotive parts that were friction stir atTower Automotive. who use the process also for the engine tunnel of the Ford GT. A spin-off of this company is called Friction Stir Link. Inc. and successfully exploits the FSW process. *e.g.* for the flatbed trailer "Revolution" of Fontaine Trailers. In Japan FSW is applied to suspension struts at Showa Denko and for joining of aluminium sheets to galvanized steel brackets for the boot (trunk) lid of the Mazda MX-5. Friction stir spot welding is successfully used for the bonnet (hood) and rear doors of the Mazda RX-8 and the boot lid of theToyota Prius. Wheels are friction stir welded at Simmons Wheels. UT Alloy Works and Fundo. Rear seats for the Volvo V70 are friction stir welded at Sapa. HVAC pistons at Halla Climate Control and exhaust gas recirculation coolers at Pierburg. Tailor welded blanks are friction stir welded for the Audi R8 at Riftec. The B-column of the Audi R8 Spider is friction stir welded from two extrusions at Hammerer Aluminium Industries in Austria.

Railways

Fig. The high-strength low-distortion body of Hitachi's A-train *British Rail Class 395* is friction stir welded from longitudinal aluminium extrusions

Since 1997 roof panels were made from aluminium extrusions at Hydro Marine Aluminium with a bespoke 25m long FSW machine. *e.g.* for DSB class SA-SD trains of Alstom LHB Curved side and roof panels for the Victoria line trains of London Underground. side panels for Bombardier's Electrostar trains at Sapa Group and side panels for Alstom's British Rail Class 390 Pendolino trains are made at Sapa Group Japanese commuter and express A-trains. and British Rail Class 395 trains are friction stir welded byHitachi. while Kawasaki applies friction stir spot welding to roof panels and Sumitomo Light Metal produces Shinkansen floor panels. Innovative FSW floor panels are made by Hammerer Aluminium Industries in Austria for the Stadler KISS double decker rail cars. to obtain an internal height of 2 m on both floors and for the new car bodies of the Wuppertal Suspension Railway.

Heat sinks for cooling high-power electronics of locomotives are made at Sykatek. EBG. Austerlitz Electronics. EuroComposite. Sapa and Rapid Technic. and are the most common application of FSW due to the excellent heat transfer.

Fabrication

Fig. The lids of 50-mm-thick copper canisters for nuclear waste are attached to the cylinder by friction stir welding at SKB

Façade panels and athode sheets are friction stir welded at AMAG and Hammerer Aluminium Industries including friction stir lap welds of copper to aluminium. Bizerba meat slicers. Ökolüfter HVAC units and Siemens X-ray vacuum vessels are friction stir welded at Riftec. Vacuum valves and vessels are made by FSW at Japanese and Swiss companies. FSW is also used for the encapsulation of nuclear waste at SKB in 50-mm-thick copper canisters. Pressure vessels from ø1m semispherical forgings of 38.1mm thick aluminium alloy 2219 at Advanced Joining Technologies and Lawrence Livermore Nat Lab. Friction stir processing is applied to ship propellers at Friction Stir Link. Inc. and to hunting knives by DiamondBlade. Bosch uses it in Worcester for the production of heat exchangers.

Robotics

KUKA Robot Group has adapted its KR500-3MT heavy-duty robot for friction stir welding via the DeltaN FS tool. The system made its first public appearance at the EuroBLECH show in November 2012.

Personal Computers

Apple applied friction stir welding on the 2012 iMac to effectively join the bottom to the back of the device.

AUTOMOTIVE ENGINEERING

Modern automotive engineering. along with aerospace engineering and marine engineering. is a branch of automobile engineering. incorporating elements of mechanical.electrical. electronic. software and safety engineering as applied to the design. manufacture and operation of motorcycles. automobiles. buses and trucks and their respective engineering subsystems.

DISCIPLINES

Automobile Engineering

Some of the engineering attributes and disciplines that are of importance to the automotive engineer and many of the other aspects are included in it:

Safety engineering: Safety engineering is the assessment of various crash scenarios and their impact on the vehicle occupants. These are tested against very stringent governmental regulations. Some of these requirements include: seat belt and air bag functionality testing. front and side impact testing. and tests of rollover resistance. Assessments are done with various methods and tools. including Computer crash simulation (typically finite element analysis). crash test dummies. and partial system sled and full vehicle crashes.

Fuel economy/emissions: Fuel economy is the measured fuel efficiency of the vehicle in miles per gallon or kilometers per litre.Emissions testing includes the measurement of vehicle emissions. including hydrocarbons. nitrogen oxides (NOx). carbon monoxide (CO). carbon dioxide (CO2). and evaporative emissions.

Vehicle dynamics: Vehicle dynamics is the vehicle's response of the following attributes: ride. handling. steering. braking. comfort and traction. Design of the chassis systems of suspension. steering. braking. structure (frame). wheels and tires. and traction control are highly leveraged by the vehicle dynamics engineer to deliver the vehicle dynamics qualities desired.

NVH engineering (noise. vibration. and harshness): NVH is the customer's feedback (both tactile [felt] and audible [heard]) from the vehicle. While sound can be interpreted as a rattle. squeal. or hoot; a tactile response can be seat vibration. or a buzz in thesteering wheel. This feedback is generated by components either rubbing. vibrating. or rotating. NVH response can be classified in various ways: powertrain NVH. road noise. wind noise. component noise. and squeak and rattle. Note. there are both good and bad NVH qualities. The NVH engineer works to either eliminate bad NVH. or change the "bad NVH" to good (*i.e.*. exhaust tones).

Vehicle Electronics: Automotive electronics is an increasingly important aspect of automotive engineering. Modern vehicles employ dozens of electronic systems. These systems are responsible for operational controls such as the throttle. brake and steering controls; as well as many comfort and convenience systems such as the HVAC. infotainment. and lighting systems. It would not be possible for automobiles to meet modern safety and fuel economy requirements without electronic controls.

Performance: Performance is a measurable and testable value of a vehicles ability to perform in various conditions. Performance can be considered in a wide variety of tasks. but it's generally associated with how quickly a car can accelerate (*e.g.* standing start 1/4 mile elapsed time. 0–60 mph. etc.). its top speed. how short and quickly a car can come to a complete stop from a set speed (*e.g.* 70-0 mph). how much g-force a car can generate without losing grip. recorded lap times. cornering speed. brake fade. etc. Performance can also reflect the amount of control in inclement weather (snow. ice. rain).

Shift quality: Shift quality is the driver's perception of the vehicle to an automatic transmission shift event. This is influenced by the powertrain (engine. transmission). and the vehicle (driveline. suspension. engine and powertrain mounts. etc.) Shift feel is both a tactile (felt) and audible (heard) response of the vehicle. Shift quality is experienced as various events: Transmission shifts are felt as an upshift at acceleration (1–2). or a downshift maneuver in passing (4–2). Shift engagements of the vehicle are also evaluated. as in Park to Reverse. etc. SEANDurability/ corrosion engineering: Durability and corrosion engineering is the evaluation testing of a vehicle for its useful life. Tests include mileage accumulation. severe driving conditions. and corrosive salt baths.

Package/ ergonomics engineering: Package engineering is a discipline that designs/analyzes the occupant accommodations (seat roominess). ingress/ egress to the vehicle. and the driver's field of vision (gauges and windows).

The package engineer is also responsible for other areas of the vehicle like the engine compartment. and the component to component placement. Ergonomics is the discipline that assesses the occupant's access to the steering wheel. pedals. and other driver/passenger controls.

Climate control: Climate control is the customer's impression of the cabin environment and level of comfort related to the temperature and humidity. From the windshield defrosting. to the heating and cooling capacity. all vehicle seating positions are evaluated to a certain level of comfort.

Drivability: Drivability is the vehicle's response to general driving conditions. Cold starts and stalls. RPM dips. idle response. launch hesitations and stumbles. and performance levels.

Cost: The cost of a vehicle Programme is typically split into the effect on the variable cost of the vehicle. and the up-front tooling and fixed costs associated with developing the vehicle. There are also costs associated with warranty reductions. and marketing.

Programme timing: To some extent Programmes are timed with respect to the market. and also to the production schedules of the assembly plants. Any new part in the design must support the development and manufacturing schedule of the model.

Assembly feasibility: It is easy to design a module that is hard to assemble. either resulting in damaged units. or poor tolerances. The skilled product development engineer works with the assembly/manufacturing engineers so that the resulting design is easy and cheap to make and assemble. as well as delivering appropriate functionality and appearance.

Quality management: Quality control is an important factor within the production process. as high quality is needed to meet customer requirements and to avoid expensiverecall campaigns. The complexity of components involved in the production process requires a combination of different tools and techniques for quality control. Therefore. theInternational Automotive Task Force (IATF). a group of the world's leading manufacturers and trade organizations. developed the standard ISO/TS 16949. This standard defines the design. development. production. and when relevant. installation and service requirements. Furthermore. it combines the principles of ISO 9001 with aspects of various regional and national automotive standards such as AVSQ (Italy). EAQF (France). VDA6 (Germany) and QS-9000 (USA). In order to further minimize risks related to product failures and liability claims of automotive electric and electronic systems. the quality discipline functional safety according to ISO/IEC 17025 is applied.Since the 1950s. the comprehensive business approach total quality management. TQM. helps to continuously improve the production process of automotive products and components. Some of the companies who have implemented TQM include Ford Motor Company. Motorola and Toyota Motor Company.

5

Machine Tool

A machine tool is a machine for shaping or machining metal or other rigid materials. usually by cutting. boring. grinding. shearing. or other forms of deformation. Machine tools employ some sort of tool that does the cutting or shaping. All machine tools have some means of constraining the workpiece and provide a guided movement of the parts of the machine.

Thus the relative movement between the workpiece and the cutting tool (which is called the toolpath) is controlled or constrained by the machine to at least some extent. rather than being entirely "offhand" or "freehand".

Fig. A lathe is an example of a machine tool

The precise definition of the term *machine tool* varies among users. While all machine tools are "machines that help people to make things". although not all factory machines are machine tools.Today machine tools are typically powered other than by human muscle (e.g.. electrically. hydraulically. or via line shaft). used to make manufactured parts (components) in various ways that include cutting or certain other kinds of deformation. With their inherent precision. machine tools enabled the economical production of interchangeable parts.

NOMENCLATURE AND KEY CONCEPTS. INTERRELATED

Many historians of technology consider that true machine tools were born when the toolpath first became guided by the machine itself in some way. at least to some extent. so that direct. freehand human guidance of the toolpath (with hands. feet. or mouth) was no longer the only guidance used in the cutting or forming process. In this view of the definition. the term. arising at a time when all tools up till then had been hand tools. simply provided a label for "tools that were machines instead of hand tools". Early lathes. those prior to the late medieval period. and modern woodworking lathes and potter's wheels may or may not fall under this definition. depending on how one views the headstock spindle itself; but the earliest historical records of a lathe with direct mechanical control *of the cutting tool's path* are of a screw-cutting lathe dating to about 1483.This lathe "produced screw threads out of wood and employed a true compound slide rest".

The mechanical toolpath guidance grew out of any of various root concepts:

- First is the spindle concept itself. which constraints workpiece or tool movement to rotation around a fixed axis. This ancient concept predates machine tools per se; the earliest lathes and potter's wheels incorporated it for the workpiece. but the movement of the tool itself on these machines was entirely freehand.
- The machine slide. which has many forms. such as dovetail ways. box ways. or cylindrical column ways. Machine slides constrain tool or workpiece movement linearly. If a stop is added. the *length* of the line can also be accurately controlled. (Machine slides are essentially a subset of linear bearings. although the language used to classify these various machine elements includes connotative boundaries; some users in some contexts would contradistinguish elements in ways that others might not.)
- Tracing. which involves following the contours of a model or template and transferring the resulting motion to the toolpath.
- Cam operation. which is related in principle to tracing but can be a step or two removed from the traced element's matching the reproduced element's final shape. For example. several cams. no one of which directly matches the desired output shape. can actuate a complex toolpath by creating component vectors that add up to a net toolpath.

Abstractly programmable toolpath guidance began with mechanical solutions. such as in musical box cams and Jacquard looms. The convergence of programmable mechanical control with machine tool toolpath control was delayed many decades. in part because the programmable control methods of musical boxes and looms lacked the rigidity for machine tool toolpaths. Later. electromechanical solutions (such as servos) and soon electronic solutions (including computers) were added. leading to numerical control and computer numerical control.

When considering the difference between freehand toolpaths and machine-constrained toolpaths. the concepts of accuracy and precision. efficiency. and productivity become important in understanding *why* the machine-constrained option adds value. After all. humans are generally quite talented in their freehand movements; the drawings. paintings. and sculptures of artists such as Michelangelo or Leonardo da Vinci. and of countless other talented people. show that human freehand toolpath has great potential.

The valuethat machine tools added to these human talents is in the areas of rigidity (constraining the toolpath despite thousands of newtons (pounds) of force fighting against the constraint). accuracy and precision. efficiency. and productivity. With a machine tool. toolpaths that no human muscle could constrain can be constrained; and toolpaths that are technically possible with freehand methods. but would require tremendous time and skill to execute. can instead be executed quickly and easily. even by people with little freehand talent (because the machine takes care of it). The latter aspect of machine tools is often referred to by historians of technology as "building the skill into the tool". in contrast to the toolpath-constraining skill being in the *person* who wields the tool. As an example. it is *physically possible* to make interchangeable screws. bolts. and nuts entirely with freehand toolpaths. But it is *economically practical* to make them only with machine tools. In the 1930s. the U.S. National Bureau of Economic Research (NBER) referenced the definition of a machine tool as "any machine operating by other than hand power which employs a tool to work on metal".

The narrowest colloquial sense of the term reserves it only for machines that perform metal cutting—in other words. the many kinds of [conventional] machining and grinding. These processes are a type of deformation that produces swarf. However. economists use a slightly broader sense that also includes metal deformation of other types that squeeze the metal into shape without cutting off swarf. such as rolling. stamping with dies. shearing. swaging. riveting. and others. Thus presses are usually included in the economic definition of machine tools. For example. this is the breadth of definition used by Max Holland in his history of Burgmaster and Houdaille. which is also a history of the machine tool industry in general from the 1940s through the 1980s; he was reflecting the sense of the term used by Houdaille itself and other firms in the industry. Many reports on machine tool export and import and similar economic topics use this broader definition.The colloquial sense implying [conventional] metal cutting is also growing obsolete because of changing technology over the decades. The many more recently developed processes labeled "machining". such as electrical discharge machining. electrochemical machining. electron beam machining. photochemical machining. and ultrasonic machining. or even plasma cutting and water jet cutting. are often performed by machines that could most logically be called machine tools. In addition. some of the newly developed additive manufacturing processes. which are not about cutting away material but rather about adding it. are done by machines that are likely to end up labeled. in some cases. as machine tools. In fact. machine tool builders are already developing machines that include both subtractive and additive manufacturing in one work envelope.and retrofits of existing machines are underway.

The natural language use of the terms varies. with subtle connotative boundaries. Many speakers resist using the term "machine tool" to refer to woodworking machinery(joiners. table saws. routing stations. and so on). but it is difficult to maintain any true logical dividing line. and therefore many speakers are fine with a broad definition. It is common to hear machinists refer to their machine tools simply as "machines". Usually the mass noun "machinery" encompasses them. but sometimes it is used to imply only those machines that are being excluded from the definition of "machine tool". This is why the machines in a food-processing plant. such as conveyors. mixers. vessels. dividers. and so on. may be labeled "machinery". while the machines in the factory's tool and die department are instead called "machine tools" in contradistinction. As for the 1930s NBER definition quoted above. one could argue that its specificity to metal is obsolete. as it is quite common today for particular lathes. milling machines. and machining centers (definitely machine tools) to work exclusively on plastic cutting jobs throughout their whole working lifespan. Thus the NBER definition above could be expanded to say "which employs a tool to work on metal *or other materials of high hardness*". And its specificity to "operating by other than hand power" is also problematic. as machine tools can be powered by people if appropriately set up. such as with a treadle (for a lathe) or a hand lever (for a shaper). Hand-powered shapers are clearly "the 'same thing' as shapers with electric motors except smaller". and it is trivial to power a micro lathe with a hand-cranked belt pulley instead of an electric motor. Thus one can question whether power source is truly a key distinguishing concept; but for economics purposes. the NBER's definition made sense. because most of the commercial value of the existence of machine tools comes about via those that are powered by electricity. hydraulics. and so on. Such are the vagaries of natural language and controlled vocabulary. both of which have their places in the business world.

HISTORY

Forerunners of machine tools included bow drills and potter's wheels. which had existed in ancient Egypt prior to 2500 BC. and lathes. known to have existed in multiple regions of Europe since at least 1000 to 500 BC. But it was not until the later Middle Ages and the Age of Enlightenment that the modern concept of a machine tool—a class of machines used as tools in the making of metal parts. and incorporating machine-guided toolpath—began to evolve. Clockmakers of the Middle Ages and renaissance men such as Leonardo da Vinci helped expand humans' technological milieu Towards the preconditions for industrial machine tools. During the 18th and 19th centuries. and even in many cases in the 20th. the builders of machine tools tended to be the same people who would then use them to produce the end products (manufactured goods). However. from these roots also evolved an industry of machine tool builders as we define them today. meaning people who specialize in building machine tools for sale to others.

Historians of machine tools often focus on a handful of major industries that most spurred machine tool development. In order of historical emergence. they have been firearms(small arms and artillery); clocks; textile machinery; steam engines (stationary. marine. rail. and otherwise); sewing machines; bicycles; automobiles; and aircraft. Others could be included in this list as well. but they tend to be connected with the root causes already listed. For example. rolling-element bearings are an industry of themselves. but this industry's main drivers of development were the vehicles already listed—trains. bicycles. automobiles. and aircraft; and other industries. such as tractors. farm implements. and tanks. borrowed heavily from those same parent industries.

Machine tools filled a need created by textile machinery during the Industrial Revolution in England in the middle to late 1700s. Until that time machinery was made mostly from wood. often including gearing and shafts. The increase in mechanization required more metal parts. which were usually made of cast iron or wrought iron. Cast iron could be cast in molds for larger parts. such as engine cylinders and gears. but was difficult to work with a file and could not be hammered. Red hot wrought iron could be hammered into shapes. Room temperature wrought iron was worked with a file and chisel and could be made into gears and other complex parts; however. hand working lacked precision and was a slow and expensive process.

James Watt was unable to have an accurately bored cylinder for his first steam engine. trying for several years until John Wilkinson invented a suitable boring machine in 1774. boring Boulton and Watt's first commercial engine in 1776.

The advance in the accuracy of machine tools can be traced to Henry Maudslay and refined by Joseph Whitworth. That Maudslay had established the manufacture and use of master plane gages in his shop (Maudslay and Field) located on Westminster Road south of the Thames River in London about 1809. was attested to by James Nasmyth who was employed by Maudslay in 1829 and Nasmyth documented their use in his autobiography.

The process by which the master plane gages were produced dates back to antiquity but was refined to an unprecedented degree in the Maudslay shop. The process begins with three plates each given an identification (ex.. 1.2 and 3). The first step is to rub plates 1 and 2 together with a marking medium (called bluing today) revealing the high spots which would be removed by hand scraping with a steel scraper. until no irregularities were visible. This would not produce absolutely true plane surfaces but a "ball and socket" fit. as this mechanical fit. like two perfect planes. can slide over each other and reveal no high spots. Next. plate number 3 would be compared and scraped to conform to plate number 1. In this manner plates number 2 and 3 would be identical. Next plates number 2 and 3 would be checked against each other to determine what condition existed. either both plates were "balls" or "sockets". These would then be scraped until no high spots existed and then compared to plate number 1. After repeating this process. comparing and scraping the three plates together. they would automatically generate exact true plane surfaces accurate to within millionths of an inch.

The traditional method of producing the surface gages used an abrasive powder rubbed between the plates to remove the high spots. but it was Whitworth who contributed the refinement of replacing the grinding with hand scraping. Sometime after 1825 Whitworth went to work for Maudslay and it was there that Whitworth perfected the hand scraping of master surface plane gages. In his paper presented to the British Association for the Advancement of Science at Glasgow in 1840. Whitworth pointed out the inherent inaccuracy of grinding due to no control and thus unequal distribution of the abrasive material between the plates which would produce uneven removal of material from the plates.

With the creation of master plane gages of such high accuracy. all critical components of machine tools (*i.e.*. guiding surfaces such as machine ways) could then be compared against them and scraped to the desired accuracy.

The first machine tools offered for sale (*i.e.*. commercially available) were constructed by Matthew Murray in England around 1800. Others. such as Henry Maudslay. James Nasmyth. and Joseph Whitworth. soon followed the path of expanding their entrepreneurship from manufactured end products and millwright work into the realm of building machine tools for sale.Important early machine tools included the slide rest lathe. screw-cutting lathe. turret lathe. milling machine. pattern tracing lathe. shaper. and metal planer. which were all in use before 1840. With these machine tools the decades old objective of producing interchangeable parts was finally realized. An important early example of something now taken for granted was the standardization of screw fasteners such as nuts and bolts. Before about the beginning of the 19th century. these were used in pairs. and even screws of the same machine were generally not interchangeable. Methods were developed to cut screw thread to a greater precision than that of the feed screw in the lathe being used. This led to the bar length standards of the 19th and early 20th centuries.

American production of machine tools was a critical factor in the Allies' victory in World War II. Production of machine tools tripled in the United States in the war. No war was more industrialized than World War II. and it has been written that the war was won as much by machine shops as by machine guns.The production of machine tools is concentrated in about 10 countries worldwide: China. Japan. Germany. Italy. South Korea. Taiwan. Switzerland. USA. Austria. Spain and a few others. Machine tool innovation continues in several public and private research centers worldwide.

DRIVE POWER SOURCES

"all the turning of the iron for the cotton machinery built by Mr. Slater was done with hand chisels or tools in lathes turned by cranks with hand power". David WilkinsonMachine tools can be powered from a variety of sources. Human and animal power (via cranks. treadles. treadmills. or treadwheels) were used in the past. as was water power (via water wheel); however. following the development of high-pressure steam engines in the mid 19th century. factories increasingly used steam power. Factories also used hydraulic and pneumatic power. Many small workshops continued to use water. human and animal power until electrification after 1900.

Today most machine tools are powered by electricity; however. hydraulic and pneumatic power are sometimes used. but this is uncommon.

AUTOMATIC CONTROL

Machine tools can be operated manually. or under automatic control. Early machines used flywheels to stabilize their motion and had complex systems of gears and levers to control the machine and the piece being worked on. Soon after World War II. the numerical control (NC) machine was developed. NC machines used a series of numbers punched on paper tape or punched cards to control their motion. In the 1960s. computers were added to give even more flexibility to the process. Such machines became known as computerized numerical control (CNC) machines. NC and CNC machines could precisely repeat sequences over and over. and could produce much more complex pieces than even the most skilled tool operators.

Before long. the machines could automatically change the specific cutting and shaping tools that were being used. For example. a drill machine might contain a magazine with a variety of drill bits for producing holes of various sizes. Previously. either machine operators would usually have to manually change the bit or move the work piece to another station to perform these different operations. The next logical step was to combine several different machine tools together. all under computer control. These are known asmachining centers. and have dramatically changed the way parts are made. From the simplest to the most complex. most machine tools are capable of at least partial self-replication. and produce machine parts as their primary function.

BROACHING (METALWORKING)

Broaching is a machining process that uses a toothed tool. called a broach. to remove material. There are two main types of broaching:*linear* and *rotary*. In linear broaching. which is the more common process. the broach is run linearly against a surface of the workpiece to effect the cut. Linear broaches are used in a broaching machine. which is also sometimes shortened to *broach*. In rotary broaching. the broach is rotated and pressed into the workpiece to cut an axis symmetric shape. A rotary broach is used in a lathe or screw machine. In both processes the cut is performed in one pass of the broach. which makes it very efficient.

Broaching is used when precision machining is required. especially for odd shapes. Commonly machined surfaces include circular and non-circular holes. splines. keyways. and flat surfaces. Typical workpieces include small to medium sized castings. forgings. screw machine parts. and stampings. Even though broaches can be expensive. broaching is usually favored over other processes when used for high-quantity production runs.

Broaches are shaped similar to a saw. except the height of the teeth increases over the length of the tool. Moreover. the broach contains three distinct sections: one for roughing. another for semi-finishing. and the final one for finishing. Broaching is an unusual machining process because it has the feedbuilt into the tool. The profile of the machined surface is always the inverse of the profile of the broach. The rise per tooth (RPT). also known as the *step* or feed per tooth. determines the amount of material removed and the size of the chip. The broach can be moved relative to the workpiece or vice-versa. Because all of the features are built into the broach no complex motion or skilled Labour is required to use it. A broach is effectively a collection of single-point cutting tools arrayed in sequence. cutting one after the other; its cut is analogous to multiple passes of a shaper.

PROCESS

The process depends on the type of broaching being performed. Surface broaching is very simple as either the workpiece is moved against a stationary surface broach. or the workpiece is held stationary while the broach is moved against it.Internal broaching is more involved. The process begins by clamping the workpiece into a special holding fixture. called a *workholder*. which mounts in the broaching machine. The broaching machine *elevator*. which is the part of the machine that moves the broach above the workholder. then lowers the broach through the workpiece. Once through. the broaching machine's *puller*. essentially a hook. grabs the *pilot* of the broach.

The elevator then releases the top of the pilot and the puller pulls the broach through the workpiece completely. The workpiece is then removed from the machine and the broach is raised back up to reengage with the elevator. The broach usually only moves linearly. but sometimes it is also rotated to create a spiral spline or gun-barrel rifling.

Cutting fluids are used for three reasons;

1. to cool the workpiece and broach
2. to lubricate cutting surfaces
3. to flush the chips from the teeth.

Fortified petroleum cutting fluids are the most common. however heavy duty water soluble cutting fluids are being used because of their superior cooling. cleanliness. and non-flammability.

USAGE

Fig. An example of a broached workpiece. Here the broaching profile is a spline.

Broaching was originally developed for machining internal keyways. However. it was soon discovered that broaching is very useful for machining other surfaces and shapes for high volume workpieces.

Because each broach is specialized to cut just one shape either the broach must be specially designed for the geometry of the workpiece or the workpiece must be designed around a standard broach geometry. A customized broach is usually only viable with high volume workpieces. because the broach can cost US$15.000 to US$30.000 to produce.

Broaching speeds vary from 20 to 120 surface feet per minute (SFPM). This results in a complete cycle time of 5 to 30 seconds. Most of the time is consumed by the return stroke. broach handling. and workpiece loading and unloading.

The only limitations on broaching are that there are no obstructions over the length of the surface to be machined. the geometry to be cut does not have curves in multiple planes. and that the workpiece is strong enough to withstand the forces involved.

Specifically for internal broaching a hole must first exist in the workpiece so the broach can enter.

Also. there are limits on the size of internal cuts. Common internal holes can range from 0.125 to 6 in (3.2 to 152.4 mm) in diameter but it is possible to achieve a range of 0.05 to 13 in (1.3 to 330.2 mm). Surface broaches' range is usually 0.075 to 10 in (1.9 to 254.0 mm). although the feasible range is 0.02 to 20 in (0.51 to 508.00 mm).

Tolerances are usually ± 0.002 in (± 0.05 mm). but in precise applications a tolerance of ± 0.0005 in (± 0.01 mm) can be held. Surface finishes are usually between 16 and 63 microinches (ìin). but can range from 8 to 125 ìin. There may be minimal burrs on the exit side of the cut.

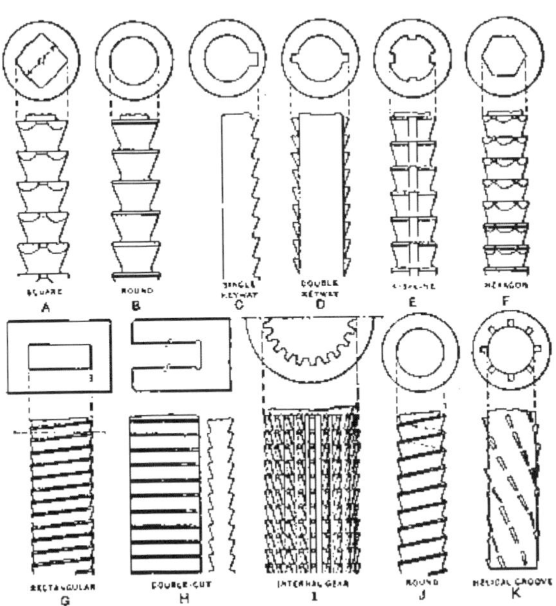

Broaching works best on softer materials. such as brass. bronze. copper alloys. aluminium. graphite. hard rubbers. wood. composites. and plastic. However. it still has a goodmachinability rating on mild steels and free machining steels. When broaching. the machinability rating is closely related to the hardness of the material. For steels the ideal hardness range is between 16 and 24 Rockwell C (HRC); a hardness greater than HRC 35 will dull the broach quickly. Broaching is more difficult on harder materials. stainless steel and titanium. but is still possible.

TYPES

Broaches can be categorized by many means:

- Use: internal. or surface
- Purpose: single. or combination
- Motion: push. pull. or stationary
- Construction: solid. built-up. hollow or shell
- Function: roughing. sizing. or burnishing

If the broach is large enough the costs can be reduced by using a *built-up* or *modular* construction. This involves producing the broach in pieces and assembling it. If any portion wears out only that section has to be replaced. instead of the entire broach.

Most broaches are made from high speed steel (HSS) or an alloy steel; TiN coatings are common on HSS to prolong life. Except when broaching cast iron. tungsten carbide is rarely used as a tooth material because the cutting edge will crack on the first pass.

Surface broaches

The *slab broach* is the simplest surface broach. It is a general purpose tool for cutting flat surfaces.

Slot broaches (G and H) are for cutting slots of various dimensions at high production rates. Slot broaching is much quicker than milling when more than one slot needs to be machined. because multiple broaches can be run through the part at the same time on the same broaching machine.

Contour broaches are designed to cut concave. convex. cam. contoured. and irregular shaped surfaces.*Pot broaches* are cut the inverse of an internal broach; they cut the outside diameter of a cylindrical workpiece.

They are named after the pot looking fixture in which the broaches are mounted; the fixture is often referred to as a "pot". The pot is designed to hold multiple broaching tools concentrically over its entire length.

The broach is held stationary while the workpiece is pushed or pulled through it. This has replaced hobbing for some involute gears and cutting external splines and slots. *Straddle broaches* use two slab broaches to cut parallel surfaces on opposite sides of a workpiece in one pass. This type of broaching holds closer tolerances than if the two cuts were done independently. It is named after the fact that the broaches "straddle" the workpiece on multiple sides.

Internal broaches

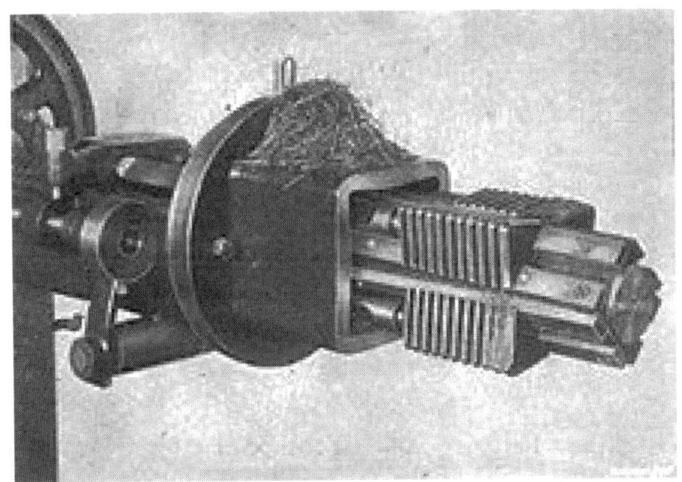

Fig. A modular broach

Solid broaches are the most common type; they are made from one solid piece of material. For broaches that wear out quickly *shell*broaches are used; these broaches are similar to a solid broach. except there is a hole through the center where it mounts on an arbor. Shell broaches cost more initially. but save cost overall if the broach must be replaced often because the pilots are on the mandrel and do not have to be reproduced with each replacement.

Modular broaches are commonly used for large internal broaching applications. They are similar to shell broaches in that they are a multi-piece construction. This design is used because it is cheaper to build and resharpen and is more flexible than a solid design.

A common type of internal broach is the *keyway* broach (C and D). It uses a special fixture called a *horn* to support the broach and properly locate the part with relation to the broach.

A *concentricity broach* is a special type of spline cutting broach which cuts both the minor diameter and the spline form to ensure precise concentricity. The *cut-and-recut broach* is used to cut thin-walled workpieces. Thin-walled workpieces have a tendency to expand during cutting and then shrink Afterwards. This broach overcomes that problem by first broaching with the standard roughing teeth. followed by a "breathing" section. which serves as a pilot as the workpiece shrinks. The teeth after the "breathing" section then include roughing. semi-finishing. and finishing teeth.

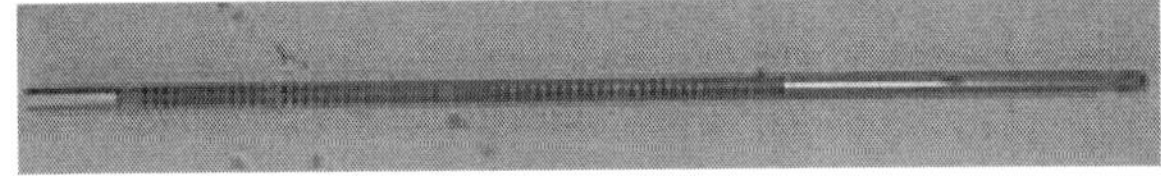

An internal broach for cutting splines

The finishing teeth

The semi-finishing teeth

The roughing teeth

The front pilot

The slot in the tip of the broach where the broaching machine latches on to the broach to pull it through the workpiece

Design

For defining the geometry of a broach an internal type is shown below. Note that the geometries of other broaches are similar.

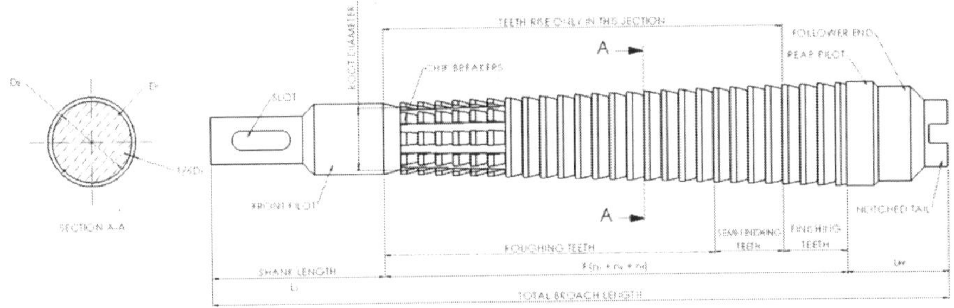

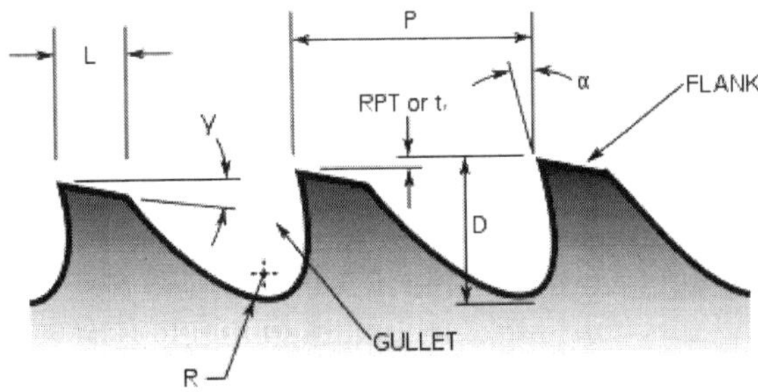

where:

- P = pitch
- RPT = rise per tooth
- n_r = number of roughing teeth
- n_s = number of semi-finishing teeth

- n_f = number of finishing teeth
- t_r = RPT for the roughing teeth
- t_s = RPT for the semi-finishing teeth
- t_f = RPT for the finishing teeth
- L_s = Shank length
- L_{RP} = Rear pilot length
- D_1 = Diameter of the tooth tip
- D_2 = Diameter of the tooth root
- D = Depth of a tooth (0.4P)
- L = Land (behind the cutting edge) (0.25P)
- R = Radius of the gullet (0.25P)
- $\acute{a}$ = Hook angle or rake angle
- $\tilde{a}$ = Back-off angle or clearance angle
- L_w = Length of the workpiece (not shown)

The most important characteristic of a broach is the rise per tooth (RPT). which is how much material is removed by each tooth. The RPT varies for each section of the broach. which are the roughing section (t_r). semi-finishing section (t_s). and finishing section (t_f). The roughing teeth remove most of the material so the number of roughing teeth required dictates how long the broach is. The semi-finishing teeth provide surface finish and the finishing teeth provide the final finishing. The finishing section's RPT (t_f) is usually zero so that as the first finishing teeth wear the later ones continue the sizing function. For free-machining steels the RPT ranges from 0.006 to 0.001 in (0.152 to 0.025 mm). For surface broaching the RPT is usually between 0.003 to 0.006 in (0.076 to 0.152 mm) and for diameter broaching is usually between 0.0012 to 0.0025 in (0.030 to 0.064 mm). The exact value depends on many factors. If the cut is too big it will impart too much stress into the teeth and the workpiece; if the cut is too small the teeth rub instead of cutting. One way to increase the RPT while keeping the stresses down is with *chip breakers*. They are notches in the teeth designed to break the chip and decrease the overall amount of material being removed by any given tooth. For broaching to be effective. the workpiece should have 0.020 to 0.025 in (0.51 to 0.64 mm) more material than the final dimension of the cut.

The *hook* ($\acute{a}$) angle is a parameter of the material being cut. For steel. it is between 15 and 20° and for cast iron it is between 6 and 8°. The *back-off* ($\tilde{a}$) provides clearance for the teeth so that they don't rub on the workpiece; it is usually between 1 and 3°.

When radially broaching workpieces that require a deep cut per tooth. such as forgings or castings. a *rotor-cut* or *jump-cut* design can be used; these broaches are also known as *free egress* or *nibbling* broaches. In this design the RPT is designated to two or three rows of teeth. For the broach to work the first tooth of that cluster has a wide notch. or undercut. and then the next tooth has a smaller notch (in a three tooth design) and the final tooth has no notch. This allows for a deep cut while keeping stresses. forces. and power requirements low.

There are two different options for achieving the same goal when broaching a flat surface. The first is similar to the rotor-cut design. which is known as a *double-cut* design. Here four teeth in a row have the same RPT. but each progressive tooth takes only a portion of the cut due to notches in the teeth. The other option is known as a *progressive* broach. which completely machines the center of the workpiece and then the rest of the broach machines outward from there. All of these designs require a broach that is longer than if a standard design were used.

For some circular broaches. *burnishing teeth* are provided instead of finishing teeth. They are not really teeth. as they are just rounded discs that are 0.001 to 0.003 in (0.025 to 0.076 mm) oversized. This results in burnishing the hole to the proper size. This is primarily used on non-ferrous and cast iron workpieces.

The pitch defines the tooth construction. strength. and number of teeth in contact with the workpiece. The pitch is usually calculated from workpiece length. so that the broach can be designed to have at least two teeth in contact with the workpiece at any time; the pitch remains constant for all teeth of the broach.

BROACHING MACHINES

Fig. The hydraulic cylinder of a horizontal broaching machine.

Broaching machines are relatively simple as they only have to move the broach in a linear motion at a predetermined speed and provide a means for handling the broach automatically. Most machines are hydraulic. but a few specialty machines are mechanically driven. The machines are distinguished by whether their motion is horizontal or vertical. The choice of machine is primarily dictated by the stroke required. Vertical broaching machines rarely have a stroke longer than 60 in (1.5 m).

Vertical broaching machines can be designed for push broaching. pull-down broaching. pull-up broaching. or surface broaching. Push broaching machines are similar to an arbor press with a guided ram; typical capacities are 5 to 50 tons. The two ram pull-down machine is the most common type of broaching machine. This style machine has the rams under the table. Pull-up machines have the ram above the table; they usually have more than one ram. Most surface broaching is done on a vertical machine.

Horizontal broaching machines are designed for pull broaching. surface broaching. continuous broaching. and rotary broaching. Pull style machines are basically vertical machines laid on the side with a longer stroke. Surface style machines hold the broach stationary while the workpieces are clamped into fixtures that are mounted on a conveyor system. Continuous style machines are similar to the surface style machines except adapted for internal broaching.

Horizontal machines used to be much more common than vertical machines. however today they represent just 10% of all broaching machines purchased. Vertical machines are more popular because they take up less space.

ROTARY BROACHING

A somewhat different design of cutting tool that can achieve the irregular hole or outer profile of a broach is called a *rotary broach* or*wobble broach*. One of the biggest advantages to this type of broaching is that it does not require a broaching machine. but instead is used on lathes. milling machines. screw machines or Swiss lathes.

Rotary broaching requires two tooling components: a tool holder and a broach. The leading (cutting) edge of the broach has a contour matching the desired final shape. The broach is mounted in a special tool holder that that allows it to freely rotate. The tool holder is special because it holds the tool so that its axis of rotation is inclined slightly to the axis of rotation of the work. A typical value for this misalignment is 1°. This angle is what produces a rotating edge for the broach to cut the workpiece. Either the workpiece or the tool holder is rotated. If the tool holder is rotated. the misalignment causes the broach to appear as though it is "wobbling". which is the origin of the term *wobble broach*.

For internal broaching the sides of the broach are drafted inward so it becomes thinner; for external broaching the sides are drafted outward. to make the pocket bigger. This draft keeps the broach from jamming; the draft must be larger than the angle of misalignment. If the work piece rotates. the broach is pressed against it. is driven by it. and rotates synchronously with it. If the tool holder rotates. the broach is pressed against the workpiece. but is driven by the tool holder.

Ideally the tool advances at the same rate that it cuts. The ideal rate of cut is defined as:Rate of cut [inches per rotation (IPR)] = (diameter of tool [inches]) × sin(Angle of misalignment [degrees])

If it advances much faster. then the tool becomes choked; conversely. if it advances much slower. then an interrupted or zig-zag cut occurs. In practice the rate of cut is slightly less than the ideal rate so that the load is released on the non-cutting edge of the tool.

There is some spiraling of the tool as it cuts. so the form at the bottom of the workpiece may be rotated with respect to the form at the top of the hole or profile. Spiraling may be undesirable because it binds the body of the tool and prevents it from cutting sharply. One solution to this is to reverse the rotation in mid cut. causing the tool to spiral in the opposite direction. If reversing the machine is not practical. then interrupting the cut is another possible solution.In general. a rotary broach will not cut as accurately as a push or pull broach. However. the ability to use this type of cutting tool on common machine tools is highly advantageous.

DRILL

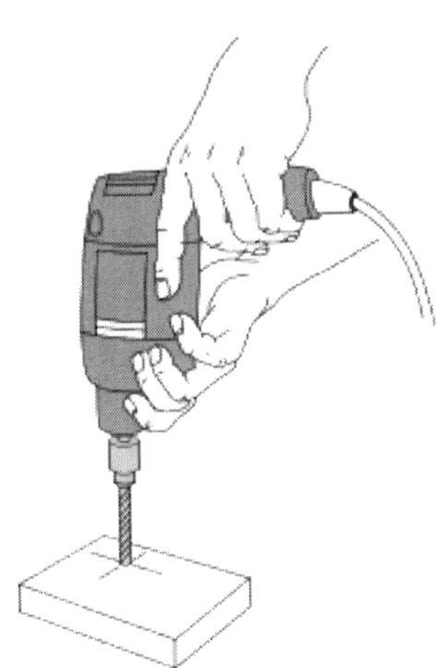

Fig. Drill scheme

A drill is a tool fitted with a cutting tool attachment or driving tool attachment. usually a drill bit or driver bit. used for boring holes in various materials or fastening various materials together with the use of fasteners. The attachment is gripped by a chuck at one end of the drill and rotated while pressed against the target material. The tip. and sometimes edges. of the cutting tool does the work of cutting into the target material. This may be slicing off thin shavings (twist drills or auger bits). grinding off small particles (oil drilling). crushing and removing pieces of the workpiece (SDS masonry drill). countersinking. counterboring. or other operations.

Drills are commonly used in woodworking. metalworking. construction and do-it-yourself projects. Specially designed drills are also used in medicine. space missions and other applications. Drills are available with a wide variety of performance characteristics. such as powerand capacity.

HISTORY

Fig. A wooden drill handle and other carpentry tools found on board the 16th century carrack *Mary Rose.*

Around 35.000 BCE. Homo sapiens discovered the benefits of the application of rotary tools. This would have rudimentarily consisted of a pointed rock being spun between the hands to bore a hole through another material. This led to the hand drill. a smooth stick. that was sometimes attached to flint point. and was rubbed between the palms. This was used by many ancient civilizations around the world including the Mayans. The earliest perforated artifacts. such as bone. ivory. shells and antlers found. are from the Upper Paleolithicera.

Bow drill (strap-drills) are the first machine drills. as they convert a back-and forth motion to a rotary motion. and they can be traced back to around 10.000 years ago. It was discovered that tying a cord around a stick. and then attaching the ends of the string to the ends of a stick(a bow). allowed a user to drill quicker and more efficiently. Mainly used to create fire. bow-drills were also used in ancient woodwork. stonework and dentistry. Archeologist discovered a Neo-lithic grave yard in Mehrgrath. Pakistan dating from the time of theHarappans. around 7.500-9.000 years ago. containing 9 adult bodies with a total of 11 teeth that had been drilled. There arehieroglyphs depicting Egyptian carpenters and bead makers in a tomb at Thebes using bow-drills. The earliest evidence of these tools being used in Egypt dates back to around 2500 BCE. The usage of bow-drills was widely spread through Europe. Africa. Asia and North America. during ancient times and is still used today. Over the years many slight variations of bow and strap drills have developed for the various uses of either boring through materials or lighting fires.

The core drill was developed in ancient Egypt by 3000 BC. The pump drill was invented during Roman times. it consists of a vertical spindle aligned by a piece of horizontal wood and a flywheel to maintain accuracy and momentum.

The hollow-borer tip. first used around the 13th century. consisted of a stick with a tubular shaped piece of metal on the end. such as copper. This allowed a hole to be drilled while only actually grinding the outer section of it. This completely separates the inner stone or wood from the rest. allowing the drill to pulverize less material to create a similar sized hole.

While the pump-drill and the bow-drill were used in Western Civilization to bore smaller holes for a larger part of human history. the Auger was used to drill larger holes starting sometime between Roman and Medieval ages. The auger allowed for more torque for larger holes. It is uncertain when the Brace and Bit was invented however the earliest picture found so far dates from the 15th century. It is a type of hand crank drill that consists of two parts as seen in the picture. The brace. on the upper half. where the user holds and turns it and on the lower part is the bit. The bit is interchangeable as bits wear down. The auger uses a rotating helical screw similar to the Archimedean screw shaped bit that is common today. The gimlet is also worth mentioning as it is scaled down version of an auger.

In the East. churn drills were invented as early as 221 BC during the Chinese Qin Dynasty. capable of reaching a depth of 1500 m. Churn drills in ancient China were built of wood and Labour-intensive. but were able to go through solid rock. The churn drill appears in Europe during the 12th century. In 1835 Isaac Singer is reported to have built a steam powered churn drill based off the method the Chinese used. Also worth briefly discussing are the early drill presses. they were machine tools that derived from bow-drills but were powered by windmills and water wheels. Drill presses consisted of the powered drills that could be raised or lowered into a material. allowing for less force by the user. The next great advancement in drilling technology. the electric motor. led to the invention of the electric drill. It is credited to Arthur James Arnot and William Blanch Brain ofMelbourne. Australia who patented the electric drill in 1889. In 1895. the first portable handheld drill was created by brothers.

Wilhem and Carl Fein. from Stuttgart Germany. In 1917 the first trigger switch. pistol-grip portable drill was patented by Black and Decker. This was the start of the modern drill era. Over the last century the electric drill has been created to the variety of types. and multiple sizes for an assortment of specific uses.

TYPES

There are many types of drills: some are powered manually. others use electricity (electric drill) or compressed air (*pneumatic drill*) as the motive power. and a minority are driven by an internal combustion engine (for example. earth drilling augers).

Drills with a percussive action (hammer drills) are mostly used in hard materials such as masonry(brick. concrete and stone) or rock.

Drilling rigs are used to bore holes in the earth to obtain water or oil. Oil wells. water wells. or holes for geothermal heating are created with large drilling rigs. Some types of hand-held drills are also used to drive screws and other fasteners. Some small appliances that have no motor of their own may be drill-powered. such as small pumps. grinders. etc.

Fig. Carpenter using a crank-powered brace to drill a hole

Hand tools

A variety of hand-powered drills have been employed over the centuries. Here are a few. starting with approximately the oldest:

- Bow drill
- Brace and bit
- Gimlet
- Hand drill. also known as an "eggbeater" drill

- Breast drill. similar to an "eggbeater" drill. it has a flat chest piece instead of a handle
- Push drill. a tool using a spiral ratchet mechanism
- Pin chuck. a small hand-held jeweler's drill

Fig. An old hand drill or "eggbeater" drill. The hollow wooden handle. with screw-on cap. is used to store drill bits

Pistol-grip (corded) drill

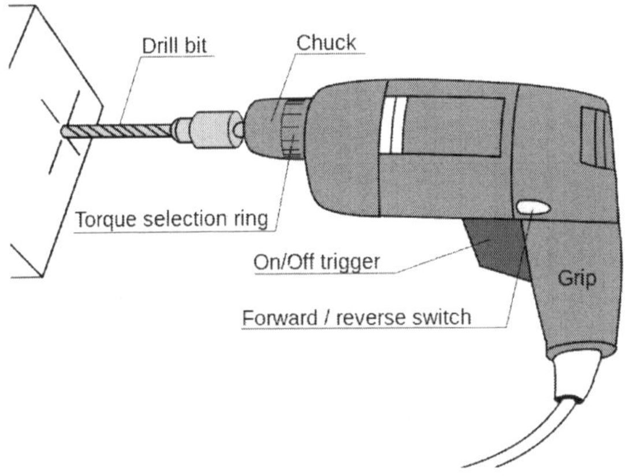

Fig. Anatomy of a pistol-grip corded drill.

Drills with pistol grips are the most common type in use today. and are available in a huge variety of subtypes. A less common type is the right-angle drill. a special tool used by tradesmen such as plumbers and electricians. The motor used in corded drills is often a universal motor due to its high power.

For much of the 20th century. many attachments could commonly be purchased to convert corded electric hand drills into a range of other power tools. such as orbital sanders and power saws. more cheaply than purchasing conventional. self-contained versions of those tools (the greatest saving being the lack of an additional electric motor for each device). As the prices of power tools and suitable electric motors have fallen. however. such attachments have become much less common. A similar practice is currently employed for cordless tools where the battery. the most expensive component. is shared between various motorised devices. as opposed to a single electric motor being shared between mechanical attachments.

Fig. Drills can also be used at an angle to join two boards.

Hammer drill

The hammer drill is similar to a standard electric drill. with the exception that it is provided with a hammer action for drilling masonry. The hammer action may be engaged or disengaged as required. Most electric hammer drills are rated (input power) at between 600 and 1100 watts. The efficiency is usually 50-60% *i.e.* 1000 watts of input is converted into 500-600 watts of output (rotation of the drill and hammering action).

The hammer action is provided by two cam plates that make the chuck rapidly pulse forward and backward as the drill spins on its axis. This pulsing (hammering) action is measured in Blows Per Minute (BPM) with 10.000 or more BPMs being common. Because the combined mass of the chuck and bit is comparable to that of the body of the drill. the energy transfer is inefficient and can sometimes make it difficult for larger bits to penetrate harder materials such as poured concrete. The operator experiences considerable vibration. and the cams are generally made from hardened steel to avoid them wearing out quickly. In practice. drills are restricted to standard masonry bits up to 13 mm (1/2 inch) in diameter. A typical application for a hammer drill is installing electrical boxes. conduit straps or shelves in concrete.

In contrast to the cam-type hammer drill. a rotary/pneumatic hammer drill accelerates only the bit. This is accomplished through a piston design. rather than a spinning cam. Rotary hammers have much less vibration and penetrate most building materials. They can also be used as "drill only" or as "hammer only" which extends their usefulness for tasks such as chipping brick or concrete. Hole drilling progress is greatly superior to cam-type hammer drills. and these drills are generally used for holes of 19 mm (3/4 inch) or greater in size. A typical application for a rotary hammer drill is boring large holes for lag bolts in foundations. or installing large lead anchors in concrete for handrails or benches.A standard hammer drill accepts 6 mm (1/4 inch) and 13 mm (1/2 inch) drill bits.

while a rotary hammer uses SDS or Spline Shank bits. These heavy bits are adept at pulverising the masonry and drill into this hard material with relative ease.However. there is a big difference in cost. In the UK a cam hammer typically costs £12 or more. while a rotary/pneumatic costs £35 or more. In the US a typical hammer drill costs between $70 and $120. and a rotary hammer between $150 and $500 (depending on bit size). For DIY use or to drill holes less than 13 mm (1/2 inch) in size. the hammer drill is most commonly used.

Rotary hammer drill

Fig. A rotary hammer drill used in construction

The rotary hammer drill (also known as a rotary hammer. roto hammer drill or masonry drill) combines a primary dedicated hammer mechanism with a separate rotation mechanism. and is used for more substantial material such as masonry or concrete. Generally. standard chucks and drills are inadequate and chucks such as SDS and carbide drills that have been designed to withstand the percussive forces are used. Some styles of this tool are intended for masonry drilling only and the hammer action cannot be disengaged. Other styles allow the drill to be used without the hammer action for normal drilling. or hammering to be used without rotation for chiselling.

Cordless drills

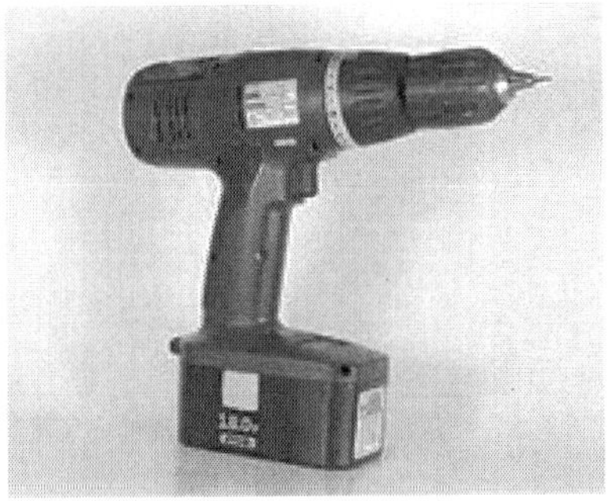

Fig. Cordless drill

A cordless drill is an electric drill which uses rechargeable batteries. These drills are available with similar features to an AC mains-powered drill. They are available in the hammer drill configuration and most have a clutch. which aids in driving screws into various substrates while not damaging them. Also available are right angle drills. which allow a worker to drive screws in a tight space. While 21st century battery innovations allow significantly more drilling. large diameter holes (typically 12–25 mm (0.5–1.0 in) or larger) may drain current cordless drills quickly.

For continuous use. a worker will have one or more spare battery packs charging while drilling. and quickly swap them instead of having to wait an hour or more for recharging. although there are now Rapid Charge Batteries that can charge in 10–15 minutes.Early cordless drills used interchangeable 7.2 V battery packs. Over the years battery voltages have increased. with 18 V drills being most common. but higher voltages are available. such as 24 V. 28 V. and 36 V. This allows these tools to produce as much torque as some corded drills.

Common battery types of are nickel-cadmium (NiCd) batteries and lithium-ion batteries. with each holding about half the market share. NiCd batteries have been around longer. so they are less expensive (their main advantage). but have more disadvantages compared to lithium-ion batteries. NiCd disadvantages are limited life. self-discharging. environment problems upon disposal. and eventually internally short circuiting due to dendrite growth. Lithium-ion batteries are becoming more common because of their short charging time. longer life. absence of memory effect. and low weight. Instead of charging a tool for an hour to get 20 minutes of use. 20 minutes of charge can run the tool for an hour. Lithium-ion batteries also hold a charge for a significantly longer time than nickel-cadmium batteries. about two years if not used. vs. 1 to 4 months for a nickel-cadmium battery.

Drill press

Fig. A drill press

Fig. Woman operating drill press (boring machine). boring wooden reels for winding barbed wire. 1917.

A drill press (also known as a pedestal drill. pillar drill. or bench drill) is a fixed style of drill that may be mounted on a stand or bolted to the floor or workbench. Portable models with a magnetic base grip the steel workpieces they drill. A drill press consists of a base. column (or pillar). table. spindle (or quill). and drill head. usually driven by an induction motor. The head has a set of handles (usually 3) radiating from a central hub that. when turned. move the spindle and chuck vertically. parallel to the axis of the column. The table can be adjusted vertically and is generally moved by a rack and pinion; however. some older models rely on the operator to lift and reclamp the table in position. The table may also be offset from the spindle's axis and in some cases rotated to a position perpendicular to the column. The size of a drill press is typically measured in terms of *swing*. Swing is defined as twice the *throat distance*. which is the distance from the center of the spindle to the closest edge of the pillar. For example. a 16-inch (410 mm) drill press has an 8-inch (200 mm) throat distance.

A drill press has a number of advantages over a hand-held drill:

- Less effort is required to apply the drill to the workpiece. The movement of the chuck and spindle is by a lever working on a rack and pinion. which gives the operator considerable mechanical advantage
- The table allows a vise or clamp to be used to position and restrain the work. making the operation much more secure
- The angle of the spindle is fixed relative to the table. allowing holes to be drilled accurately and consistently

- Drill presses are almost always equipped with more powerful motors compared to hand-held drills. This enables larger drill bits to be used and also speeds up drilling with smaller bits.

For most drill presses—especially those meant for woodworking or home use—speed change is achieved by manually moving a belt across a stepped pulley arrangement. Some drill presses add a third stepped pulley to increase the number of available speeds. Modern drill presses can. however. use a variable-speed motor in conjunction with the stepped-pulley system. Medium-duty drill presses such as those used in machine shop (tool room) applications are equipped with a continuously variable transmission.

This mechanism is based on variable-diameter pulleys driving a wide. heavy-duty belt. This gives a wide speed range as well as the ability to change speed while the machine is running. Heavy-duty drill presses used for metalworking are usually of the gear-head.

Drill presses are often used for miscellaneous workshop tasks other than drilling holes. This includes sanding. honing. and polishing. These tasks can be performed by mounting sanding drums. honing wheels and various other rotating accessories in the chuck. This can be unsafe in some cases. as the chuck arbor. which may be retained in the spindle solely by the friction of a taper fit. may dislodge during operation if the side loads are too high.

Geared head drill press

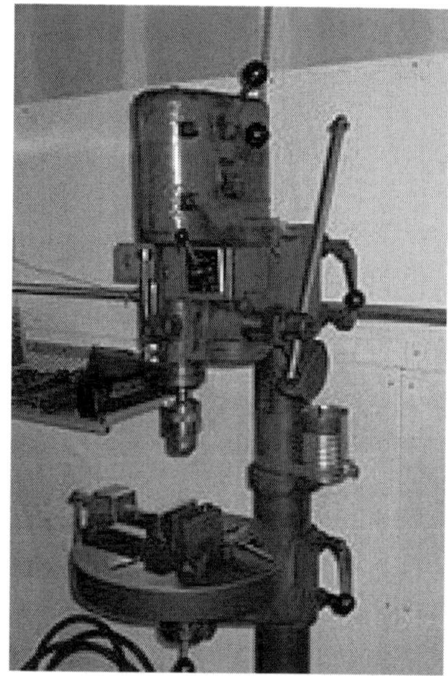

Fig. Geared head drill press. Shift levers on the head and a two speed motor control immediately in front of the quill handle select one of eight possible speeds

A geared head drill press is a drill press in which power transmission from the motor to the spindle is achieved solely through spur gearing inside the machine's head. No friction elements (*e.g.*. belts) of any kind are used. which assures a positive drive at all times and minimizes maintenance requirements. Gear head drills are intended for metalworking applications where the drilling forces are higher and the desired speed (RPM) is lower than that used for woodworking.

Levers attached to one side of the head are used to select different gear ratios to change the spindle speed. usually in conjunction with a two- or three-speed motor. Most machines of this type are designed to be operated on three-phase electric power and are generally of more rugged construction than equivalently sized belt-driven units. Virtually all examples have geared racks for adjusting the table and head position on the column.

Geared head drill presses are commonly found in tool rooms and other commercial environments where a heavy duty machine capable of production drilling and quick setup changes is required. In most cases. the spindle is machined to accept Morse taper tooling for greater flexibility. Larger geared head drill presses are frequently fitted with power feed on the quill mechanism. with an arrangement to disengage the feed when a certain drill depth has been achieved or in the event of excessive travel. Some gear-head drill presses have the ability to perform tapping operations without the need for an external tapping attachment. This feature is commonplace on larger gear head drill presses. A clutch mechanism drives the tap into the part under power and then backs it out of the threaded hole once the proper depth is reached. Coolant systems are also common on these machines to prolong tool life under production conditions.

Fig. Radial arm drill press.

Radial arm drill press

Fig. Radial arm drill press controls

A radial arm drill press is a large geared head drill press in which the head can be moved along an arm that radiatesfrom the machine's column. As it is possible to swing the arm relative to the machine's base. a radial arm drill press is able to operate over a large area without having to reposition the workpiece. This saves considerable time because it is much faster to reposition the drill head than it is to unclamp. move. and then re-clamp the workpiece to the table.

The size of work that can be handled may be considerable. as the arm can swing out of the way of the table. allowing anoverhead crane or derrick to place a bulky workpiece on the table or base. A vise may be used with a radial arm drill press. but more often the workpiece is secured directly to the table or base. or is held in a fixture.

Power spindle feed is nearly universal with these machines and coolant systems are common. Larger size machines often have power feed motors for elevating or moving the arm. The biggest radial arm drill presses are able to drill holes as large as four inches (101.6 millimeters) diameter in solid steel or cast iron. Radial arm drills are specified by the diameter of the column and the length of the arm. The length of the arm is usually the same as the maximum throat distance. The Radial Arm Drill pictured in this article is a 9-inch column x 3-foot arm. The maximum throat distance of this drill would be approximately 36". giving a swing of 72" (6 feet)..

Mill drill

Mill drills are a lighter alternative to a milling machine. They combine a drill press (belt driven) with the X/Y coordinate abilities of the milling machine's table and a locking collet that ensures that the cutting tool will not fall from the spindle when lateral forces are experienced against the bit. Although they are light in construction. they have the advantages of being space-saving and versatile as well as inexpensive. being suitable for light machining that may otherwise not be affordable.

Accessories

Drills are often used simply as motors to drive a variety of applications. in much the same way that tractors with generic PTOs are used to power ploughs. mowers. trailers. etc.

Accessories available for drills include:

- Screw-driving tips of various kinds - flathead. Philips. etc. for driving screws in or out
- Water pumps
- Nibblers for cutting metal sheet
- Rotary sanding discs
- Rotary polishing discs

GEAR SHAPER

A gear shaper is a machine tool for cutting the teeth of internal or external gears. The name shaper relates to the fact that the cutter engages the part on the forward stroke and pulls away from the part on the return stroke. just like the clapper box on a planer shaper.

The cutting tool is also gear shaped having the same pitch as the gear to be cut. However number of cutting teeth must be less than that of the gear to be cut for internal gears. For external gears the number of teeth on the cutter is limited only by the size of the shaping machine. For larger gears the blank is sometimes gashed to the rough shape to make shaping easier.

The principal motions involved in rotary gear shaper cutting are of the following:

1. *Cutting Motion*: The downward linear motion of the cutter spindle together with the cutter.
2. *Return Stroke*: The upward linear travel of the spindle and cutter to withdraw the latter to its starting position.
3. *Indexing Motion*: Slow speed continuous rotation of the cutter spindle and work spindle to provide circular feed. the two speeds being regulated through the change gears such that against each rotation of the cutter the gear blank revolves through n/N revolution. where "n" is the number of teeth of the cutter. and "N" is the number of teeth to be cut on the blank.

4. *Completion of Cutting Operation*: The indexing and reciprocating motions continue until the required number of teeth to the required depth are cut all along the periphery of the gear blank.

HOBBING

Fig. A hob — the cutter used for hobbing.

Hobbing is a machining process for gear cutting. cutting splines. and cutting sprockets on a hobbing machine. which is a special type of milling machine. The teeth or splines are progressively cut into the workpiece by a series of cuts made by a cutting tool called a hob. Compared to other gear forming processes it is relatively inexpensive but still quite accurate. thus it is used for a broad range of parts and quantities.It is the most widely used gear cutting process for creating spur and helical gears and more gears are cut by hobbing than any other process since it is relatively quick and inexpensive.A type of skiving that is analogous to the hobbing of external gears can be applied to the cutting of internal gears. which are skived with a rotary cutter (rather than shaped or broached).

PROCESS

Hobbing uses a hobbing machine with two skew spindles. one mounted with a blank workpiece and the other with the hob. The angle between the hob's spindle and the workpiece's spindle varies. depending on the type of product being produced. For example. if a spur gear is being produced. then the hob is angled equal to the helix angle of the hob; if a helical gear is being produced then the angle must be increased by the same amount as the helix angle of the helical gear. The two shafts are rotated at a proportional ratio. which determines the number of teeth on the blank; for example. if the gear ratio is 40:1 the hob rotates 40 times to each turn of the blank. which produces 40 teeth in the blank. Note that the previous example only holds true for a single threaded hob; if the hob has multiple threads then the speed ratio must be multiplied by the number of threads on the hob. The hob is then fed up into workpiece until the correct tooth depth is obtained. Finally the hob is fed through the workpiece parallel to the blank's axis of rotation.Up to five teeth can be cut into the workpiece at the same time. Often multiple gears are cut at the same time. For very large gears the blank can be gashed to the rough shape first to make hobbing easier.

EQUIPMENT

Fig. A horizontal hobbing machine

Fig. A horizontal hobbing machine

Modern hobbing machines. also known as *hobbers*. are fully automated machines that come in many sizes. because they need to be able to produce anything from tiny instrument gears up to 10 ft (3.0 m) diameter marine gears. Each gear hobbing machine typically consists of a chuck andtailstock. to hold the workpiece or a spindle. a spindle on which the hob is mounted. and a drive motor.

For a tooth profile which is a theoretical involute. the fundamental rack is straight-sided. with sides inclined at the pressure angle of the tooth form. with flat top and bottom. The necessaryaddendum correction to allow the use of small-numbered pinions can either be obtained by suitable modification of this rack to a cycloidal form at the tips. or by hobbing at other than the theoretical pitch circle diameter. Since the gear ratio between hob and blank is fixed. the resulting gear will have the correct pitch on the pitch circle. but the tooth thickness will not be equal to the space width.Hobbing machines are characterised by the largest module or pitch diameter it can generate. For example. a 10 in (250 mm) capacity machine can generate gears with a 10 in pitch diameter and usually a maximum of a 10 in face width. Most hobbing machines are vertical hobbers. which means the blank is mounted vertically. Horizontal hobbing machines are usually used for cutting longer workpieces; *i.e.* cutting splines on the end of a shaft.

Hob

Fig. A gear hob in a hobbing machine with a finished gear.

The *hob* is a cutting tool used to cut the teeth into the workpiece. It is cylindrical in shape withhelical cutting teeth. These teeth have grooves that run the length of the hob. which aid in cutting and chip removal. There are also special hobs designed for special gears such as the spline and sprocket gears. The cross-sectional shape of the hob teeth are almost the same shape as teeth of a rack gearthat would be used with the finished product. There are slight changes to the shape for generating purposes. such as extending the hob's tooth length to create a clearance in the gear's roots. Each hob tooth is relieved on the back side to reduce friction.

Most hobs are single-thread hobs. but double-. and triple-thread hobs increase production rates. The downside is that they are not as accurate as single-thread hobs. Depending on type of gear teeth to be cut. there are custom made hobs and general purpose hobs. Custom made hobs are different from other hobs as they are suited to make gears with modified tooth profile. The tooth profile is modified to add strength and reduce size and gear noise.

This list outlines types of hobs:

- Roller chain sprocket hobs
- Worm wheel hobs
- Spline hobs
- Chamfer hobs
- Spur and helical gear hobs
- Straight side spline hobs
- Involute spline hobs
- Serration hobs
- Semitopping gear hobs

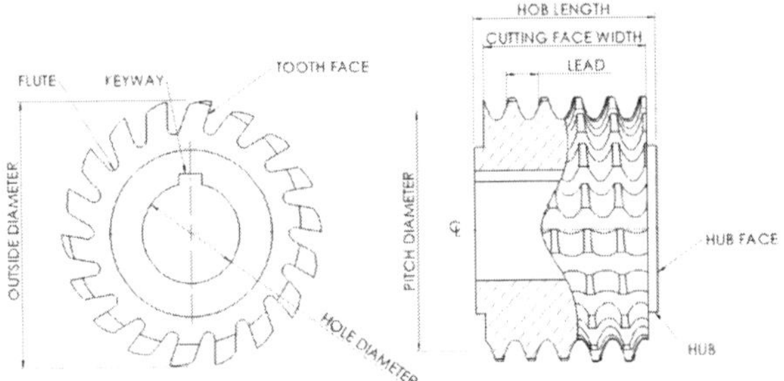

USES

Hobbing is used to make following types of finished goods:

- Cycloid gears
- Helical gears
- Involute gears
- Ratchets
- Splines
- Sprockets
- Spur gears
- Worm gears

Hobbing is used to produce most throated worm wheels. but certain tooth profiles cannot be hobbed. If any portion of the hob profile is perpendicular to the axis then it will have no cutting clearance generated by the usual backing off process. and it will not cut well.

Cycloidal forms

For cycloidal gears (as used in BS975-2 Specification for fine pitch gears) and cycloidal-type gears each module. ratio and number of teeth in the pinion requires a different hobbing cutter so the technique is only suitable for large volume production.To circumvent this problem a special war-time emergency circular arc gear standard was produced giving a series of close to cycloidal forms which could be cut with a single hob for each module for eight teeth and upwards to economize on cutter manufacturing resources. A variant on this is still included in BS978-2a (Gears for instruments and clockwork mechanisms. Cycloidal type gears. Double circular arc type gears).Tolerances of concentricity of the hob limit the lower modules which can be cut practically by hobbing to about 0.5 module.

HISTORY

Many manufacturing firms that maintain museums of how products were produced in times past will have examples of manual gear hobs that helped to produce gears prior to the gears of the 19th century and earlier. Along with these completely manual gear hobs will be samples of some of the first semi-automated gear hobs. and finally examples of more recent technology that demonstrates the fully automated process that modern gear hobs use to produce gears today. A few producers of gear hobs also have interesting literature on the history of gear hobs. including details about how modern gear hobs can produce thousands of gears in a single hour.

AUTOMATIC LATHE

Fig. Fay automatic lathe. 1921.

An automatic lathe is a lathe (usually a metalworking lathe) whose actions are controlled automatically. Although all electronically controlled (CNC) lathes are automatic. they are usually not called by that name. as explained under "General nomenclature". The first kinds of automatic lathes were mechanically automated ones. from the 1870s until the advent of NC and CNC in the 1950s and 1960s. CNC has not yet entirely displaced mechanically automated machines. The latter type of machine tool is no longer being newly built. but many existing examples remain in service.

GENERAL NOMENCLATURE

Because of the historical path of development of machine tool technology. the natural language terminology used to name automatic lathes. at least in English. is not hierarchical in quite the way that a manufacturing layperson might expect. Retronymy (and. in other respects. lack of retronymy) have shaped the nomenclature. However. it is easy enough to understand once a bit of history is known.

The term "automatic lathe" is still most often used in manufacturing in its earlier sense. referring to automated lathes of non-CNC types. The first kinds of automatic lathes were mechanically automated ones (whose control is via cams or tracers and pantographs). Thus. before electronic automation via numerical control. programmable logic controllers. and so on. the "automatic" in the term "automatic machine tool" always referred implicitly to *mechanical* automation.

The earliest mechanically automated lathes were geometric lathes. These included Rose engine lathes and others. In industrial contexts during the Machine Age. the term "automatic lathe" referred to mechanical screw machines and chuckers. of which a large variety of types. brands. and models were built.

Since the maturation of CNC. the implicit dichotomy of "manual versus automatic" still exists. but because CNC is so ubiquitous. the term "automatic" has lost some of its distinguishing power. All CNC machine tools are automatic. but (perhaps *therefore*) the usage of the machining industries does not routinely call them by that term. The term "automatic". when it is used at all. still usually refers implicitly to cam-operated machines. Thus a "plain old" 2-axis CNC lathe is not referred to as an "automatic lathe" (even though it is. literally speaking. automatic). However. within the machining subspecialty of Swiss-style CNC turning centers. the word "automatic" is often used freely for cam-op and CNC alike.

Small- to medium-sized cam-operated automatic lathes were (and still are) usually called screw machines or automatic screw machines. These machines work on parts that (as a rough guide only) are usually less than 80 millimetres (3.1 in) in diameter and less than 300 millimetres (12 in) long. Screw machines almost invariably do *bar work*. which means that an entire length of bar stock (anywhere from 1 to 4 m (3.3 to 13.1 ft) in length) passes through the spindle and is gripped by the chuck (which is usually a collet chuck). As the part is being machined. the entire length of bar stock is turning with the spindle. When the part is done. it is "parted off" from the bar. the chuck un-clamps. the bar is fed forward. and the chuck then closes again. ready for the next cycle. The bar-feeding can happen by various means. including pulling-finger tools that grab the bar and pull or roller bar feed that pushes the bar from behind.

Larger cam-operated automatic lathes were (and still are) usually called automatic chucking lathes. automatic lathes. automatic chuckers. automatics. or chuckers. The "chucker" part of the name comes from the fact that the workpieces are usually discrete blanks. held in a bin called a "magazine". and each one takes a turn at being chucked(gripped by the machine for being worked on) and cut. (This is analogous to the way that each round of ammunition in the magazine of a semi-automatic pistol gets its turn at being chambered.) The blanks are either individual forgings or castings. or they are pre-sawed pieces of billet. However. some members of this family of machine tools turn bar work or work on centers (for example. the Fay automatic lathe). Regarding bar work of large diameter (for example. 150 millimetres (5.9 in) or more). it is merely an academic point whether it is called "screw machine work" or just "automatic work".

SCREW MACHINE

Fig. Brown and Sharpe *Single Spindle* screw machine. Model 2G Sq Base. four-slide machine. $1D_2$ cap or $1D_4$ Air Feed.

Screw machines. being the class of automatic lathes for small- to medium-sized parts. are used in the high-volume manufacture of a vast variety of turned components.

Screw machine nomenclature

Speaking with reference to the normal definition of the term *screw machine*. all screw machines are fully automated. whether mechanically (via cams) or by CNC (computerized control). which means that once they are set up and started running. they continue running and producing parts with very little human intervention. This has been true since the 1870s. Mechanical automation came first. beginning in the 1870s; computerized control (via first NC and then CNC) came later. beginning in the 1950s.

Fig. Brown and Sharpe No. 1 wire feed screw machine. B&S persisted in calling manually operated turret lathes "screw machines" long after most machinists were reserving that term to refer specifically to cam-op automatics.

The name *screw machine* is somewhat of a misnomer. because screw machines spend much of their time making things that are not screws and that in many cases are not even threaded. However. the archetypal use for which screw machines were named was screw-making.

The definition of the term *screw machine* has changed with changing technology. Any use of the term prior to the 1840s. if it occurred. would have referred ad hoc to any machine tool used to produce screws. that is. there would have been no established differentiation from the term *screw-cutting lathe*. When turret lathes were developed in the 1840s. the term *screw machine* was applied to them in overlapping usage with the term *turret lathe*. In 1860. when some of the movements. such as turret indexing. were mechanically automated. the term *automatic screw machine* was applied. and the term *hand screw machine* or *manual screw machine* wasretronymously applied to the earlier machines. Within 15 years. the entire part-cutting cycle had been mechanically automated. and machines of the 1860 type were retronymously called *semi-automatic*. From that time on. machines with fully automated cycles were usually called *automatic screw machines*. and eventually. in the usage of most people in the machining industries. the term *screw machine* no longer was used to refer to manual or semi-automatic turret lathes. having become reserved for one class of machine. the fully mechanically automated type.

This narrow meaning of *screw machine* remained stable from about the 1890s until the 1950s. (Brown and Sharpe continued to call some of their hand-operated turret lathe models "screw machines". but most machinists reserved the term for automatics.) Within this class called *screw machines* there were variations. such as single-spindle versus multispindle. horizontal-turret versus vertical-turret. etc. With the advent of NC. screw machines diverged into two classes. mechanical and NC. This distinction continues today with mechanical screw machines and CNC screw machines. However. in shop-floor jargon. the term *screw machine* by itself is still often understood in context to imply a mechanical screw machine. so the retronym *mechanical screw machine* is not consistently used.

AUTOMATIC CHUCKER

An automatic chucking machine is very similar to an automatic screw machine. except it handles larger work. which due to its size is more often chucking work and less often bar work. The Fay automatic lathe was a variant that specialized in turning work on centers. While a screw machine is limited to around 80 millimetres (3.1 in) practice. automatic chuckers are available that can handle up to 300 millimetres (12 in) chucks. The chucks are air-operated. Many of these machines are multispindle (more than one main spindle). Well-known brands of such machines have included National-Acme. Hardinge. New Britain. New Britain-Gridley. Acme-Gridley. Davenport.

Bullard Mult-Au-Matic (a vertical multispindle variant). Thomas Ryder and Son. and others.Automatic chuckers are a class of machine tool that relatively few machinists get a chance to work with. Thus some of these models and brands are obscure outside of narrow industry niches. such as OEM parts suppliers to the automotive industry.

They are limited in their economic niches to high-volume production of large parts. which tends to occur only at relatively few companies (compared to smaller work that may be done by countless small businesses). The market for such machine tools generally does not include the neighborhood job shop or tool and die shop.

A related characteristic of cam-operated chuckers is that they are fading into history faster than most other non-CNC machine tool classes. This is because the few companies that have them tend to be forced to continually adapt to the latest state of the art (which today is all CNC) in order to compete and thus survive. Cam-op chuckers may end up in scrap yards more easily than other types of non-CNC machine tools.

Unlike with "Grandpa's South Bend lathe" or "Dad's old Bridgeport knee mill". virtually no one can afford to keep and use them for sentimental reasons alone. As has happened with most Non-digital commercial typesetting machinery (such as old Linotype machines). it seems likely that within a few decades the only examples of these machines still extant will be a few museum pieces and a few obscure pockets of abandoned inventory.

This is not because they are "primitive" by any means—in fact. they are mechanical marvels with ingenious design and high build quality. The change simply reflects the fact that CNC and CAD/CAM have become so advanced and flexible that it will be hard to compete with them.

CHOICE OF MACHINES AND CONTROL TYPE

Mechanical screw machines have been replaced to some extent by CNC lathes (turning centers) and CNC screw machines. However. they are still commonly in operation. and for high-volume production of turned components it is still often true that nothing is as cost-efficient as a mechanical screw machine.

In the hierarchy of manufacturing machines. the screw machine sits at the top when large product volumes are needed. An engine lathe sits at the bottom. taking the least amount of time to set up but the most amount of skilled Labour and time to actually produce a part. A turret lathe has traditionally been one step above an engine lathe. needing greater set-up time but being able to produce a higher volume of product and usually requiring a lower-skilled operator once the set-up process is complete. Screw machines may require an extensive set-up. but once they are running. a single operator can monitor the operation of several machines.The advent of the CNC lathe (or more properly. CNC turning center) has blurred these distinct levels of production to some extent. The CNC turning center most appropriately fits in the mid-range of production. replacing the turret lathe.

However. it is often possible to produce a single component with a CNC turning center more quickly than can be done with an engine lathe. To some extent too. the CNC turning center has stepped into the region traditionally occupied by the (mechanical) screw machine. CNC screw machines do this to an even greater degree. but they are expensive. In some cases they are vital. yet in others a mechanical machine can match or beat overall performance and profitability. It is not unusual for cam-op automatic lathes to beat CNCs on cycle time. CNC offers many benefits. not least CAD/CAM integration. but the CNC itself usually does not give any inherent speed advantage within the context of an automatic lathe cycle in terms of speeds and feeds or tool-changing speed. There are many variables involved in answering the question of which is best for a particular part at a particular company.

(Overhead is part of the calculation—not least because most cam-op machines are long since paid for. whereas a late-model CNC machine has hefty monthly payments). Businesses relying on cam-op machines are still competing even in today's CNC-filled environment; they just need to be vigilant and smart about keeping it that way. In the multispindle segment. some machine tool builders also build hybrid machines that are part CNC and part old-school control (some stations are CNC while others are cam-op or actuated with simple hydraulic cycles). This lets shops with certain mixes of work derive competitive advantage from the lower cost compared with all-CNC machines.The variety of machines that allow profitable production within certain niches reflects the variety of work that exists: some high-volume work remains the province of cam-op; full CNC with all the bells and whistles outcompetes on some flexible low-volume work; and hybrid machines may yield the lowest unit price on mixes in between.

DESIGN

Fig. Close up view of a Brown and Sharpe *Single Spindle*screw machine. Notice the six station turret. the front and rear slides. and the two vertical slides. Also notice the black shaft just over the turret for use of swing stop.

An automatic lathe may have a single spindle or multiple spindles. Each spindle contains a bar or blank of material that is being machined simultaneously. A common configuration is six spindles. The cage that holds these six bars of materialindexes after each machining operation is complete. The indexing is reminiscent of a Gatling gun.\Each station may have multiple tools that cut the material in sequence. The tools are usually arranged in several axes. such as turret (rotary indexing). horizontal slide (linear indexing). and vertical slide (linear indexing). The linear groups are called "gangs". The operation of all these tools is similar to that on a turret lathe.By way of example: a bar of material is fed forward through the spindle. The face of the bar is machined (facing operation). The outside of the bar is machined to shape (turning operation). The bar is drilled or bored. and finally. the part is cut off (parting operation).

Fig. View of *Lead Cam* and *Seconds Gear Box* for a Brown and Sharpe screw machine. Sq-base 542 Series.

In a single-spindle machine. these four operations would most likely be performed sequentially. with four cross-slides each coming into position in turn to perform their operation. In a multi-spindle machine. each station corresponds to a stage in the production sequence through which each piece is then cycled. all operations occurring simultaneously. but on different pieces of work. in the manner of an assembly line.

OPERATIONS

Form tools

For the machining of complex shapes. it is common to use form tools. This contrasts with the cutting that is performed on an engine lathe where the cutting tool is usually a single-point tool. A form tool has the form or contour of the final part but in reverse. so it cuts the material leaving the desired component shape. This contrasts to a single-point tool. which cuts on one point at a time and the shape of the component is dictated by the motion of the tool rather than its shape.

Threading

Unlike on a lathe. single-point threading is rarely if ever performed; it is too time-consuming for the short cycle times that are typical of screw machines. A self-releasing die head can rapidly cut or roll-form threads on outside diameters. A Non--releasing tap holder with a tap can quickly cut inside diameters but it requires single spindle machines to reverse into high speed in order for the tap to be removed from the work. Threading and tapping speed (low speed) is typically 1/5 the high speed.

Rotary broaching

Rotary broaching is another common operation. The broach holder is mounted stationary while its internal live spindle and end cutting broach tool are driven by the workpiece. As the broach is fed into or around the workpiece. the broach's contact points are constantly changing. easily creating the desired form. The most common form made this way is a hexagonal socket in the end of a cap screw.

History

Fig. Charles Vander Woerd's machine for the American Watch Company. one of the earliest automatic screw machines.

Fig. A view inside the enclosure of a CNC Swiss-style screw machine.

The history of geometric lathes is discussed elsewhere. and concerns such applications as engraving and printing (especially of paper currency). jewelry making. and artistic pursuits.

The history of automatic lathes in industrial contexts began with screw machines. and that history can only be truly understood within the context of screw making in general. Thus the discussion below begins with a simple overview of screw making in prior centuries. and how it evolved into 19th-. 20th-. and 21st-century practice.

Humans have been making screws since ancient times. For most of those centuries. screw making generally involved custom cutting of the threads of each screw by hand (via whittling or filing). Other ancient methods involved wrapping wire around a mandrel (such as a stick or metal rod) or carving a tree branch that had been spirally wrapped by a vine.

Various machine elements that potentially lent themselves to screw making (such as the lathe. the leadscrew. the slide rest. gears. slide rests geared direct to spindles. and "change gear" gear trains) were developed over the centuries. with some of those elements being quite ancient. Various sparks of inventive power during the Middle Ages and Renaissance combined some of these elements into screw-making machines that presaged the industrial era to follow. For example. various medieval inventors whose names are lost to history clearly worked on the problem. as shown by Wolfegg Castle's *Medieval Housebook* (written circa 1475–1490). and Leonardo da Vinciand Jacques Besson left us with drawings of screw-cutting machines from the 1500s; not all of these designs are known to have been built. but clearly similar machines were a reality during Besson's lifetime. However. it was not until the era of 1760–1800 that these various elements were brought together successfully to create (in contemporaneous parallel) two new types of machine tool: the screw-cutting lathe (for low-volume. toolroom-style production of *machine* screws. with easy selection of various pitches) and the first high-volume-production. specialized. single-purpose machine tools for the production of screws. which were created to produce *wood* screws [meaning screws made of metal for use in wood] at high volume and low unit price. Screw-cutting lathes fed into the just-dawning evolution of modern machine shop practice. whereas the wood-screw-making machines fed into the just-dawning evolution of the modern hardware industry. that is. the concept of one factory supplying the needs of thousands of customers. who consumed screws in growing quantities for carpentry. cabinet making. and other trades. but did not make the hardware themselves (purchasing it instead from capital-intensive specialist makers for lower unit cost than they could achieve on their own). These two classes of machine tools simultaneously took the various classes of screws and moved them. for the first time. from the category of expensive. hand-made. seldom-used objects into the category of affordable. often-interchangeable commodity. (The interchangeability developed gradually. from intra-company to inter-company to national to international).

Between 1800 and 1840. on the machine-screw side. it became common practice to build all of the relevant screw-cutting machine elements into engine lathes. so the term "screw-cutting lathe" ceased to stand in contradistinction to other metalworking lathe types as a "special" kind of lathe. Meanwhile. on the wood-screw side. hardware manufacturers had developed for their own in-house use the first fully automatic [mechanically automated] special-purpose machine tools for the making of screws. The 1760–1840 development arc was a tremendous technological advance. but later advancements would make screws even cheaper and more prevalent yet again. These began in the 1840s with the adaptation of the engine lathe with a turret-head toolholder to create the turret lathe. This development greatly reduced the time. effort. and skill needed from the machine operator to produce each machine screw. Single-pointing was forgone in Favour of die head cutting for such medium- and high-volume repetitive production. Then. in the 1870s. the turret lathe's part-cutting cycle (sequence of movements) was automated by being put under cam control. in a way very similar to how music boxes and player pianos can play a tune automatically. According to Rolt (1965). the first person to develop such a machine was Christopher Miner Spencer. a New England inventor. Charles Vander Woerd may have contemporarily independently invented a machine similar to Spencer's. However. the wood-screw-making machines of the 1840s and 1850s [special-purpose factory production machine tools as opposed to small-machine-shop machine tools]. such as those developed by Cullen Whipple of the New England Screw Company and Thomas J. Sloan of the American Screw Company. had anticipated the machines of Spencer and Vander Woerd in various ways. albeit approaching the problem of automated screw production from a different commercial angle. All of the above machine tools (*i.e.*. screw-cutting lathes; suitably equipped engine lathes and bench lathes; turret lathes; turret-lathe-derived screw machines; and wood-screw-factory screw machines) were sometimes called "screw machines" during this era (logically enough. given that they were machines tailored to screw making). The nomenclatural evolution whereby the term "screw machine".

Spencer patented his idea in 1873; unfortunately. his patent attorney failed to protect the most significant part. the cam drum. which Spencer called the "brain wheel".Therefore many other people quickly took up the idea. Later important developers of fully automatic lathes (large and small) included S. L. Worsley. who developed a single-spindle machine for Brown and Sharpe; Edwin C. Henn. Reinhold Hakewessel. and George O. Gridley. who developed multiple-spindle variants and who were involved with a succession of corporations (Acme. National. National-Acme. Windsor Machine Company. Acme-Gridley. New Britain-Gridley); Edward P. Bullard Jr. who led the development of the Bullard Mult-Au-Matic; F.C. Fay and Otto A. Schaum. who developed the Fay automatic lathe; Ralph Flanders and his brother Ernest. who further refined the Fay lathe and who developed the automatic screw thread grinder; and many others. Meanwhile. engineers in Switzerland were also developing clever new manually and automatically controlled lathes during this same era. The technological developments in America and Switzerland flowed rapidly into other industrialized countries (via routes such as machine tool exports; trade journal articles and advertisements; trade shows. from world's fairs to regional events; and the turnover and emigration of engineers. setup hands. and operators). There. local innovators also developed further creative tooling for the machines and built clone machine models.

The development of numerical control was the next major leap in the history of automatic lathes—and it is also what changed the paradigm of what the "manual versus automatic" distinction even meant. Beginning in the 1950s. NC lathes began to take over the jobs that formerly were done by manual lathes and cam-op screw machines. although the displacement of the older technology by CNC has been a long. gradual arc that even today is not a total eclipse. By the 1980s. true CNC screw machines (as opposed to simpler CNC lathes). Swiss-style and non-Swiss. had begun to make serious inroads into the realm of cam-op screw machines. Similarly. CNC chuckers were developed. eventually evolving even into CNC rotary transfer machines. Very few people outside of automotive manufacturing are familiar with these machine tools. because they simply have no economic reason to come into contact with this segment of the machine tool industry. Today CNC lathes and their offspring (turn-mills. mill-turns. rotary transfers) are technological wonders with a blizzard of axes and accessories under CNC control. Their sophistication. accuracy and precision. metal-removal speed. tool-changing speed. degree of automation. and degree of networking with the rest of the enterprise are formidable.

MILLING (MACHINING)

Milling is the machining process of using rotary cutters to remove material from a workpiece advancing (or *feeding*) in a direction at an angle with the axis of the tool. It covers a wide variety of different operations and machines. on scales from small individual parts to large. heavy-duty gang milling operations. It is one of the most commonly used processes in industry and machine shops today for machining parts to precise sizes and shapes.

Milling can be done with a wide range of machine tools. The original class of machine tools for milling was the milling machine (often called a mill). After the advent ofcomputer numerical control (CNC). milling machines evolved into machining centers (milling machines with automatic tool changers. tool magazines or carousels. CNC control. coolant systems. and enclosures). generally classified as vertical machining centers (VMCs) and horizontal machining centers (HMCs). The integration of milling intoturning environments and of turning into milling environments. begun with live tooling for lathes and the occasional use of mills for turning operations. led to a new class of machine tools. multitasking machines (MTMs). which are purpose-built to provide for a default machining strategy of using any combination of milling and turning within the same work envelope.

Process

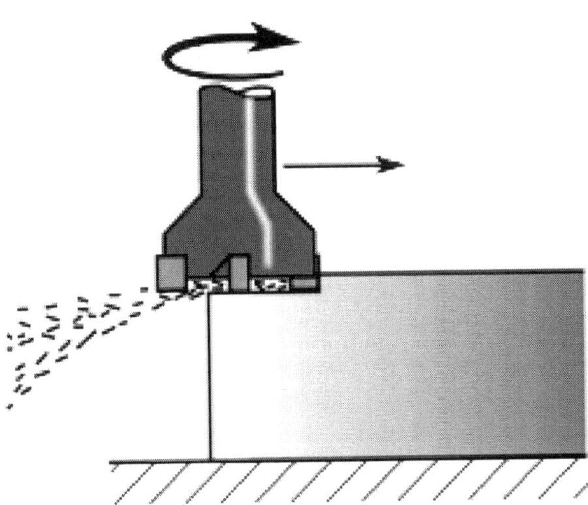

Fig. Face milling process (cutter rotation axis is vertical)

Milling is a cutting process that uses a milling cutter to remove material from the surface of a workpiece. The milling cutter is a rotarycutting tool. often with multiple cutting points. As opposed to drilling. where the tool is advanced along its rotation axis. the cutter in milling is usually moved perpendicular to its axis so that cutting occurs on the circumference of the cutter. As the milling cutter enters the workpiece. the cutting edges (flutes or teeth) of the tool repeatedly cut into and exit from the material. shaving off chips (swarf) from the workpiece with each pass.

The cutting action is shear deformation; the metal is pushed off the workpiece in tiny clumps that hang together to more or less extent (depending on the metal type) to form chips. This makes metal cutting a bit different (in its mechanics) from slicing softer materials with a blade.

The milling process removes material by performing many separate. small cuts. This is accomplished by using a cutter with many teeth. spinning the cutter at high speed. or advancing the material through the cutter slowly; most often it is some combination of these three approaches.

The speeds and feeds used are varied to suit a combination of variables. The speed at which the piece advances through the cutter is called feed rate. or just feed; it is most often measured in length of material per full revolution of the cutter.

There are two major classes of milling process:

- In face milling. the cutting action occurs primarily at the end corners of the milling cutter. Face milling is used to cut flat surfaces (faces) into the workpiece. or to cut flat-bottomed cavities.
- In peripheral milling. the cutting action occurs primarily along the circumference of the cutter. so that the cross section of the milled surface ends up receiving the shape of the cutter. In this case the blades of the cutter can be seen as scooping out material from the work piece. Peripheral milling is well suited to the cutting of deep slots. threads. and gear teeth.

Milling cutters

Many different types of cutting tools are used in the milling process. Milling cutters such as endmills may have cutting surfaces across their entire end surface. so that they can be drilled into the workpiece (plunging). Milling cutters may also have extended cutting surfaces on their sides to allow for peripheral milling. Tools optimized for face milling tend to have only small cutters at their end corners.

The cutting surfaces of a milling cutter are generally made of a hard and temperature-resistant material. so that they wear slowly. A low cost cutter may have surfaces made ofhigh speed steel. More expensive but slower-wearing materials include cemented carbide. Thin film coatings may be applied to decrease friction or further increase hardness.

They are cutting tools typically used in milling machines or machining centres to perform milling operations (and occasionally in other machine tools). They remove material by their movement within the machine (*e.g.*. a ball nose mill) or directly from the cutter's shape (*e.g.*. a form tool such as a hobbing cutter).

Surface finish

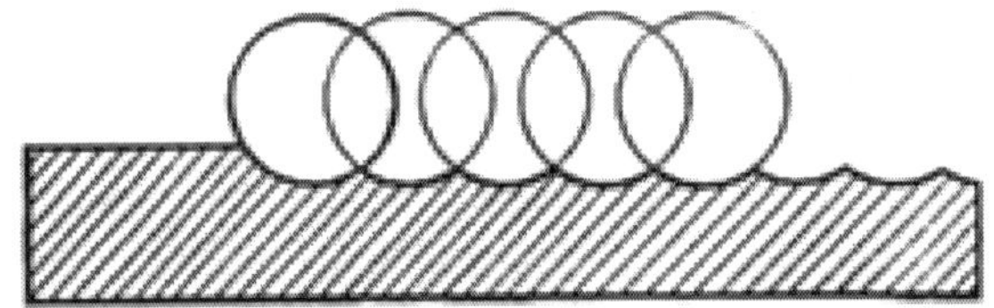

Fig. A diagram of revolution ridges on a surface milled by the side of the cutter. showing the position of the cutter for each cutting pass and how it corresponds with the ridges (cutter rotation axis is perpendicular to image plane)

As material passes through the cutting area of a milling machine. the blades of the cutter take swarfs of material at regular intervals. Surfaces cut by the side of the cutter (as in peripheral milling) therefore always contain regular ridges. The distance between ridges and the height of the ridges depend on the feed rate. number of cutting surfaces. the cutter diameter. With a narrow cutter and rapid feed rate. these revolution ridges can be significant variations in the surface height.

The face milling process can in principle produce very flat surfaces. However. in practice the result always shows visible trochoidal marks following the motion of points on the cutter's end face.

These revolution marks give the characteristic finish of a face milled surface. Revolution marks can have significant roughness depending on factors such as flatness of the cutter's end face and the degree of perpendicularity between the cutter's rotation axis and feed direction. Often a final pass with a slow feed rate is used to compensate for a poor milling setup. in order to reduce the roughness of revolution marks. In a precise face milling operation. the revolution marks will only be microscopic scratches due to imperfections in the cutting edge.

Gang milling

Gang milling refers to the use of two or more milling cutters mounted on the same arbor (that is. ganged) in a horizontal-milling setup. All of the cutters may perform the same type of operation. or each cutter may perform a different type of operation. For example. if several workpieces need a slot. a flat surface. and an angular groove. a good method to cut these (within a non-CNC context) would be gang milling. All the completed workpieces would be the same. and milling time per piece would be minimized.

Gang milling was especially important before the CNC era. because for duplicate part production. it was a substantial efficiency improvement over manual-milling one feature at an operation. then changing machines (or changing setup of the same machine) to cut the next op. Today. CNC mills with automatic tool change and 4- or 5-axis control obviate gang-milling practice to a large extent.

EQUIPMENT

Milling is performed with milling cutters attached to a milling machine.

Types and nomenclature

Mill orientation is the primary classification for milling machines. The two basic configurations are vertical and horizontal. However. there are alternate classifications according to method of control. size. purpose and power source.

Mill orientation

- Watch video

Vertical mill

In the vertical mill the spindle axis is vertically oriented. Milling cutters are held in the spindle and rotate on its axis. The spindle can generally be extended (or the table can be raised/lowered. giving the same effect). allowing plunge cuts and drilling. There are two subcategories of vertical mills: the bed mill and the turret mill.

- A turret mill has a stationary spindle and the table is moved both perpendicular and parallel to the spindle axis to accomplish cutting. The most common example of this type is the Bridgeport. Turret mills often have a quill which allows the milling cutter to be raised and lowered in a manner similar to a drill press. This type of machine provides two methods of cutting in the vertical (Z) direction: by raising or lowering the quill. and by moving the knee.
- In the bed mill. however. the table moves only perpendicular to the spindle's axis. while the spindle itself moves parallel to its own axis.

Turret mills are generally considered by some to be more versatile of the two designs. However. turret mills are only practical as long as the machine remains relatively small. As machine size increases. moving the knee up and down requires considerable effort and it also becomes difficult to reach the quill feed handle (if equipped). Therefore. larger milling machines are usually of the bed type.

A third type also exists. a lighter machine. called a mill-drill. which is a close relative of the vertical mill and quite popular with hobbyists. A mill-drill is similar in basic configuration to a small drill press. but equipped with an X-Y table. They also typically use more powerful motors than a comparably sized drill press. with potentiometer-controlled speed and generally have more heavy-duty spindle bearings than a drill press to deal with the lateral loading on the spindle that is created by a milling operation. A mill dril also typically raises and lowers the entire head. including motor. often on a dovetailed vertical. where a drill press motor remains stationary. while the arbor raises and lowers within a driving collar. Other differences that separate a mill-drill from a drill press may be a fine tuning adjustment for the Z-axis. a more precise depth stop. the capability to lock the X. Y or Z axis. and often a system of tilting the head or the entire vertical to allow angled cutting.

Aside from size and precision. the principal difference between these hobby-type machines and larger true vertical mills is that the X-Y table is at a fixed elevation; the Z-axis is controlled in basically the same fashion as drill press. where a larger vertical or knee mill has a vertically fixed milling head. and changes the X-Y table elevation. As well. a mill-drill often uses a standard drill press-type Jacob's chuck. rather than an internally tapered arbor that accepts collets. These are frequently of lower quality than other types of machines. but still fill the hobby role well because they tend to be benchtop machines with small footprints and modest price tags.

Horizontal mill

A horizontal mill has the same sort of *x–y* table. but the cutters are mounted on a horizontal arbor across the table. Many horizontal mills also feature a built-in rotary table that allows milling at various angles; this feature is called a *universal table*. While endmills and the other types of tools available to a vertical mill may be used in a horizontal mill. their real advantage lies in arbor-mounted cutters. called side and face mills. which have a cross section rather like a circular saw. but are generally wider and smaller in diameter. Because the cutters have good support from the arbor and have a larger cross-sectional area than an end mill. quite heavy cuts can be taken enabling rapid material removal rates.

These are used to mill grooves and slots. Plain mills are used to shape flat surfaces. Several cutters may be ganged together on the arbor to mill a complex shape of slots and planes. Special cutters can also cut grooves. bevels. radii. or indeed any section desired. These specialty cutters tend to be expensive. Simplex mills have one spindle. and duplex mills have two. It is also easier to cut gears on a horizontal mill. Some horizontal milling machines are equipped with a power-take-off provision on the table. This allows the table feed to be synchronized to a rotary fixture. enabling the milling of spiral features such as hypoid gears.

Comparative merits

The choice between vertical and horizontal spindle orientation in milling machine design usually hinges on the shape and size of a workpiece and the number of sides of the workpiece that require machining. Work in which the spindle's axial movement is normal to one plane. with an endmill as the cutter. lends itself to a vertical mill. where the operator can stand before the machine and have easy access to the cutting action by looking down upon it. Thus vertical mills are most favored for diesinking work (machining a mould into a block of metal). Heavier and longer workpieces lend themselves to placement on the table of a horizontal mill.Prior to numerical control. horizontal milling machines evolved first. because they evolved by putting milling tables under lathe-like headstocks. Vertical mills appeared in subsequent decades. and accessories in the form of add-on heads to change horizontal mills to vertical mills (and later vice versa) have been commonly used. Even in the CNCera. a heavy workpiece needing machining on multiple sides lends itself to a horizontal machining center. while diesinking lends itself to a vertical one.

GRINDING MACHINE

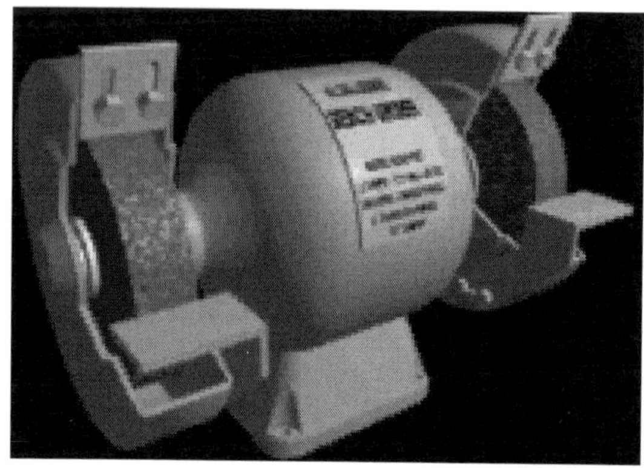

Fig. Rotating abrasive wheel on a bench grinder.

A grinding machine. often shortened to grinder. is any of various power tools or machine tools used for grinding. which is a type ofmachining using an abrasive wheel as the cutting tool. Each grain of abrasive on the wheel's surface cuts a small chip from the workpiece via shear deformation.

Grinding is used to finish workpieces that must show high surface quality (*e.g.*. low surface roughness) and high accuracy of shape and dimension. As the accuracy in dimensions in grinding is on the order of 0.000025 mm. in most applications it tends to be a finishing operation and removes comparatively little metal. about 0.25 to 0.50 mm depth. However. there are some roughing applications in which grinding removes high volumes of metal quite rapidly. Thus. grinding is a diverse field.

The grinding machine consists of a bed with a fixture to guide and hold the work piece. and a power-driven grinding wheel spinning at the required speed. The speed is determined by the wheel's diameter and manufacturer's rating. The user can control the grinding head to travel across a fixed work piece. or the work piece can be moved while the grind head stays in a fixed position.

Fine control of the grinding head or tables position is possible using a vernier calibrated hand wheel. or using the features of numerical controls.

Grinding machines remove material from the work piece by abrasion. which can generate substantial amounts of heat. To cool the work piece so that it does not overheat and go outside its tolerance. grinding machines incorporate a coolant. The coolant also benefits the machinist as the heat generated may cause burns. In high-precision grinding machines (most cylindrical and surface grinders). the final grinding stages are usually set up so that they remove about 200 nm (less than 1/10000 in) per pass - this generates so little heat that even with no coolant. the temperature rise is negligible. '

TYPES

Fig. A surface grinder.

Fig. A cylindrical grinder.

These machines include the:

- Belt grinder. which is usually used as a machining method to process metals and other materials. with the aid of coated abrasives. Sanding is the machining of wood; grinding is the common name for machining metals. Belt grinding is a versatile process suitable for all kind of applications like finishing. deburring. and stock removal.

- Bench grinder. which usually has two wheels of different grain sizes for roughing and finishing operations and is secured to a workbench or floor stand. Its uses include shaping tool bits or various tools that need to be made or repaired. Bench grinders are manually operated.
- Cylindrical grinder. which includes both the types that use centers and the centerless types. A cylindrical grinder may have multiple grinding wheels. The workpiece is rotated and fed past the wheel(s) to form a cylinder. It is used to make precision rods. tubes. bearing races. bushings. and many other parts.
- Surface grinder which includes the wash grinder. A surface grinder has a "head" which is lowered. and the workpiece is moved back and forth past the grinding wheel on a table that has a permanent magnet for use with magnetic stock. Surface grinders can be manually operated or have CNC controls. Rotary surface grinders or commonly known as "Blanchard" style grinders. the grinding head rotates and the table usually magnetic but can be vacuum or fixture. rotates in the opposite direction. this type machine removes large amounts of material and grinds flat surfaces with noted spiral grind marks. Used to make and sharpen; burn-outs. metal stamping die sets. flat shear blades. fixture bases or any flat and parallel surfaces.
- Tool and cutter grinder and the D-bit grinder. These usually can perform the minor function of the drill bit grinder. or other specialisttoolroom grinding operations.
- Jig grinder. which as the name implies. has a variety of uses when finishing jigs. dies. and fixtures. Its primary function is in the realm of grinding holes and pins. It can also be used for complex surface grinding to finish work started on a mill.
- Gear grinder. which is usually employed as the final machining process when manufacturing a high-precision gear. The primary function of these machines is to remove the remaining few thousandths of an inch of material left by other manufacturing methods (such as gashing or hobbing).

TOOL WEAR

Tool wear describes the gradual failure of cutting tools due to regular operation. It is a term often associated with tipped tools. tool bits. or drill bits that are used with machine tools.

Types of wear include:

- Flank wear in which the portion of the tool in contact with the finished part erodes. Can be described using the Tool Life Expectancy equation.
- Crater wear in which contact with chips erodes the rake face. This is somewhat normal for tool wear. and does not seriously degrade the use of a tool until it becomes serious enough to cause a cutting edge failure.

Can be caused by spindle speed that is too low or a feed rate that is too high. In orthogonal cutting this typically occurs where the tool temperature is highest. Crater wear occurs approximately at a height equaling the cutting depth of the material. Crater wear depth $\sim t_0$ t_0= cutting depth

- Built-up edge in which material being machined builds up on the cutting edge. Some materials (notably aluminum and copper) have a tendency to anneal themselves to the cutting edge of a tool. It occurs most frequently on softer metals. with a lower melting point. It can be prevented by increasing cutting speeds and using lubricant. When drilling it can be noticed as alternating dark and shiny rings.
- Glazing occurs on grinding wheels. and occurs when the exposed abrasive becomes dulled. It is noticeable as a sheen while the wheel is in motion.
- Edge wear. in drills. refers to wear to the outer edge of a drill bit around the cutting face caused by excessive cutting speed. It extends down the drill flutes. and requires a large volume of material to be removed from the drill bit before it can be corrected.

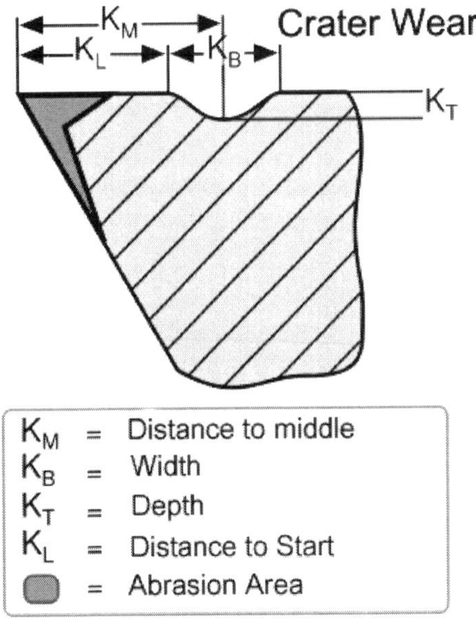

Fig. Crater wear

EFFECTS OF TOOL WEAR

Some General effects of tool wear include:

- increased cutting forces....
- increased cutting temperatures
- poor surface finish

- decreased accuracy of finished part
- May lead to tool breakage
- Causes change in tool geometry

Reduction in tool wear can be accomplished by using lubricants and coolants while machining. These reduce friction and temperature. thus reducing the tool wear.

TOOL LIFE EXPECTANCY

The Taylor's Equation for Tool Life Expectancy provides a good approximation.

$$V_c T^n = C$$

A more general form of the equation is

$$V_c T^n \times D^x S^y = C$$

where

- =cutting speed
- T=tool life
- D=depth of cut
- S=feed rate
- x and y are determined experimentally
- n and C are constants found by experimentation or published data; they are properties of tool material. workpiece and feed rate.

TEMPERATURE CONSIDERATIONS

At high temperature zones crater wear occurs. The highest temperature of the tool can exceed 700 °C and occurs at the rake face whereas the lowest temperature can be 500 °C or lower depending on the tool...

ENERGY CONSIDERATIONS

Energy comes in the form of heat from tool friction. It is a reasonable assumption that 80% of energy from cutting is carried away in the chip. If not for this the workpiece and the tool would be much hotter than what is experienced. The tool and the workpiece each carry approximately 10% of the energy. The percent of energy carried away in the chip increases as the speed of the cutting operation increases. This somewhat offsets the tool wear from increased cutting speeds. In fact. if not for the energy taken away in the chip increasing as cutting speed is increased; the tool would wear more quickly than is found.

MULTI-CRITERIA OF MACHINING OPERATION

Malakooti and Deviprasad (1989) introduced the multi-criteria metal cutting problem where the criteria could be cost per part.production time per part. and quality of surface. Also. Malakooti et al. (1990) proposed a method to rank the materials in terms of machinability. Malakooti (2013) presents comprehensive discussion about tool life and its multi-criteria problem. As as example objectives can be minimizing of Total cost (which can be measured by the total cost of replacing all tools during a production period). maximizing ofProductivity (which can be measured by the total number of parts produced per period). and maximizing of quality of cutting.

6

Production Management

INTRODUCTION TO PRODUCTION

Production means application of processes. The raw material to add the use and economic values to arrive at desired product by the best method, with out sacrificing the desired quality.

We have three ways of Production, they are:

- *Production by Disintegration*: By separating the contents of Crude oil or a mixture the desired products are produced. For example the crude oil is disintegrated into various fuel oils. Similarly salt production is also an example for product produced by disintegrated. We can use Mechanical or Chemical or both technologies to get the desired product, so that it will have desired use value.
- *Production by Integration*: In this type of Production various Components of the products are assembled together to get the desired product. In this process, Physical and Chemical Properties of the materials used may change. The examples are: Assembly of Two wheelers, Four wheelers and so on.
- *Production by Service*: Here the Chemical and Mechanical Properties of materials are improved without any physical change. The example for this is Heat Treatment of metals. In real world, a combin-ation of methods is used. In general production is the use of any process or procedure designed to transform a set of input elements into a set of output elements, which have use value and economic value.

PRODUCT DEVELOPMENT

Product development is the process of designing, creating, and marketing an idea or product. The product can either be one that is new to the marketplace or one that is new to your particular company, or, an existing product that has been improved. In many instances a product will be labeled new and improved when substantial changes have been made.

PRODUCT DEVELOPMENT PROCESS

All product development goes through a similar planning process. Although the process is a continuous one, it is crucial that companies stand back after each step and evaluate whether the new product is worth the investment to continue. That evaluation should be based on a specific set of objective criteria, not someone's gut feeling. Even if the product is wonderful, if no one buys it the company will not make a profit. Brainstorming and developing a concept is the first step in product development. Once an idea is generated, it is important to determine whether there is a market for the product, what the target market is, and whether the idea will be profitable, as well as whether it is feasible from an engineering and financial standpoint. Once the product is determined to be feasible, the idea or concept is tested on a small sample of customers within the target market to see what their reactions are.

DOCUMENTATION

Simply having an "idea"is worthless--you need to have proof of when you came up with the idea for your invention. Write down everything you can think of that relates to your invention, from what it is and how it works to how you'll make and market it. This is the first step to patenting your idea and keeping it from being stolen. You've probably heard about the "poor man's patent"--writing your idea down and mailing it to yourself in a sealed envelope so you have dated proof of your invention's conception. This is unreliable and unlikely to hold up in court. Write your idea down in an inventor's journal and have it signed by a witness. This journal will become your bible throughout the patent process. An inventor's journal can by any bound notebook whose pages are numbered consecutively and can't be removed or reinserted.

You can find specially designed inventor's journals at bookstores or you can save money and purchase a generic notebook anywhere they're sold, such as the grocery store, office supply store, stationary store, etc.

RESEARCH

You will need to research your idea from a legal and business standpoint. *Before you file a patent, you should*:

- *Complete an initial patent search*: Just because you haven't seen your invention doesn't mean it doesn't already exist. Before you hire a patent attorney or agent. You should also complete a non-patent "prior art"search. If you find any sort of artwork or design related to your idea, you cannot patent it--regardless of whether a prior patent has been filed.
- *Research your market*: Sure, your brother thinks your idea for a new lawn sprinkler is a great idea, but that doesn't mean your neighbour would buy one. More than 95 per cent of all patents never make

money for the inventor. Before you invest too much time and money into patenting your invention, do some preliminary research of your target market. Is this something people will actually buy? Once you know there's a market, make sure your product can be manufactured and distributed at a low enough cost so that your retail price is reasonable. You can determine these costs by comparing those of similar products currently on the market. This will also help you size up your competition--which you will have, no matter how unique you think your invention is.

MAKING A PROTOTYPE

A prototype is a model of your invention that puts into practice all of the things you have written in your inventor's journal. This will demonstrate the design of your invention when you present it to potential lenders and licensees. Do not file a patent before you have made a prototype.

You will almost always discover a flaw in your original design or think of a new feature you would like to add. If you patent your idea before you work out these kinks, it will be too late to include them in the patent and you will risk losing the patent rights of the new design to someone else.

Here are some general rules of thumb when prototyping your invention:

- *Begin with a drawing*: Before you begin the prototyping phase, sketch out all of your ideas into your inventor's journal.
- Create a concept mockup out of any material that will allow you to create a 3-D model of your design.
- Once you're satisfied with the mockup, create a full-working model of your idea. There are many books and kits that can help you create prototypes. If your invention is something that will cost a lot of money or is unreasonable to prototype, consider using a computer-animated virtual prototype.

FILING A PATENT

Now that you have all of the kinks worked out of your design, it's finally time to file a patent. There are two main patents you will have to choose from: a utility patent or a design patent. You can write the patent and fill out the application yourself, but do not file it yourself until you have had a skilled patent professional look it over first.

If the invention is really valuable, someone will infringe on it. If you do not have a strong patent written by a patent attorney or agent, you will be pulling your hair out later when a competitor finds a loophole that allows them to copy your idea. It's best to get the legal help now to avoid any legal problems in the future. When searching for a patent attorney or agent, remember one thing: If you see them advertised on TV, run away!

Once you are far, far away, follow these steps to choosing the best patent professional:

- *Do your homework*: Have your inventor's journal, prototype and notes with you. This will save them time, and you money. This will also help persuade them to work with you.
- *Make sure they are registered with the U.S*: Patent and Trademark Office.
- *Ask them what their technical background is*: If your invention is electronic, find a patent professional who is also an electrical engineer.
- *Discuss fees*: Keep your focus on smaller patent firms. They are less expensive and will work more closely with you. Agree to the estimated total cost before hiring your patent professional.

MARKETING YOUR INVENTION

Now it's time to figure out how you're going to bring your product to market. Create a business plan: How will you get money? Where will you manufacture the product? How will you sell it? Now is a good time to decide if you will manufacture and sell the product yourself, or license it for sale through another company. When you license your product you will probably only receive two per cent to five per cent in royalty fees. This often scares away inventors who feel they deserve more. But consider the upside: You will not have the financial burden associated with maintaining a business. This could end up making you more money in the long run.

Following these five steps will ensure an easy road to patenting your invention. Just remember that an easy road doesn't necessarily mean a short one. From the time you conceive your idea to the time you see your product on the shelf is a very long process. Most inventions take years to come to fruition. Have patience and follow due diligence in your steps to patenting your invention and your years of hard work will finally pay off.

NEW PRODUCT DEVELOPMENT

The dynamics of markets, technology, and competition have brought changes to virtually every market sector and have made new product development one of the most powerful business activities. The monumental changes that constantly impact commerce have forced companies to innovate with increasing speed, efficiency, and quality. In turn, this has made new product development one of the most complex and difficult business functions. However, firms must innovate in order to survive. The power of innovation is revealed in numerous studies, which show that companies leading their industries attribute about half of their revenues to products developed in the most recent five years. By comparison, companies at the bottom of their industries achieve approximately one-tenth of their sales from new products.

A firm's new product development efforts are shaped by its size, as well as the nature of the industry in which it operates. New products may be defined as any product, service, or idea not currently made or marketed by a company, or which the consumer may perceive as new.

Many types of new products exist, from never-seen-before products like Apple's personal communicator, to repositioned standards like Sears' shift to Sears Brand Central. Various studies suggest that between 50 and 80 per cent of new products fail—the greater the rate of new product development, the higher the failure rate.

New Product News predicts that more than 36,000 new products will be brought to market in 2005. Although there are numerous reasons why new products fail, faulty management and planning are at the core of most failures. Therefore, managing the new product development process is a key to a healthy organization.

HISTORY

The history of product innovation can be divided into three stages, beginning with the product-oriented or technology-pushed stage. In the post-World War II era Americans were coming off wartime shortages and were in the mood to buy the many goods that manufacturers produced.

Engineers, who were more product-oriented than consumer oriented, designed new products that might or might not find places in consumers' hearts and minds.

This was a product-oriented process in which the market was considered the receptacle for products that emerged from the firm's research and development efforts. However, competition escalated and consumers became more skeptical and selective about the types of products they purchased. Marketers found it increasingly difficult to rely on persuasive sales techniques to move products. Retailers grew restless when these products did not move off shelves as quickly as planned. Companies had to know more about their target markets. What were the wants and needs of the people who were buying their products? How could their firm satisfy these wants and needs?

The second stage was marked by the emergence of the market as the driver of innovation. Instead of being technology-driven, new product development evolved into a market-led process in which new products emerged from well-researched customer needs. The new product development process was placed in the hands of marketers who knew consumers' wants and needs. Customer demand "pulled" the product through the development process. Modern new product development is a blending of these two orientations into a "dual-drive" approach to innovation. Companies recognize that innovation is a complex process that requires sound investment in research and development, as well as significant marketing expertise that focuses on satisfying consumers' wants and needs.

The rapid pace of change that engulfed businesses towards the end of the twentieth century put an even greater burden on companies to build adaptive capabilities into their organizations. Global competition means there are more competitors capable of world-class performance.

This has made competition more intense, rigorous, and aggressive than ever before. Fragmenting and more sophisticated markets mean that consumers demand more from products in terms of quality, differentiation, and "meaningfulness."

New technologies have had two important outcomes in regards to innovation. First, new technologies are responsible for this new market sophistication in which consumers have more choices and are thus more demanding. Secondly, new technology has increased manufacturers' capabilities for rapid response to shifting market needs.

Finally, product life cycles have become more compressed as the skills required for developing new products increase in complexity. For example, consider the development of a new type of computer software. The expertise needed to develop the software from conception to commercialization might take years. The product's life cycle in such a competitive and turbulent environment might last only a few months.

Therefore, companies have embraced the view that new products are transient, whereas the skills and expertise needed to develop these products are a much more persistent requirement for success. Instead of the mono-approach, in which technology or markets drive innovation, new product development now requires a convergence of technology, marketing, product design, engineering, and manufacturing capabilities.

Speed, efficiency, and quality in product development are the challenges that new product development faces in today's intense competitive environment.

TYPES AND SOURCES OF NEW PRODUCTS

There are five categories of new products. New-to-the-world products or services are new inventions like in-line skates and health maintenance organizations. New category entries, such as sport utility vehicles, are products or services that are new to a firm. Additions to product lines add products or services to a firm's current markets. For example, when a powder laundry detergent offers a liquid version it is considered a line extension. Product improvements are another type of new product and are common to every product category. Repositionings target products to new markets or for new uses. Firms can obtain new products internally or externally. External sourcing means the company acquires the product or service, or obtains the rights to market the product or service, from another organization. Internal development means the firm develops the new product itself. This is riskier than external development because the company bears all of the costs associated with new product development and implementation. Collaborations, which include strategic partnerships, strategic alliances, joint ventures, and licensing agreements, occur when two or more firms work together on developing new products.

NEW PRODUCT DEVELOPMENT PROCESS

Historically, the new product development process has been conceived in discreet terms with a beginning and an end. Different companies and different industries may alter this seven-step process for different products, or the steps themselves may become blurred as companies become engaged in several stages at the same time.

The process begins with idea generation. For every successful new product, many new product ideas are conceived and discarded. Therefore, companies usually generate a large number of ideas from which successful new products emerge.

Idea screening, the second step, considers all new product ideas in the idea pool and eliminates ones that are perceived to be the least likely to succeed. Not only should the firm's manufacturing, technology, and marketing capabilities be evaluated at this stage, but also how the new idea fits with the company's vision and strategic objectives.

The third stage, concept development and testing, requires formal evaluations of the product concept by consumers, usually through some form of marketing research. New product ideas with low concept test scores are discarded or revised. While the Internet is making it easier to gather consumer data, there are limitations. As people get deluged with an increasing number of surveys and solicitations, it is possible that they will grow tired of helping marketers.

The business analysis stage is next. At this point the new product idea is analysed for its marketability and costs. After passing the first three stages an idea may be discarded once marketing and manufacturing costs are analysed, due to limited potential for profitability or commercial success. Throughout these four stages, the new idea has remained on document with a relatively small investment required.

The fifth stage, prototype development, is the first stage where new product costs begin to escalate. Because of this, many companies have placed greater emphasis on the first four stages and reduced the proportion of new products that reach the prototype stage from about 50 per cent to around 20 per cent. At this stage the concept is converted into an actual product. A customer value perspective during this phase means the product is designed to satisfy the needs expressed by consumers. Firms may use quality function deployment as they develop the prototype. QFD links specific consumer requirements such as versatility, durability, and low maintenance with specific product characteristics.

The customer value perspective requires the new product to satisfy customer needs and meet desired quality levels at specified production costs.Test marketing tests the prototype and marketing strategy in simulated or actual market situations. Because of the expense and risks associated with actual test markets, marketers use them with caution. Products that test poorly are pulled back and reconceptualized or discarded.

Commercialization, the final stage, is when the product is introduced full scale. The level of investment and risk are highest at this stage. Consumer adoption rates, timing decisions for introduction, and coordinating efforts with production, distribution, and marketing should be considered.

FACTORS INFLUENCING NEW PRODUCT DEVELOPMENT

The seven-step process assumes a definite beginning and end. However, studies suggest that what goes on before and after new products are introduced is as important as the process itself. Organizational structure, leadership, and team building influence the speed and efficiency with which new products are introduced. Structure influences efficiency, autonomy, and coordination. New product innovation requires structure that optimizes direction and guidance. Structure that facilitates internal information exchange, decision making, and materials flow is essential. A "fast-cycle" structure allows more time for planning and implementing activities to gain competitive advantage. This type of structure also cuts costs because production materials and information collect less overhead and do not accumulate as work-in-process inventory. Autonomy refers to the amount of decision making allowed at lower levels of management. The coordination of the engineering, product design, manufacturing, and marketing functions in the new product development process is vital.

Leadership influences strategy, culture, and the firm's overall ability to undertake new product development. Top management can demonstrate involvement in the development process by providing career advancement for entrepreneurial skills and encouraging broad employee participation. Clarity and vision are crucial to ensuring that new product ideas are good strategic fits for the company. The degree to which leadership allows trial and error and promotes individual initiative positively influences the development of new products. This acceptance of risk and support for an entrepreneurial spirit within the organization are crucial in order for innovation to flourish. New products emerge in a variety of ways and their development does not always proceed in rational and consistent manners. It is necessary for leadership to view the process as iterative and dynamic, and to foster adaptation and flexibility. Management flexibility and responsiveness to change also are needed. This type of leadership is particularly important to the project manager who must coordinate and integrate the various parts of the new product development process so that a coherent system emerges that produces a product with compelling value. Initiative encourages creativity and problem-solving skills. Teams provide mechanisms for breaking down functional biases created by a strict adherence to structure. The amount of interdepartmental conflict in the organization, the social cohesion among team members, and the frequency and directionality of interdepartmental communication influence team building. Through shared understanding of the objectives and purposes of the project, as well as the tasks required in the development process, teams can shape the project and influence how work gets done in the organization.

IMPROVING SPEED, EFFICIENCY, AND QUALITY

New products often fail because of unanticipated market shifts that result in missed opportunities and misused channels of distribution. Failures also occur because companies miscalculate their own technological strengths or the product's technological challenges. These potential problems often crop up in the latter stages and result in delays, redesigns, or poor quality products.

Companies are constantly seeking ways to avoid these pitfalls. One solution is new product development maps that chart the evolution of a company's product lines. This historical perspective helps the firm to identify and analyse functional capabilities in a systematic, repetitive fashion that allows for the development of linkages and the identification of resources for new endeavours. These maps can direct the firm to new market opportunities and point out technological challenges.

Aggregate plans for projects offer another solution. Rather than viewing each new product development project individually, they consider all of the new product development projects under consideration by the firm. This is particularly important in firms with hundreds of new product development projects going on at the same time. Projects are categorized according to resources required and contribution to the firm's bottom line. Aggregate project plans enable management to improve the management of new product development by providing greater control over resource allocation and utilization. These plans help to point out where capabilities need to be improved, how sequencing projects may help, and how projects fit with the firm's development strategies. Return maps graphically represent the contributions of all team members to product success in terms of time and money. Their focus is on the point at which product sales generate sufficient profit so that the firm's initial investment in development is returned. Return maps show team members the time and money needed to complete their tasks in the development process so that they may estimate and re-estimate their investment in the process. In doing this return maps show the impact of their actions on the project's overall success.

Another way to improve the speed and efficiency with which new products are introduced is to involve purchasing in the development process. When purchasing expertise is introduced into the development project team, quality may increase, time to market entry may decrease, investment in inventory may diminish, and costs may significantly decrease.

Technology continues to change and create new opportunities and threats. Customer requirements and expectations continue to shift and create new demands. Old channels of distribution are becoming obsolete and new channels are opening new opportunities. Some competitors are falling by the wayside while others are surging to the forefront by making new and unexpected moves to gain advantage. The very structure of industry is changing. A key to success in this tumultuous environment will continue to be the ability to sustain a competitive advantage through innovation. However, speed, efficiency, and quality in product development will be paramount. Building capabilities in all aspects of product creation and implementation, overcoming uncertainty and facilitating decision-making, ensuring these innovations are strategically linked to the firm's vision, and doing this on a continuous basis is the challenge of new product development in the next century.

PRODUCT AND MARKETING MIX DEVELOPMENT

Ideas passing through business analysis are given serious consideration for development. Companies direct their research and development teams to construct an initial design or prototype of the idea. Marketers also begin to construct a marketing plan for the product. Once the prototype is ready the marketer seeks customer input. However, unlike the concept testing stage where customers were only exposed to the idea, in this step the customer gets to experience the real product as well as other aspects of the marketing mix, such as advertising, pricing, and distribution options (*e.g.*, retail store, direct from company, etc.). Favorable customer reaction helps solidify the marketer's decision to introduce the product and also provides other valuable information such as estimated purchase rates and understanding how the product will be used by the customer. Reaction that is less favorable may suggest the need for adjustments to elements of the marketing mix. Once these are made the marketer may again have the customer test the product. In addition to gaining customer feedback, this step is used to gauge the feasibility of large-scale, cost effective production for manufactured products.

Market Testing

Products surviving to Step 6 are ready to be tested as real products. In some cases the marketer accepts what was learned from concept testing and skips over market testing to launch the idea as a fully marketed product. But other companies may seek more input from a larger group before moving to commercialization. The most common type of market testing makes the product available to a selective small segment of the target market (*e.g.*, one city), which is exposed to the full marketing effort as they would be to any product they could purchase. In some cases, especially with consumer products sold at retail stores, the marketer must work hard to get the product into the test market by convincing distributors to agree to purchase and place the product on their store shelves. In more controlled test markets distributors may be paid a fee if they agree to place the product on their shelves to allow for testing.

Another form of market testing found with consumer products is even more controlled with customers recruited to a "laboratory" store where they are given shopping instructions. Product interest can then be measured based on customer's shopping response.

Finally, there are several high-tech approaches to market testing including virtual reality and computer simulations. With virtual reality testing customers are exposed to a computer-projected environment, such as a store, and are asked to locate and select products. With computer simulations customers may not be directly involved at all. Instead certain variables are entered into a sophisticated computer programme and estimates of a target market's response are calculated.

Commercialization

If market testing displays promising results the product is ready to be introduced to a wider market. Some firms introduce or roll-out the product in waves with parts of the market receiving the product on different schedules. This allows the company to ramp up production in a more controlled way and to fine tune the marketing mix as the product is distributed to new areas.

MANAGING EXISTING PRODUCTS

Marketing strategies developed for initial product introduction almost certainly need to be revised as the product settles into the market. While commercialization may be the last step in the new product development process it is just the beginning of managing the product. Adjusting the product's marketing strategy is required for many reasons including:

- Changing customer tastes
- Domestic and foreign competitors
- Economic conditions
- Technological advances

To stay on top of all possible threats the marketer must monitor all aspects of the marketing mix and make changes as needed. Such efforts require the marketer to develop and refine the product's marketing plan on a regular basis. The marketing strategies change as a product moves through time leading to the concept called the Product Life Cycle (PLC). We will see that marketers make numerous revisions to their strategy as product move through different stage of the PLC.

DEVELOPING NEW PRODUCTS

By its nature marketing requires new ideas. Unlike some organizational functions, where basic processes follow a fairly consistent routine (e.g., accounting), successful marketers are constantly making adjustments to their marketing efforts. New ideas are essential for responding to changing demand by the target market and by pressure exerted by competitors. These changes are manifested in decisions in all marketing areas including the development of new products.

In addition to being responsive to changing customer tastes and competitive forces, there are many other reasons why new product development is vital. These include:

- Many new products earn higher profits than older products. This is often the case for products considered innovative or unique which, for a period of time, may enjoy success and initially face little or no competition.
- New products can help reposition the company in customer's minds. For instance, a company that traditionally sold low priced products with few features may shift customers' perceptions about the company by introducing products with more features and slightly higher pricing.
- Fierce global competition and technological developments make it much easier for competitors to learn about products and replicate them. To stay ahead of competitors marketers must innovate and often create and introduce new products on a consistent schedule.
- Companies with limited depth in a product line may miss out on more sales unless they can add new products to fill out the line.
- Some firms market seasonal products that garner their highest sales during a certain time of the year or sell cyclical products whose sales fluctuate depending on economic or market factors. Expanding the firm's product mix into new areas may help offset these fluctuations. For manufacturing firms an additional benefit is realized as new products utilize existing production capacity that is under-used when seasonal or cyclical products are not being produced.

CATEGORIES OF NEW PRODUCTS

New products can fall into one of several categories. These categories are defined by the type of market the product is entering (*i.e.*, newly created, existing but not previously targeted, existing and targeted) and the level of product innovation (*i.e.*, radically new, new, upgrade).

- *Creates New Market with Radically New Product or Product Line:* This category is represented by new breakthrough products that are so revolutionary they create an entirely new market. Recent examples include digital music players, such as Apple's iPod, that have spawned new delivery methods (downloadable music) and new media (podcasting). Highly innovative products are rare so very few new products fall into this category.

- *Enters Existing But Not Previously Targeted Market with New-Product or Product Line*: In this category a marketer introduces a new product item or product line to an existing market which they did not previously target. Often these products are similar to competitors' products already available in the market but with some level of difference (e.g., different features, lower price, etc.). Microsoft's entry into the video gaming system market with their Xbox is an example.
- *Stays in Existing and Previously Targeted Market by Enhancing Existing Product or Product Line*: Under this development category the marketer attempts to improve its current position in the market by either improving or upgrading existing products or by extending a product line by adding new products. This type of new product is seen in our earlier example of Procter and Gamble's Tide product line which contains many product variations of the basic Tide product.

HOW NEW PRODUCTS ARE OBTAINED

Marketers have several options for obtaining new products. First, products can be developed within an organization's own research operations. For some companies, such as service firms, this may simply mean the marketer designs new service options to sell to target markets. For instance, a marketer for a mortgage company may design new mortgage packages that offer borrowers different rates or payment options. At the other extreme companies may support an extensive research and development effort where engineers, scientists or others are engaged in new product discovery. A second way to obtain products is to acquire them from external sources. This can occur in several ways including:

- Purchase the Product - With this option a marketer purchases the product outright from another firm that currently owns the product. The advantage is that the product is already developed, which reduces the purchasing company's time and cost of trying to develop it themselves. On the negative side the purchase cost may be high.
- License the Product – Under this option the marketer negotiates with the owner of the product for the rights to market the product. This may be a particularly attractive option for companies who have to fill a product need quickly (*e.g.*, give a product line more depth) or it may be used as a temporary source of products while the marketer's company is developing its own product. On the negative side the arrangement may have a limited time frame at which point the licensor may decide to end the relationship leaving the marketer without a source for the product.

- Purchase Another Firm - Instead of purchasing another company's products marketers may find it easier to just purchase the whole company selling the products. One key advantage to this is that the acquisition often includes the people and resources that developed the product which may be a key consideration if the acquiring company wants to continue to develop the acquired products.

NEW PRODUCT DEVELOPMENT PROCESS

Because introducing new products on a consistent basis is important to the future success of many organizations, marketers in charge of product decisions often follow set procedures for bringing products to market. In the scientific area that may mean the establishment of ongoing laboratory research Programmes for discovering new products (*e.g.*, medicines) while less scientific companies may pull together resources for product development on a less structured timetable.

We present a 7-step process comprising the key elements of new product development. While some companies may not follow a deliberate step-by-step approach, the steps are useful in showing the information input and decision making that must be done in order to successfully develop new products. The process also shows the importance market research plays in developing products. We should note that while the 7-step process works for most industries, it is less effective in developing radically new products.

The main reason lies in the inability of the target market to provide sufficient feedback on advanced product concepts since they often find it difficult to understand radically different ideas. So while many of these steps are used to research breakthrough ideas, the marketer should exercise caution when interpreting the results.

Idea Generation

The first step of new product development requires gathering ideas to be evaluated as potential product options. For many companies idea generation is an ongoing process with contributions from inside and outside the organization.

Many market research techniques are used to encourage ideas including: running focus groups with consumers, channel members, and the company's sales force; encouraging customer comments and suggestions via toll-free telephone numbers and Web site forms; and gaining insight on competitive product developments through secondary data sources.

One important research technique used to generate ideas is brainstorming where open-minded, creative thinkers from inside and outside the company gather and share ideas. The dynamic nature of group members floating ideas, where one idea often sparks another idea, can yield a wide range of possible products that can be further pursued.

Screening

In Step 2 the ideas generated in Step 1 are critically evaluated by company personnel to isolate the most attractive options. Depending on the number of ideas, screening may be done in rounds with the first round involving company executives judging the feasibility of ideas while successive rounds may utilize more advanced research techniques. As the ideas are whittled down to a few attractive options, rough estimates are made of an idea's potential in terms of sales, production costs, profit potential, and competitors' response if the product is introduced. Acceptable ideas move on to the next step.

Concept Development and Testing

With a few ideas in hand the marketer now attempts to obtain initial feedback from customers, distributors and its own employees. Generally, focus groups are convened where the ideas are presented to a group, often in the form of concept board presentations (*i.e.*, storyboards) and not in actual working form. For instance, customers may be shown a concept board displaying drawings of a product idea or even an advertisement featuring the product. In some cases focus groups are exposed to a mock-up of the ideas, which is a physical but generally non-functional version of product idea. During focus groups with customers the marketer seeks information that may include: likes and dislike of the concept; level of interest in purchasing the product; frequency of purchase (used to help forecast demand); and price points to determine how much customers are willing to spend to acquire the product.

Business Analysis

At this point in the new product development process the marketer has reduced a potentially large number of ideas down to one or two options. Now in Step 4 the process becomes very dependent on market research as efforts are made to analyse the viability of the product ideas. (Note, in many cases the product has not been produced and still remains only an idea.) The key objective at this stage is to obtain useful forecasts of market size (*e.g.*, overall demand), operational costs (*e.g.*, production costs) and financial projections (*e.g.*, sales and profits).

Additionally, the organization must determine if the product will fit within the company's overall mission and strategy. Much effort is directed at both internal research, such as discussions with production and purchasing personnel, and external marketing research, such as customer and distributor surveys, secondary research, and competitor analysis.

IMPLEMENTING A PRODUCT DIFFERENTIATION STRATEGY

The Organization question of the VRIO Model is perhaps even more important with a product differentiation strategy than with a cost leadership strategy because of the relationship between the focal firm and customers. A successful differentiation strategy depends on creating customer preferences for the products and/or services of the focal firm.

Customer preferences are heavily influenced by customers' experiences in interacting with the focal firm. The focal firm must be able to respond quickly and accurately to customer needs.

Customers need to'feel' that the focal firm is catering to their needs. Organizational structure, management control systems, and compensation policies can all be managed to encourage customers to have a preference for the focal firm's products and/or services.

Organizational Structure

At the business level, the U-Form is used to implement product differentiation strategies just as it is to implement cost leadership strategies.

However, there are some important differences in the way the structure is used. The U-Form is used in a cost leadership strategy to exploit the efficiencies inherent in the structure due to specialization. With a product differentiation strategy, the specialization of the U-Form structure is exploited through cross-functional teams.

Management Controls

The main idea behind using management controls in the implementation of a product differentiation strategy is that of flexibility.

Not only must managers and employees have the freedom to be flexible, they should also be encouraged to be creative and adaptable. Decision making is usually more decentralized in a product differentiation strategy as compared to a cost leadership strategy.

This decentralization means that managers can make decisions and take actions that allow the focal firm to differentiate its products and/or services through a high degree of responsiveness to customers. As a matter of firm policy, decision making guidelines are broader-allowing greater flexibility. Also, managers and employees should explicitly be given the freedom and encouragement to experiment with new ideas. Managers and employees need to know that if experimentation leads to failure they will not be punished for having tried.

Compensation Policies

Compensation policies can be used to help exploit the U-form structure and reinforce the broader management controls. In the simplest of terms, compensation policies should be structured to reward managers and employees for cooperating within cross functional teams and being creative in the process. Compensation policies can be especially effective with regard to experimentation and risk taking. Promised rewards for successful experimentation and the promised absence of punishment for failed experimentation provide strong incentive to be creative.

PRODUCT DIFFERENTIATION

Product differentiation is a business level strategy in which firms attempt to create and exploit differences between their products and those offered by competitors. These differences may lead to competitive advantage if customers perceive the difference and have a preference for the difference.

A product differentiation strategy requires that a firm be able to effectively communicate with customers through advertising, public relations, sponsoring of events, etc. In fact, advertising usually plays a critical role in an effective product differentiation strategy. Ironically, a firm does not have to be able to create a product with actual differences if it can convince customers that differences exist. Firms that do create products with actual differences have a much easier time convincing customers that those differences exist. Nike's capabilities lie primarily in design and marketing. The vast majority of Nike's production of shoes and clothing is outsourced to other firms. Nike's base of differentiation is not proprietary high-tech manufacturing of superior athletic shoes. Rather, Nike's base of differentiation is a well-orchestrated marketing effort that has spanned decades.

BASES OF DIFFERENTIATION

The notion of a base of differentiation is important because it allows a firm to focus its efforts on creating and exploiting a particular difference between its products and competitors' products. Managers need to understand their own bases of differentiation and the bases of differentiation of competitors so that they can make informed strategic choices. Almost anything could be a base of differentiation. The key is that some set of customers must find value in the base of differentiation.Everything from tangible product characteristics to abstract intangible concepts like national or regional pride could potentially be a base of differentiation. Managers can create and exploit bases of differentiation from a seemingly infinite number of ideas. For example, "freedom fries" became a base of differentiation among some restaurants as a form of protest against the French who refused to join the U.S. in its war against Saddam Hussein's government in Iraq. The name change from French fries to freedom fries was the idea of small but very patriotic restaurateur.This' base of differentiation was short-lived as the attention of Americans shifted from the lack of French participation to the war itself.

Attributes of the Product or Service

- Preferences are created by actual differences in the tangible product or service offered by the focal firm vis-à-vis competitors' offerings

- Product features
- Product complexity
- Timing of product introduction
- Location

Relationship Between the Focal Firm and its Customers

- Preferences are created as the focal firm develops and exploits relationships with customers based on what the focal firm's target customers want
- Product customization
- Consumer marketing
- Product reputation

Linkages Within or Between Firms

- Preferences are created as the focal firm combines the competencies of different functions within or across organizations to produce tangible and/or intangible differences between the focal firm's offerings and those of competitors
- Linkages among functions within the focal firm
- Linkages with other firms
- Product mix
- Distribution channels
- Service and support

VALUE OF DIFFERENTIATION

Neutralizing Threats. Here is a brief description of how product differentiation can neutralize the threats of the forces in the Five Forces Model along with an example of each one. If the focal firm's product differentiation strategy is effective:

Threat of Entry

- Would-be entrants face the costs of overcoming customers' preferences for the focal firm's products and/or services
- *Example*: Toyota was protected from Hyundai's entry into the U.S. market because Hyundai had to enter at a low price and advertise heavily to attract customers away from Toyota's well-established Corolla.

Threat of Rivalry

- Customers have, to some extent, segmented themselves based on their preferences for the products of the several competing firms in a market. Thus, the rivalry is generally lower among firms competing in a market of differentiated products.
- *Example*: Allen Edmonds men's dress shoes sell for around $300.

Most models have thick leather soles that conform comfortably to the foot. Once a customer wears Allen Edmonds shoes, he tends to be very loyal to the brand. Cole Hahn is a competitor at the high end of the market. Some people prefer Cole Hahn, some prefer Allen Edmonds and once the customer decides on a preference, there is little competition remaining between Cole Hahn and Allen Edmonds. Product differentiation attenuates rivalry for Allen Edmonds because competition for customers is minimized due to customers' selfselected segmentation.

Threat of Substitutes

- Customers will find the focal firm's products and services substantially more attractive than substitute products
- *Example*: Printing digital photographs on a personal printer at home may be viewed as a substitute for professional printing at a photo shop. Photo shops that advertise that their digital prints are superior to what can be printed at home are attempting to create a preference for their product. Shops that successfully convince customers that their product is superior are insulated from the competitive pressure of the in-home substitute.

Threat of Suppliers

- The power of suppliers may be mitigated in two ways. First, the focal firm will likely be able to pass supplier price increases along to customers who have a preference for the focal firm's differentiated product. Second, a firm that enjoys the strong preference of customers will usually have more bargaining power with suppliers compared to competitors that do not have differentiated products and services.
- *Example*: Recent spikes in the price of beef are easily passed on to customers of high-end steak houses like Ruth's Chris and Spencer's. McDonald's, Wendy's, and Burger King's customers are more sensitive to price increases that make the $.99 burger a thing of the past.

Threat of Buyers

- The power of buyers is reduced because the focal firm enjoys a quasimonopoly. By definition, if a firm has a highly differentiated product, then the firm is the only firm in that market that can offer that particular product. Customers with a preference for the focal firm's products and services must buy from the focal firm, thus reducing the power of buyers.
- Daimler-Chrysler's Crossfire sports car has allowed dealers to enjoy a quasi-monopoly as evidenced by the "local market adjustment" that

dealers are able to tack onto the price of the car. The car is different from other cars and a set of customers has a strong preference for the car. There are a limited number of the cars being built. These factors serve to greatly reduce the power of buyers of the Crossfire.

Exploiting Opportunities

A product differentiation strategy can be used to exploit opportunities in several different ways. The textbook focuses on how product differentiation can be used to exploit opportunities based on the type of industry in which the focal firm operates. In addition to industry-type opportunities, there are many other opportunities that arise in the external environment that firms can exploit. In a sense, a firm is exploiting an opportunity in the external environment any time it is able to fill some customer need in a new or different way.

SCOPE OF PRODUCTION MANAGEMENT

In fact, we apply Principles of Management; and functions of Management in our day-to-day life. We all know, from morning till night, we plan our activities; we coordinate available resources and control our activities to achieve certain goals. So also any organization must follow the Principles of Management for its survival and growth. The same is applicable to production Management also. Reading and learning Production Management will enable one to be capable of solving the problems of the organization, may be an Educational Institution, Production Shop, Hospital, Departmental shop or even a barber shop. The problems a manager face in various organizations are more or less similar to that of Production department but smaller in magnitude. Hence the knowledge of Production Management will help any professional Manager to tackle the problems of his business easily.

For example: The Production Management consists of Planning, selection of materials, planning of processes, Routing, Scheduling and controlling the activities etc., Take the example of an Educational Institution/University. Here also selection of raw students, Planning of the Course Work, Educating the students and conducting the examination. Therefore this knowledge will enable one to apply the principles of Production Management to any field of life without restriction. Here, we have to remember that this is also applicable to the management of a service organization and the management of a Project.

Here it is better to distinguish between product, Service and Project, so as to help the reader to know on which particular aspect of Production Management to put much emphasis, in managing a service organization or a project.

- *Product*: Manufacturing system often produces standardized products in large volumes. The plant and machinery have a finite capacity. The facilities constitute fixed costs, which are allocated to the products produced. Variable costs, such as, labour cost and materials costs. While manufacturing the product use value and economic values are added to the product. Hence the product is a store of values added during manufacture. Because the input costs and output costs are measurable, the productivity can be measured with certain degree of accuracy. Product can be transported to the markets and stored physically until it is sold.

- *Service*: Service system present more uncertainty with respect to capacity and costs. Services are produced and consumed in the presence of the customer. We cannot store the service physically. Because of this the service organizations, such as Hotels, Hospitals, Transport Organizations and many other service organizations the capacity must be sufficiently or consciously managed to accommodate a highly variable demand. Sometimes services like legal practice and medical practice involve Professional or intellectual judgments, which cannot be easily standardized. Because of this the calculation of cost and productivity is difficult.
- *Project*: Project system does not produce standardized products. The Plant, Machinery, Men and Materials are often brought to project site and the project is completed. The project is of big size and remains in the site itself after completion. As the costs can be calculated and allocated to the project with considerable accuracy, Productivity can be measured. Once the project is completed, all the resources are removed from site.

OBJECTIVE OF PRODUCTION MANAGEMENT

The objective of Production Management is to produce the desired product or specified product by specified methods so that the optimal utilization of available resources is met with. Hence the production management is responsible to produce the desired product, which has marketability at the cheapest price by proper planning, the manpower, material and processes. Production management must see that it will deliver right goods of right quantity at right place and at right price. When the objective is achieved, we say that we have effective Production Management system.

BENEFITS DERIVED FROM EFFICIENT PRODUCTION MANAGEMENT

The efficient Production Management will give benefits to the various parts of the society.

They are:

- Consumer benefits from improved industrial Productivity, increased use value in the product. Products are available to him at right place, at right price, at right time, in desired quantity and of desired quality.

- *Investors*: They get increased security for their investments, adequate market returns, and creditability and good image in the society.
- Employee gets adequate Wages, Job security, improved working conditions and increased Personal and Job satisfaction.
- *Suppliers*: Will get confidence in management and their bills can be realised with out any delay.
- *Community*: community enjoys Benefits from economic and social stability.
- The Nation will achieve prospects and security because of increased Productivity and healthy industrial atmosphere.

PRODUCT PRESENTATION

Non-store retailers have a real challenge when it comes to product presentation. If a product is largely standardised and its tangible features wholly understood, for example a CD or a book, then the presentation of the product is less problematic. If the benefits of a product are mainly functional rather than aesthetic, then again a photographic image and a wealth of product performance detail is likely to be sufficient.

However, for goods where the aesthetics and the sensory elements of the product are important, for example, fresh food, clothing and cosmetics, then a two-dimensional image may not adequately represent its benefits. Representing the product in use may help, for example showing clothing modelled or home furnishings in room settings, but problems concerning the match between customers' own self-image and that of the photographic image can arise. Some mail order companies are adopting magazine type layouts, to offer a more lifestyle approach to product presentation and to transfer media familiarity to shopping formats.

Internet sites are considered by Din (2000) to be visually lacking in stimulation, with too much written text and essentially offering the customer little more than the pages of a catalogue. The product offer is often presented on websites in a list type of format, and can be organised according to retail categorisation rather than being consumer orientated.

For example, Tesco have used the term 'dry goods' on their Web site, which is a trade term for packaged goods like sugar and flour and not a term that would necessarily be understood by customers. However, unlike static pages, the internet does allow some moving imagery to be lodged in the Web site, such as a fashion show or a live product demonstration.

In addition, the opportunity to deal directly with internet customers offers the possibility of tailoring the Web site image to individual customers. Home shopping retailer Land's End, for example, has experimented with displaying merchandise in a variety of ways, according to the demographics of the on-line customer.

Internet shopping via the mobile phone clearly offers market opportunities, given the popularity of the handset as a communication medium with its convenience, easy access and low cost. However, product presentation on a mobile handset is challenging: transmission bandwidth can make screen information slow to receive and limited in scope. Mobile shopping requires a handset that incorporates a mini-web browser (the Wireless Application Protocol or WAP), which is accessed via the phone keypad, and in itself presents difficulties with site navigation.

The web pages written for a PC (in hypertext mark-up language, HTML) may continue to be too complex for mobiles, which have to be written in wireless mark-up language (WML), and so compatibility and consistency between the two media becomes an issue.

However, in the spring of 2000, mobile phone retailer Carphone Warehouse was preparing to pre-install a shopping and information portal in every WAP phone sold, confident in the viability of the mobile as a means of trading information-based service products, such as travel and entertainment tickets. An indication of the potential for this method of shopping is the willingness of grocery retailer Waitrose to become involved in WapWorld, the mobile phone portal company founded by Sir Bob Geldof.

Interactive TV offers much more flexibility in product presentation, in particular through links from TV programming and interactive advertisements to websites. The first interactive TV advertisement in the UK aired by Open, for example, was for 'Chicken Tonight' cooking sauces, which linked the advertisement to recipes, related product and vouchers.

Although this is an interesting development, it raises a complex issue concerning the blurring of the distinction between programming and advertising and the freedom of viewers to 'surf away' from other advertisements and programming, which is an issue of concern for the Independent Television Commission.

THE SELLING ENVIRONMENT

Creating an atmosphere within the brick walls that represent the store is not easy, but creating an atmosphere on the flat and static page of a catalogue or on a Web site is even more difficult. The principles behind a store design and a non-store format design are, however, essentially the same. The layout must be logical and easy to browse around, products should be easy to locate within the sub-sections of the format, there should be links between complementary merchandise, and there should be consistency between the merchandise and the retailer's brand image.

For example, internet retailer BagsOfTime.com offers a wide range of impulse and emergency products, with a one-hour delivery promise within London. The Web site is easy to navigate, and despite a wide range of goods on offer, which includes shirts, sandwiches, toiletry items and a large selection of gifts, there is a consistent image across the site. When the on-line customer reaches the pay point, they are presented with a list of further impulse items, in a way completely comparable to the impulse items presented at a retail store checkout.

PRICING

Home shopping retailers have the potential to offer goods at competitive prices because they do not have the expense of running a portfolio of stores. However, in traditional mail order retailing, much of this saving is offset by the need to finance the high stock holding level that is necessary to guarantee good service, as well as the funding of long customer credit terms.

In theory, an internet retailer can reduce these two costs: payment is usually taken at the point of product dispatch (if not earlier) and arrangements could be made for direct delivery from a supplier. However, skimping on infrastructure seems to be one of the commonest reasons for internet retailing failure, and so virtual retailing at very pared down prices becomes a risky business.

Nevertheless, price comparison is very easy to make between alternative internet offers, with shopping portals such as Yahoo Shopping and Shopsmart offering to undertake this process in an extremely convenient manner for the shopper, free of charge. It is difficult to justify a premium pricing policy without the benefit of the store environment as an arena for adding value to the shopping process.

One further issue with home shopping media is pricing flexibility. Catalogues have a comparatively long lead-time, and price changes have to be communicated separately once the catalogue has been issued. Store retailing offers much more immediacy in terms of price changes, and discounted items can be visibly promoted in a much more effective way, for example by moving the goods to the front of the store.

Internet retailing, again in theory, offers price flexibility, as an immediate medium, but promoting offers is more complex, requiring flexibility in the web page design. One of the most complex issues regarding pricing is consistency when a retailer is using more than one shopping channel. Next, the UK clothing specialist, for example, does not discount products in its stores outside the strictly controlled end of season sales periods in order to protect the integrity of its catalogue, which offers a high proportion of products that are identical to the range found in the stores.

SERVICE

Both customer service and stock service are important when carrying out a retail transaction. Dealing with live people in real time is one aspect of store shopping that eventually may be its salvation. Information about the product, its applications and uses, demonstrations and trials are available on demand within a shop. Also the stock position is immediately apparent and if a product variant is not in stock, the position can be established immediately and/or alternatives offered.Therefore the store arena offers the opportunity as a stage for delivering an excellent standard of customer service. In addition, the quality of the service is relatively easy to measure in this environment. Poor quality service can be detected through visible signs of customer disatisfaction or via customer complaints. It is much more difficult and in many cases impossible to evaluate levels and frequencies of poor customer service with an impersonal medium.

Customer service through non-store channels is not only different, but provides more opportunities for service implementation. A customer has to make a contact, for example by telephone or e-mail, in order to find out any information about the product that is not immediately apparent. The stock position may be communicated, but this information has to be accurate and therefore continually to be updated.

If the communication is via e-mail the customer has to wait for a response. Following transactions the customer waits for the product to be delivered whereas in store retailing the customer (usually) departs with the product. Again the delivery promise must be rigidly adhered to in order to prevent customer dissatisfaction. The infrastructure that supports the product communication is absolutely vital to the success of any non-store retailer.

One of the most frequent causes of internet shopping dissatisfaction ('cyber-shopping rage') is poor response times to enquiries and poor order fulfilment, and in such cases all the convenience advantage of the shopping format for the customer is lost. Some internet retailers who have become aware of these problems have taken steps to prevent customer loss by incorporating service orientation in the Web site design, for example by including e-mails contact points and 'phone-me' options.

Some sites also allow customers to access real-time stock availability and delivery information, so there is no need for them to wait for an order acknowledgement or delivery arrangement.

One feature of home shopping that is attractive to consumers is the ease with which goods can be returned. Catalogue retailers accept that around one-third of customer purchases will be returned, and in some departments, such as clothing and footwear, this proportion can be considerably higher, as the customer will order two or more sizes to try, only ever intending to purchase one. Reducing the amount of returns is a way of improving retail productivity, whether store or non-store based, but internet retailers have to accept that returns are a necessary evil of home shopping, and make adequate provision for this service, clearly setting out the returns policy for the customer.

One of many problems cited in the demise of on-line clothing retailer Boo.com was an indiscriminate returns policy and an inadequate infrastructure to deal with returned goods. Again, multi-channel retailers have to consider how flexible their various outlets will be in terms of offering a multi-channel service, as well as a multi-channel selling strategy. Nordstrom, the highly service orientated US department store, allows catalogue returns to be taken back to the store, but many retailers are not able to offer this flexibility.

CONVENIENCE

One of the most oft-quoted sayings in the retail industry is the following: 'There are three factors for success in retailing; these are location, location and location' (anon.). Perhaps the most pleasant and convenient location for a consumer is at home. Traffic jams, weather and crowds can be avoided, prices can quickly be compared between outlets, and heavy and bulky shopping is delivered rather than having to be carried and loaded.

In addition the consumer gains privacy and personal efficiency as they browse through non-store outlets that are geared to their individual needs. In a convenience orientated society, home shopping clearly purports to offer a set of tangible benefits.

However, home shopping is only convenient if it delivers its promised service; if it does not, then it is highly inconvenient and risks high levels of customer frustration. The infrastructure behind the non-store outlet must therefore not only support the product offer but also the stated or assumed service offer.

7

Advances in Production Planning and Control Management

ASPECTS OF PLANNING

EVENT PLANNING

Event planning is the process of planning a festival, ceremony, competition, party, or convention. Event planning includes budgeting, establishing dates and alternate dates, selecting and reserving the event site, acquiring permits, and coordinating transportation and parking.

Event planning also includes some or all of the following, depending on the event: developing a theme or motif for the event, arranging for speakers and alternate speakers, coordinating location support, arranging decor, tables, chairs, tents, event support and security, catering, police, fire, portable toilets, parking, signage, emergency plans, health care professionals, and cleanup.

Event Planning is a relatively new career field. There is now training that helps one trying to break into the career field. There must be training for an event planner to handle all the pressure and work efficiently. This career deals with a lot of communication and organization aspects. There are many different names for an event planner such as a conference coordinator, a convention planner, a special event coordinator, and a meeting manager.

Steps to Planning an Event

The first step to planning an event is determining its purpose, whether it is for a wedding, company, birthday, festival, graduation or any other event requiring extensive planning. From this the event planner needs to choose entertainment, location, guest list, speakers, and content. The location for events is endless, but with event planning they would likely be held at hotels, convention centres, reception halls, or outdoors depending on the event. Once the location is set the coordinator/planner needs to prepare the event with staff, set up the entertainment, and keep contact with the client. After all this is set the event planner has all the smaller details to address like set up of the event such as food, drinks, music, guest list, budget, advertising and marketing, decorations, all this preparation is what is needed for an event to run smoothly.An event planner needs to be able to manage their time wisely for the event, and the length of preparation needed for each event so it is a success.

Working Conditions

Event planners work is considered either stressful or energizing. This line of work is also considered fast paced and demanding. Planners face deadlines and communicating with multiple people at one time. Planners spend most of their time in offices, but when meeting with clients the work is usually on-site at the location where the event is taking place. Some physical activity is required such as carrying boxes of materials and decorations or supplies needed for the event. Also, long working hours can be a part of the job. The day the event is taking place could start as early as 5:00 a.m. and then work until midnight. Working on weekends is sometimes required, which is when many events take place.

Publications and Resources

Many business-to-business trade publications exist to help event planning and production professionals become educated about the issues and trends in their industry. Many are controlled circulation publications available at no cost to qualified event professionals. Qualification is based on multiple variables like job title, company type, industry segment or geographic region, and is at the publisher's discretion.

FINANCIAL PLAN

In general usage, a financial plan can be a budget, a plan for spending and saving future income. This plan allocates future income to various types of expenses, such as rent or utilities, and also reserves some income for short-term and long-term savings. A financial plan can also be an investment plan, which allocates savings to various assets or projects expected to produce future income, such as a new business or product line, shares in an existing business, or real estate.In business, a financial plan can refer to the three primary financial statements created within a business plan. Financial forecast or financial plan can also refer to an annual projection of income and expenses for a company, division or department. A financial plan can also be an estimation of cash needs and a decision on how to raise the cash, such as through borrowing or issuing additional shares in a company. While a financial plan refers to estimating future income, expenses and assets, a financing plan or finance plan usually refers to the means by which cash will be acquired to cover future expenses, for instance through earning, borrowing or using saved cash.

MARKETING PLAN

. It can be for a product or service, a brand, or a product line. Marketing plans cover between one and five years. A marketing plan may be part of an overall business plan. Solid marketing strategy is the foundation of a well-written marketing plan. While a marketing plan contains a list of actions, a marketing plan without a sound strategic foundation is of little use.

The Marketing Planning Process

Marketing process can be realised by the marketing mix in step 4. The last step in the process is the marketing controlling. In most organizations, "strategic planning" is an annual process, typically covering just the year ahead. Occasionally, a few organizations may look at a practical plan which stretches three or more years ahead.

To be most effective, the plan has to be formalized, usually in written form, as a formal "marketing plan." The essence of the process is that it moves from the general to the specific, from the overall objectives of the organization down to the individual action plan for a part of one marketing programme. It is also an interactive process, so that the draft output of each stage is checked to see what impact it has on the earlier stages, and is amended.

Marketing Planning Aims and Objectives

Behind the corporate objectives, which in themselves offer the main context for the marketing plan, will lie the "corporate mission," which in turn provides the context for these corporate objectives. In a sales-oriented organization, the marketing planning function designs incentive pay plans to not only motivate and reward frontline staff fairly but also to align marketing activities with corporate mission. bn

This "corporate mission" can be thought of as a definition of what the organization is, of what it does: "Our business is ...". This definition should not be too narrow, or it will constrict the development of the organization; a too rigorous concentration on the view that "We are in the business of making meat-scales," as IBM was during the early 1900s, might have limited its subsequent development into other areas. On the other hand, it should not be too wide or it will become meaningless; "We want to make a profit" is not too helpful in developing specific plans. Abell suggested that the definition should cover three dimensions: "customer groups" to be served, "customer needs" to be served, and "technologies" to be utilized. Thus, the definition of IBM's "corporate mission" in the 1940s might well have been: "We are in the business of handling accounting information [customer need] for the larger US organizations [customer group] by means of punched cards [technology]."

Perhaps the most important factor in successful marketing is the "corporate vision." Surprisingly, it is largely neglected by marketing textbooks, although not by the popular exponents of corporate strategy - indeed, it was perhaps the main theme of the book by Peters and Waterman, in the form of their "Superordinate Goals." "In Search of Excellence" said: "Nothing drives progress like the imagination. The idea precedes the deed." If the organization in general, and its chief executive in particular, has a strong vision of where its future lies, then there is a good chance that the organization will achieve a strong position in its markets. This will be not least because its strategies will be consistent and will be supported by its staff at all levels. In this context, all of IBM's marketing activities were underpinned by its philosophy of "customer service," a vision originally promoted by the charismatic Watson dynasty. The emphasis at this stage is on obtaining a complete and accurate picture.

A "traditional" - albeit product-based - format for a "brand reference book" was suggested by Godley more than three decades ago:

1. *Financial data*: Facts for this part will come from management accounting, costing and finance parts.
2. *Product data*: From production, research and development.
3. *Sales and distribution data*: Sales, packaging, distribution parts.
4. *Advertising, sales promotion, merchandising data*: Information from these departments.
5. *Market data and miscellany*: From market research, who would in most cases performanceas a source for this information. His sources of data, however, assume the resources of a very large organization. In most organizations they would be obtained from a much smaller set of people.

It is apparent that a marketing audit can be a complex process, but the aim is simple: "it is only to identify those existing factors which will have a significant impact on the future plans of the company." It is clear that the basic material to be input to the marketing audit should be comprehensive. Accordingly, the best approach is to accumulate this material continuously, as and when it becomes available; since this avoids the otherwise heavy workload involved in collecting it as part of the regular, typically annual, planning process itself - when time is usually at a premium.Even so, the first task of this annual process should be to check that the material held in the current facts book or facts files actually is comprehensive and accurate, and can form a sound basis for the marketing audit itself. The structure of the facts book will be designed to match the specific needs of the organization, but one simple format - suggested by Malcolm McDonald - may be applicable in many cases.

This splits the material into three groups:

1. *Review of the marketing environment*: A study of the organization's markets, customers, competitors and the overall economic, political, cultural and technical environment; covering developing trends, as well as the current situation.

2. *Review of the detailed marketing activity*: A study of the company's marketing mix; in terms of the 7 Ps -
3. *Review of the marketing system*: A study of the marketing organization, marketing research systems and the current marketing objectives and strategies. The last of these is too frequently ignored. The marketing system itself needs to be regularly questioned, because the validity of the whole marketing plan is reliant upon the accuracy of the input from this system, and 'garbage in, garbage out' applies with a vengeance.
   - Portfolio planning. In addition, the coordinated planning of the individual products and services can contribute towards the balanced portfolio.
   - 80:20 rule. To achieve the maximum impact, the marketing plan must be clear, concise and simple. It needs to concentrate on the 20 per cent of products or services, and on the 20 per cent of customers, which will account for 80 per cent of the volume and 80 per cent of the profit.
   - 7 P's: Product, Place, Price and Promotion, Physical Environment, People, Process. The 7 P's can sometimes divert attention from the customer, but the framework they offer can be very useful in building the action plans.

It is only at this stage that the active part of the marketing planning process begins. This next stage in marketing planning is indeed the key to the whole marketing process. The "marketing objectives" state just where the company intends to be at some specific time in the future. James Quinn succinctly defined objectives in general as: Goals state what is to be achieved and when results are to be accomplished, but they do not state 'how' the results are to be achieved. They typically relate to what products will be where in what markets. They are essentially about the match between those "products" and "markets." Objectives for pricing, distribution, advertising and so on are at a lower level, and should not be confused with marketing objectives.

They are part of the marketing strategy needed to achieve marketing objectives. To be most effective, objectives should be capable of measurement and therefore "quantifiable." This measurement may be in terms of sales volume, money value, market share, percentage penetration of distribution outlets and so on.

An example of such a measurable marketing objective might be "to enter the market with product Y and capture 10 per cent of the market by value within one year." As it is quantified it can, within limits, be unequivocally monitored, and corrective action taken as necessary.The marketing objectives must usually be based on the organization's financial objectives; converting these financial measurements into the related marketing measurements.He went on to explain his view of the role of "policies," with which strategy is most often confused: "Policies are rules or guidelines that express the 'limits' within which action should occur."Simplifying somewhat, marketing strategies can be seen as the means, or "game plan," by which marketing objectives will be achieved and, in the framework that we have chosen to use, are generally concerned with the 8 P's.

Examples are:

1. *Price:* The amount of money needed to buy products
2. *Product*: The actual product
3. *Promotion*: Getting the product known
4. *Placement*: Where the product is located
5. *People*: Represent the business
6. *Physical environment:* The ambiance, mood, or tone of the environment
7. *Process* - How do people obtain your product
8. *Packaging*: How the product will be protected

In principle, these strategies describe how the objectives will be achieved. The 7 P's are a useful framework for deciding how the company's resources will be manipulated to achieve the objectives. It should be noted, however, that they are not the only framework, and may divert attention from the real issues. The focus of the strategies must be the objectives to be achieved - not the process of planning itself. Only if it fits the needs of these objectives should you choose, as we have done, to use the framework of the 7 P's.

The strategy statement can take the form of a purely verbal description of the strategic options which have been chosen. Alternatively, and perhaps more positively, it might include a structured list of the major options chosen. One aspect of strategy which is often overlooked is that of "timing."

Exactly when it is the best time for each element of the strategy to be implemented is often critical. Taking the right action at the wrong time can sometimes be almost as bad as taking the wrong action at the right time. Timing is, therefore, an essential part of any plan; and should normally appear as a schedule of planned activities.Having completed this crucial stage of the planning process, you will need to re-check the feasibility of your objectives and strategies in terms of the market share, sales, costs, profits and so on which these demand in practice.

As in the rest of the marketing discipline, you will need to employ Judgement, experience, market research or anything else which helps you to look at your conclusions from all possible angles.

Detailed Plans and Programmes

At this stage, you will need to develop your overall marketing strategies into detailed plans and programme. Although these detailed plans may cover each of the 7 P's, the focus will vary, depending upon your organization's specific strategies. A product-oriented company will focus its plans for the 7 P's around each of its products. A market or geographically oriented company will concentrate on each market or geographical area. Each will base its plans upon the detailed needs of its customers, and on the strategies chosen to satisfy these needs.

Again, the most important element is, indeed, that of the detailed plans, which spell out exactly what programmes and individual activities will take place over the period of the plan. Without these specified - and preferably quantified - activities the plan cannot be monitored, even in terms of success in meeting its objectives.It is these programmes and activities which will then constitute the "marketing" of the organization over the period. As a result, these detailed marketing programmes are the most important, practical outcome of the whole planning process.

These plans must therefore be:

- *Clear*: They should be an unambiguous statement of 'exactly' what is to be done.
- *Quantified*: The predicted outcome of each activity should be, as far as possible, quantified, so that its performance can be monitored.
- *Focused*: The temptation to proliferate activities beyond the numbers which can be realistically controlled should be avoided. The 80:20 Rule applies in this context too.
- *Realistic*: They should be achievable.
- *Agreed*: Those who are to implement them should be committed to them, and agree that they are achievable. The resulting plans should become a working document which will guide the campaigns taking place throughout the organization over the period of the plan. If the marketing plan is to work, every exception to it must be questioned; and the lessons learned, to be incorporated in the next year's planning.

Content of the Marketing Plan

A marketing plan for a small business typically includes Small Business Administration Description of competitors, including the level of demand for the product or service and the strengths and weaknesses of competitors

- Description of the product or service, including special features
- Marketing budget, including the advertising and promotional plan
- Description of the business location, including advantages and disadvantages for marketing
- Pricing strategy
- Market Segmentation

Measurement of Progress

The final stage of any marketing planning process is to establish targets so that progress can be monitored. Accordingly, it is important to put both quantities and timescales into the marketing objectives and into the corresponding strategies. Changes in the environment mean that the forecasts often have to be changed. Along with these, the related plans may well also need to be changed. Continuous monitoring of performance, against predetermined targets, represents a most important aspect of this. However, perhaps even more important is the enforced discipline of a regular formal review.

Again, as with forecasts, in many cases the best planning cycle will revolve around a quarterly review. Best of all, at least in terms of the quantifiable aspects of the plans, if not the wealth of backing detail, is probably a quarterly rolling review - planning one full year ahead each new quarter. Of course, this does absorb more planning resource; but it also ensures that the plans embody the latest information, and - with attention focused on them so regularly - forces both the plans and their implementation to be realistic. Plans only have validity if they are actually used to control the progress of a company: their success lies in their implementation, not in the writing'.

Performance Analysis

The most important elements of marketing performance, which are normally tracked, are:

Sales Analysis

Most organizations track their sales results; or, in non-profit organizations for example, the number of clients. The more sophisticated track them in terms of 'sales variance' - the deviation from the target figures - which allows a more immediate picture of deviations to become evident.

'Micro-analysis', which is a nicely pseudo-scientific term for the normal management process of investigating detailed problems, then investigates the individual elements which are failing to meet targets.

Market Share Analysis

Few organizations track market share though it is often an important metric. Though absolute sales might grow in an expanding market, a firm's share of the market can decrease which bodes ill for future sales when the market starts to drop.

Where such market share is tracked, there may be a number of aspects which will be followed:

- Overall market share
- Segment share - that in the specific, targeted segment
- Relative share -in relation to the market leaders
- Annual fluctuation rate of market share

Expense Analysis

The key ratio to watch in this area is usually the 'marketing expense to sales ratio'; although this may be broken down into other elements.

Financial Analysis

The "bottom line" of marketing activities should at least in theory, be the net profit.

There are a number of separate performance figures and key ratios which need to be tracked:

- Gross contribution<>net profit
- Gross profit<>return on investment
- Net contribution<>profit on sales

There can be considerable benefit in comparing these figures with those achieved by other organizations; using, for instance, the figures which can be obtained from 'The Centre for Interfirm Comparison'.

The most sophisticated use of this approach, however, is typically by those making use of PIMS, initiated by the General Electric Company and then developed by Harvard Business School, but now run by the Strategic Planning Institute.

The performance analyses concentrate on the quantitative measures which are directly related to short-term performance. But there are a number of indirect measures, essentially tracking customer attitudes, which can also indicate the organization's performance in terms of its longer-term marketing strengths and may accordingly be even more important indicators.

Some useful measures are:

- *Market research*: Including customer panels
- *lost business*: The orders which were lost because, for example, the stock was not available or the product did not meet the customer's exact requirements
- *Customer complaints*: How many customers complain about the products or services, or the organization itself, and about what

Use of Marketing Plans

A formal, written marketing plan is essential; in that it provides an unambiguous reference point for activities throughout the planning period. However, perhaps the most important benefit of these plans is the planning process itself. This typically offers a unique opportunity, a forum, for information-rich and productively focused discussions between the various managers involved. The plan, together with the associated discussions, then provides an agreed context for their subsequent management activities, even for those not described in the plan itself.

Budgets as Managerial Tools

The classic quantification of a marketing plan appears in the form of budgets. Because these are so rigorously quantified, they are particularly important. They should, thus, represent an unequivocal projection of actions and expected results. What is more, they should be capable of being monitored accurately; and, indeed, performance against budget is the main management review process. The purpose of a marketing budget is, thus, to pull together all the revenues and costs involved in marketing into one comprehensive document. It is a managerial tool that balances what is needed to be spent against what can be afforded, and helps make choices about priorities. It is then used in monitoring performance in practice.The marketing budget is usually the most powerful tool by which you think through the relationship between desired results and available means. Its starting point should be the marketing strategies and plans, which have already been formulated in the marketing plan itself; although, in practice, the two will run in parallel and will interact. At the very least, the rigorous, highly quantified, budgets may cause a rethink of some of the more optimistic elements of the plans.

STRATEGIC PLANNING

Strategic planning is an organization's process of defining its strategy, or direction, and making decisions on allocating its resources to pursue this strategy, including its capital and people. Various business analysis techniques can be used in strategic planning, including SWOT analysis, PEST analysis, STEER analysis, and EPISTEL. Strategic planning is the formal consideration of an organization's future course.

All strategic planning deals with at least one of three key questions:

1. "What do we do?"
2. "For whom do we do it?"
3. "How do we excel?"

In business strategic planning, the third question is better phrased "How can we beat or avoid competition?". In many organizations, this is viewed as a process for determining where an organization is going over the next year or more -typically 3 to 5 years, although some extend their vision to 20 years.In order to determine where it is going, the organization needs to know exactly where it stands, then determine where it wants to go and how it will get there. The resulting document is called the "strategic plan." It is also true that strategic planning may be a tool for effectively plotting the direction of a company; however, strategic planning itself cannot foretell exactly how the market will evolve and what issues will surface in the coming days in order to plan your organizational strategy. Therefore, strategic innovation and tinkering with the 'strategic plan' have to be a cornerstone strategy for an organization to survive the turbulent business climate.

Mission, Vision and Values

- *Mission*: Defines the fundamental purpose of an organization or an enterprise, succinctly describing why it exists and what it does to achieve its Vision.
- *Vision*: Defines the desired or intended future state of an organization or enterprise in terms of its fundamental objective and/or strategic direction. Vision is a long term view, sometimes describing how the organization would like the world in which it operates to be. For example a charity working with the poor might have a vision statement which read "A world without poverty" It is sometimes used to set out a 'picture' of the organization in the future. A vision statement provides inspiration, the basis for all the organization's planning. It could answer the question: "Where do we want to go?"
- *Values*: Beliefs that are shared among the stakeholders of an organization. Values drive an organization's culture and priorities.
- *Strategy*: Strategy narrowly defined, means "the art of the general". A combination of the ends for which the firm is striving and the means by which it is seeking to get there.

Mission Statements and Vision Statements

Organizations sometimes summarize goals and objectives into a mission statement and/or a vision statement. Others begin with a vision and mission and use them to formulate goals and objectives. While the existence of a shared mission is extremely useful, many strategy specialists question the requirement for a written mission statement.

However, there are many models of strategic planning that start with mission statements, so it is useful to examine them here:

- A Mission statement tells you the fundamental purpose of the organization. It defines the customer and the critical processes. It informs you of the desired level of performance.
- A Vision statement outlines what the organization wants to be, or how it wants the world in which it operates to be. It concentrates on the future. It is a source of inspiration. It provides clear decision-making criteria.

An advantage of having a statement is that it creates value for those who get exposed to the statement, and those prospects are managers, employees and sometimes even customers. Statements create a sense of direction and opportunity. They both are an essential part of the strategy-making process. Many people mistake vision statement for mission statement, and sometimes one is simply used as a longer term version of the other.

The Vision should describe why it is important to achieve the Mission. A Vision statement defines the purpose or broader goal for being in existence or in the business and can remain the same for decades if crafted well. A Mission statement is more specific to what the enterprise can achieve itself. Vision should describe what will be achieved in the wider sphere if the organization and others are successful in achieving their individual missions.

A mission statement can resemble a vision statement in a few companies, but that can be a grave mistake. It can confuse people. The mission statement can galvanize the people to achieve defined objectives, even if they are stretch objectives, provided it can be elucidated in SMART terms. A mission statement provides a path to realise the vision in line with its values. These statements have a direct bearing on the bottom line and success of the organization. Which comes first? The mission statement or the vision statement? That depends. If you have a new start up business, new programme or plan to re engineer your current services, then the vision will guide the mission statement and the rest of the strategic plan. If you have an established business where the mission is established, then many times, the mission guides the vision statement and the rest of the strategic plan.

Either way, you need to know your fundamental purpose - the mission, your current situation in terms of internal resources and capabilities and external conditions, and where you want to go - the vision for the future. It's important that you keep the end or desired result in sight from the start..

Features of an effective vision statement include:

- Clarity and lack of
- Vivid and clear picture
- Description of a bright future
- Memorable and engaging wording
- Realistic aspirations
- Alignment with organizational values and culture

To become really effective, an organizational vision statement must become assimilated into the organization's culture. Leaders have the responsibility of communicating the vision regularly, creating narratives that illustrate the vision, acting as role-models by embodying the vision, creating short-term objectives compatible with the vision, and encouraging others to craft their own personal vision compatible with the organization's overall vision. In addition, mission statements need to be subjected to an internal assessment and an external assessment.

The internal assessment should focus on how members inside the organization interpret their mission statement. The external assessment — which includes all of the businesses stakeholders — is valuable since it offers a different perspective. These discrepancies between these two assessments can give insight on the organization's mission statement effectiveness.Another approach to defining Vision and Mission is to pose two questions. Firstly, "What aspirations does the organization have for the world in which it operates and has some influence over?", and following on from this, "What can the organization do or contribute to fulfill those aspirations?". The succinct answer to the first question provides the basis of the Vision Statement. The answer to the second question determines the Mission Statement.

Methodologies

There are many approaches to strategic planning but typically a three-step process may be used:

1. *Situation*: Evaluate the current situation and how it came about.
2. *Target*: Define goals and/or objectives
3. *Path*: Map a possible route to the goals/objectives

One alternative approach is called Draw-See-Think:

- *Draw*: What is the ideal image or the desired end state?
- *See*: What is today's situation? What is the gap from ideal and why?
- *Think*: What specific actions must be taken to close the gap between today's situation and the ideal state?
- *Plan*: What resources are required to execute the activities?

An alternative to the Draw-See-Think approach is called See-Think-Draw:

- *See*: What is today's situation?
- *Think*: Define goals/objectives
- *Draw*: Map a route to achieving the goals/objectives

In other terms strategic planning can be as follows:

- *Vision*: Define the vision and set a mission statement with hierarchy of goals and objectives
- *SWOT*: Analysis conducted according to the desired goals
- *Formulate*: Formulate actions and processes to be taken to attain these goals
- *Implement*: Implementation of the agreed upon processes
- *Control*: Monitor and get feedback from implemented processes to fully control the operation

Situational Analysis

When developing strategies, analysis of the organization and its environment as it is at the moment and how it may develop in the future, is important. The analysis has to be executed at an internal level as well as an external level to identify all opportunities and threats of the external environment as well as the strengths and weaknesses of the organizations.

There are several factors to assess in the external situation analysis:

- Markets
- Competition
- Technology
- Supplier markets
- Labour markets

- The economy
- The regulatory environment

It is rare to find all seven of these factors having critical importance. It is also uncommon to find that the first two - markets and competition - are not of critical importance. Analysis of the external environment normally focuses on the customer. Management should be visionary in formulating customer strategy, and should do so by thinking about market environment shifts, how these could impact customer sets, and whether those customer sets are the ones the company wishes to serve. Analysis of the competitive environment is also performed, many times based on the framework suggested by Michael Porter.

Goals, Objectives and Targets

Strategic planning is a very important business activity. It is also important in the public sector areas such as education. It is practiced widely informally and formally. Strategic planning and decision processes should end with objectives and a roadmap of ways to achieve those objectives.

One of the core goals when drafting a strategic plan is to develop it in a way that is easily translatable into action plans. Most strategic plans address high level initiatives and over-arching goals, but don't get articulated into day-to-day projects and tasks that will be required to achieve the plan. Terminology or word choice, as well as the level a plan is written, are both examples of easy ways to fail at translating your strategic plan in a way that makes sense and is executable to others. Often, plans are filled with conceptual terms which don't tie into day-to-day realities for the staff expected to carry out the plan. The following terms have been used in strategic planning: desired end states, plans, policies, goals, objectives, strategies, tactics and actions.

Definitions vary, overlap and fail to achieve clarity. The most common of these concepts are specific, time bound statements of intended future results and general and continuing statements of intended future results, which most models refer to as either goals or objectives. One model of organizing objectives uses hierarchies.

The items listed may be organized in a hierarchy of means and ends and numbered as follows: Top Rank Objective, Second Rank Objective, Third Rank Objective, etc. From any rank, the objective in a lower rank answers to the question "How?" and the objective in a higher rank answers to the question "Why?" The exception is the Top Rank Objective: there is no answer to the "Why?" question. That is how the TRO is defined.

People typically have several goals at the same time. "Goal congruency" refers to how well the goals combine with each other. Does goal A appear compatible with goal B? Do they fit together to form a unified strategy? "Goal hierarchy" consists of the nesting of one or more goals within other goals. One approach recommends having short-term goals, medium-term goals, and long-term goals. In this model, one can expect to attain short-term goals fairly easily: they stand just slightly one's reach. At the other extreme, long-term goals appear very difficult, almost impossible to attain. Strategic management jargon sometimes refers to "Big Hairy Audacious Goals" in this context. Using one goal as a stepping-stone to the next involves goal sequencing. A person or group starts by attaining the easy short-term goals, then steps up to the medium-term, then to the long-term goals. Goal sequencing can create a "goal stairway". In an organizational setting, the organization may co-ordinate goals so that they do not conflict with each other. The goals of one part of the organization should mesh compatibly with those of other parts of the organization.

FUNCTIONS OF PRODUCTION PLANNING

- Product selection and design
- Process selection and planning
- Facility location
- Facility layout and materials handling
- Capacity planning
- Systems and procedures
- Estimating quantity/costs of production, men
- Routing operation sequence
- Job scheduling and loading

FUNCTIONS OF PRODUCTION CONTROL

- Inventory control: MRP; JIT
- Time management
- Quality control
- Maintenance and Replacement
- Cost reduction and cost control
- Dispatch
- Expediting/Follow-up/Progressing

SCOPE OF PRODUCTION PLANNING AND CONTROL

- *Material*: RM, components, spares; right quantity; right time
- Methods
- Machines and equipments
- Manpower
- Routing
- Estimating
- Loading and sceduling
- Dispatching
- Expediting

- Inspection
- Evaluating
- Cost control

PHASES IN PRODUCTION PLANNING AND CONTROL SYSTEM

- *Planning*:
  - Pre-planning
  - Product planning and development;
  - Demand forecasting;
  - Resource planning;
  - Facilities planning;
  - Plant location and layout
- Active planning
  - Quantity planning;
  - Product mix;
  - Routing;
  - Scheduling;
  - Material planning;
  - Process planning;
  - Capacity planning;
  - Tool planning

BENEFITS OF PRODUCTION PLANNING AND CONTROL

- Higher quality
- Better resource utilization
- Reduced inventory
- Reduced manufacturing cycle time
- Faster delivery
- Better customer services
- Lower production costs
- Lower capital investment
- Higher customer service
- Improved sales turnover
- Improved market share
- Improved profitability
- Competitive advantage
- Flexibility
- Dependability
- Lower prices

LIMITATIONS OF PRODUCTION PLANNING AND CONTROL

- Based on assumptions

- Resistance to change
- Time consuming
- Difficult due to rapid environment changes

MEASURING EFFECTIVENESS OF PRODUCTION PLANNING AND CONTROL

- Delivery
- Inventory levels
- Production/Operations Management

REQUIREMENTS FOR EFFECTIVE PRODUCTION PLANNING AND CONTROL

- Sound organisational structure
- Delegation of authority
- Reliable, up-to-date feedback
- Standardisation
- Trained people
- Flexibility to adapt
- Appropriate management policies
- Accurate assessment of manufacturing/procurement lead times
- Adequate plant capacity

AGGREGATE PRODUCTION PLANNING

Aggregate production planning refers to the process of deciding the overall quantities of products to be manufactured or produced in a plant or other manufacturing facility during a medium term planning period such as a month, or a quarter.The aggregate plan output consist of the total quantities of each product or a group of product to be manufactured in the plan period of going into details of scheduling of different manufacturing activities required to achieve the planned production levels. The aggregate production will also not specify details such as the dates when material ordered against individual customer order will be ready for delivery.

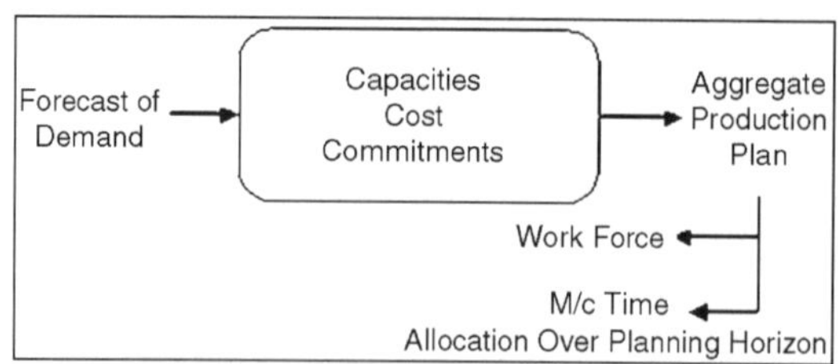

The aggregate production plan is prepared as a means of setting overall production targets and as input for planning availability of other inputs and supporting activities to meet the production targets.The aggregate plans then form the basis of more detailed production, including such as daily and weekly production schedules and customer delivery schedules. Such production plan are further detailed out as machine loading schedules.

MANAGEMENT OPTIONS TO MEET FLUCTUATING DEMAND

- Build inventories in slack periods in anticipation of higher demands later in planning horizon.
- Carry backorders or tolerate lost sales during peak periods.
- Use over time in peak periods, under time in slack periods to vary output, while holding Workforce and facilities constant.
- Vary capacity by changing size of Workforce through hiring and firing.
- Vary capacity through changes in plant and equipment
- Subcontracting may be resolved. Each option involves cost. Aim in aggregate production planning is to choose best option.

KINDS OF COSTS INVOLVED

- Procurement Costs
- Production Costs
- Inventory holding Costs
- Shortage losses associated with backorders and lost sales
- Costs of increasing/decreasing Workforce
- Cost of overtime/under time
- Cost of changing production rates

MASTER PRODUCTION SCHEDULING

The master production scheduling process translates a business plan into a dynamic and comprehensive product manufacturing schedule. Master Production Scheduling helps your management team balance and integrate the needs of marketing, manufacturing, finance and most importantly your customers.

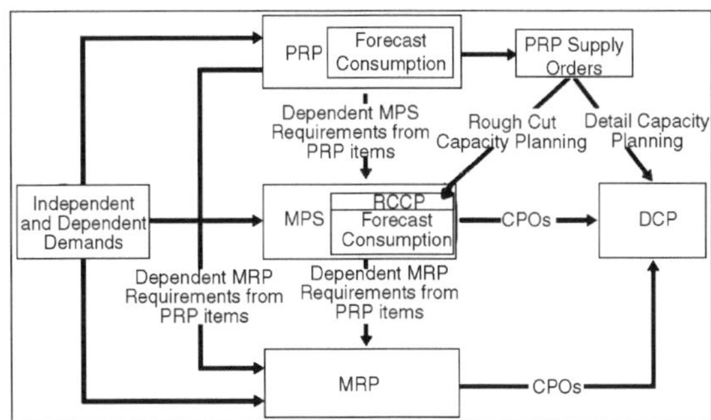

Fig. The Planning Hierarchy

POWERFUL SCHEDULING TOOLS

Master scheduling requires ongoing analysis, measurement and adjustment to achieve revenue goals and ensure profitability through the careful allocation of materials and resources. MPS gives you a set of powerful tools for resource planning and scheduling, analysis, and performance measurement.

PLANNER 'S WORKBENCH

A Planner's Workbench provides the means for consolidating all planning and scheduling functions onto one easy-to-use screen.

The workbench gives you immediate access to information in all areas necessary for successful planning/scheduling including sales demand, committed production, and purchased and planned supply. This allows planners, analysts, and Programme managers to react quickly and easily to any exceptions that occur.

COMPLETE PLANNING VISIBILITY

To help resolve any conflicts, MPS takes a variety of variables into account, including available inventory, forecasted sales, actual backlog, and firm planned production, among others.

"WHAT IF " SIMULATION

A "What If" simulation capability ensures the best possible manufacturing scenario by allowing you to analyse the effects of alternate scenarios, using either current or simulated data.

SCHEDULING CYCLES

And because no single view of your supply and demand data can satisfy all of your planning needs, MPS enables you to create and maintain an unlimited number of planning scenarios. One for near-term deliveries, another for long-range production capacities, and so on. Each cycle provides a unique view of the information necessary to help you develop the correct priorities for your factory.

INSTANT AVAILABLE - TO - PROMISE INFORMATION

Your customer has an emergency requirement for an item that is in critical demand. Can you make the shipment? Our on-line Available-To-Promise feature allows you to instantly investigate the current product availability. You'll have up-to-the-minute item information at hand to make critical delivery commitments.

PERFORMANCE MEASUREMENT

MPS can give you an on-line "snapshot" estimation of the profit or loss that your build plan will yield. Performance analysis can be based on current or simulated data. This helps you focus on areas of maximum payback and set priorities before committing critical resources.

PLANNING BASICS

Essentials of Planning

Planning is not done off hand. It is prepared after careful and extensive research.

For a comprehensive business plan, management has to:

- Clearly define the target/goal in writing.
  - It should be set by a person having authority.
  - The goal should be realistic.
  - It should be specific.
  - Acceptability
  - Easily measurable
- Identify all the main issues which need to be addressed.
- Review past performance.
- Decide budgetary requirement.
- Focus on matters of strategic importance.
- What are requirements and how will they be met?
- What will be the likely length of the plan and its structure?
- Identify shortcomings in the concept and gaps.
- Strategies for implementation.
- Review periodically.

Applications

In Organizations

Planning is also a management process, concerned with defining goals for future organizational performance and deciding on the tasks and resources to be used in order to attain those goals. To meet the goals, managers may develop plans such as a business plan or a marketing plan. Planning always has a purpose.

The purpose may be achievement of certain goals or targets. The planning helps to achieve these goals or target by using the available time and resources. To minimize the timing and resources also require proper planning. The concept of planning is to identify what the organization wants to do by using the four questions which are "where are we today in terms of our business or strategy planning? Where are we going? Where do we want to go? How are we going to get there?..."

In Public Policy

Planning refers to the practice and the profession associated with the idea of planning an idea yourself. In many countries, the operation of a town and country planning system is often referred to as "planning" and the professionals which operate the system are known as "planners".

It is a conscious as well as sub-conscious activity. It is "an anticipatory decision making process" that helps in coping with complexities. It is deciding future course of action from amongst alternatives. It is a process that involves making and evaluating each set of interrelated decisions. It is selection of missions, objectives and "translation of knowledge into action." A planned performance brings better results compared to an unplanned one. A manager's job is planning, monitoring and controlling. Planning and goal setting are important traits of an organization. It is done at all levels of the organization.

Planning includes the plan, the thought process, action, and implementation.Planning gives more power over the future. Planning is deciding in advance what to do, how to do it, when to do it, and who should do it. It bridges the gap from where the organization is to where it wants to be. The planning function involves establishing goals and arranging them in logical order.

THE PLANNING PROCESS

Planning is one those things that we all know is good for us, but that no one wants to take the time to do. While it may seem that planning only takes time away from running your business, operating a business without a plan is like going to a grocery store without a list and trying to remember all the items that are needed. One comes out of the store having forgotten something critical—and having purchased a number of items that are totally frivolous and may never be used. It is the same for a business operating without a plan. Critical issues do not get addressed - and some tasks get done that have no relationship to the direction the business needs to go. For a business, however, the consequences of these unaddressed issues can range from inconvenience to bankruptcy.

Part of this reluctance is due to how complicated the process is viewed. Yet a complicated plan is almost as useless as none. The real question is how to make something simple that fits your business' needs. Can a good grocery list system be devised that isn't unnecessarily burdensome for all involved? Of course. Let's take a look as what planning really entails. The word "plan" originated from then Medieval Latin word planus which meant a level or flat surface. This evolved in French into being a map or a drawing of any object made by projection upon a flat surface. In English this has become a more general sense of a plan of action, design or method.

Planning in its current usage in business implies a consciousness of what is happening in the business. It does not preclude creativity or instinct, but it does add a layer of awareness that spells the difference between survival and extinction in a changing environment.

Planning does involve:

- An understanding of the business' history
- An examination of the business' environment
- An assessment of the business' mission
- Goals
- A process for reaching those goals
- A process for gathering information
- A realization that planning is a continuing process that is constantly evolving

Planning does not necessarily mean trying to project the future, but being aware of a range of likely futures and being prepared for them as occur.

BUSINESS PLAN

A business plan is used when one is starting a new business or a new process or product within a business. It includes not only a description of the new business, process or product, but also a discussion of how one plans on managing the marketing, development, production, and financing of this new venture.

ORGANIZATIONAL PLAN

Organizational planning, when it does occur, too often is spurred by crisis, focused on the short term, and not well thought out. To create healthy futures, organizations must construct processes for creating their futures that are not fueled by crisis and turmoil. It can be done. One of the most confusing aspects for those who want to plan is the variety of terms that are used in conjunction with planning. How do you differentiate between a business plan, a financial plan, a marketing plan, a human resources plan, an operations plan, a strategic plan, a long-range plan and just plain general planning? The simple answer is that each area of your business needs planning so each area should have its own grocery list of what it wishes to accomplish in the future.

STRATEGIC PLAN

A strategic plan usually refers to the overall direction you wish your business to take over the longer term. Consequently, a long-range plan and a strategic plan are often used synonymously. Within that overall strategy a business will have shorter term financial goals, marketing goals, production goals, and human resource goals that will each need some type of plan if they are to be achieved.

Just because a strategic plan is longer term does not mean it is never changed, however. One of the most serious mistakes businesses make is not revising their strategic plan regularly. The environment the business is operating in is changing constantly. The plan must be revisited at regular intervals to reflect the impact on the business of these external factors.There are some universal principles that are true across all types of planning. Before tackling more specific planning models, it is wise to gain an understanding of the basic principles of general planning.

PLANNING PRINCIPLES

Any plan should include who, what, when, where, how, and why:

- Who is needed to accomplish this task?
- What needs to be done?
- When does it start and end?
- Where will it take place?
- How will it happen?
- Why must we do it?

Along with the answers to these questions there needs to be some operational plan to organize the tasks needed to achieve the goal. A helpful approach is to work backward from the goal to decide what must be done to reach it. The backward approach is a way of looking at the big picture first, and then planning all tasks, conditions, and in a logical sequence to make the big picture happen. From this a to-do list can easily be made. This list will become a checklist to ensure everything is progressing as planned. Adjustments can be made based on changing circumstances. The plan should be referenced often as a set of signposts on the journey towards the goals.

For many of us who left corporate America in favour of a smaller work environment, the idea of drafting a plan may seem offensive. After all, isn't frustration with all that busywork one of the reasons we left in the first place? We all have an aversion to doing anything on our job that doesn't immediately help the situation we are now experiencing. However, isn't it also true that a little foresight and action before the fact can help eliminate many of the problems we face each day.

Wouldn't it be nice to anticipate something like a price cut by your major competitor or a rise in the interest rate on your credit line? Of course it would. And with that anticipation comes an organized and effective response.

PLANNING ORGANIZATIONS

Planning in organizations and public policy is both the organizational process of creating and maintaining a plan; and the psychological process of thinking about the activities required to create a desired goal on some scale. As such, it is a fundamental property of intelligent behaviour.

This thought process is essential to the creation and refinement of a plan, or integration of it with other plans, that is, it combines forecasting of developments with the preparation of scenarios of how to react to them. An important, albeit often ignored aspect of planning, is the relationship it holds with forecasting. Forecasting can be described as predicting what the future will look like, whereas planning predicts what the future should look like. The term is also used to describe the formal procedures used in such an endeavor, such as the creation of documents, diagrams, or meetings to discuss the important issues to be addressed, the objectives to be met, and the strategy to be followed. Beyond this, planning has a different meaning depending on the political or economic context in which it is used. Two attitudes to planning need to be held in tension: on the one hand we need to be prepared for what may lie ahead, which may mean contingencies and flexible processes. On the other hand, our future is shaped by consequences of our own planning and actions.

AN OVERVIEW

Planning is a process for accomplishing purpose. It is a blue print of business growth and a road map of development. It helps in deciding objectives both in quantitative and qualitative terms. It is setting of goals on the basis of objectives and keeping in view the resources.

What should a Plan be?

A plan should be a realistic view of the expectations. Depending upon the activities, a plan can be long range, intermediate range or short range. It is the framework within which it must operate. For management seeking external support, the plan is the most important document and key to growth. Preparation of a comprehensive plan will not guarantee success, but lack of a sound plan will almost certainly ensure failure.

Purpose of a Plan

Just as no two organizations are alike, so also their plans. It is therefore important to prepare a plan keeping in view the necessities of the enterprise. A plan is an important aspect of business.

It serves the following three critical functions:

1. Helps management to clarify, focus, and research their business's or project's development and prospects.
2. Provides a considered and logical framework within which a business can develop and pursue business strategies over the next three to five years.
3. Offers a benchmark against which actual performance can be measured and reviewed.

Importance of the Planning Process

A plan can play a vital role in helping to avoid mistakes or recognize hidden opportunities. Preparing a satisfactory plan of the organization is essential. The planning know the business and that they have thought through its development in terms of products, management, finances, and most importantly, markets and competition. Planning helps in forecasting the future, makes the future visible to some extent. It bridges between where we are and where we want to go. Planning is looking ahead.

TYPES OF PLANS OR PLANNING

- Architectural planning
- Business plan
- Comprehensive planning
- Enterprise Architecture Planning
- Event Planning and Production
- Family planning
- Financial planning
- Infrastructure planning
- Land use planning
- Life planning
- Marketing plan
- Network resource planning
- Strategic planning
- Urban planning
- Operational planning

OBJECTIVES AND POLICIES

Objectives

The objectives are general parts of the planning process. They are the end-results towards which all business activities are directed.

They are needed in every aspect where performance and result directly and vitally affect the survival and success of the firm. In other words, the objective of the firm justifies its existence. Robert C. Appley, "Objectives are goals; they are aims which management and administration wish the organization to achieve." In other words, goals, aims and purposes are also used to signify objectives. Newman and Summer stated, "For managerial purposes, it is useful to think of objectives as the results we want to achieve. Objective covers firm's long-range plans specific departmental goals and short-term individual assignment also."

Policies

George R. Ferry, "Policy is a verbal, written or implied overall guide setting up boundaries that supply the general units and directions in which managerial action will take place." Policies are specific guidelines and constraints for managerial thinking on decision-making and action. Policies provide the framework within which decision-makers are expected to operate while making organizational decisions. They are the basic guides to be consistent in decision-making.

CAPACITY-PLANNING TECHNIQUES

There are four procedures for capacity planning; capacity planning using overall factors, capacity bills, resource profiles, and capacity requirements planning. The first three are rough-cut approaches that can be used with or without manufa-cturing resource planning systems. CRP is used in conjunction with MRP systems. Capacity using overall factors is a simple, manual approach to capacity planning that is based on the master production schedule and production standards that convert required units of finished goods into historical loads on each work centre. Bills of capacity is a procedure based on the MPS. Instead of using historical ratios, however, it utilizes the bills of material and routing sheet. Capacity requirements can then be determined by multiplying the number of units required by the MPS by the time needed to produce each. Resource profiles are the same as bills of capacity, except lead times are included so that workloads fall into the correct periods.

Capacity requirements planning is only applicable in firms using MRP or MRP II. CRP uses the information from one of the previous rough-cut methods, plus MRP outputs on existing inventories and lot sizing. The result is a tabular load report for each work centre or a graphical load profile for helping plan-production requirements. This will indicate where capacity is inadequate or idle, allowing for imbalances to be corrected by shifts in personnel or equipment or the use of overtime or added shifts. Finite capacity scheduling is an extension of CRP that simulates job order stopping and starting to produce a detailed schedule that provides a set of start and finish dates for each operation at each work centre.

A failure to understand the critical nature of managing capacity can lead to chaos and serious customer service problems. If there is a mismatch between available and required capacity, adjustments should be made. However, it should be noted that firms cannot have perfectly-balanced material and capacity plans that easily accommodate emergency orders. If flexibility is the firm's competitive priority, excess capacity would be appropriate.

MANUFACTURING PLANNING AND CONTROL

Manufacturing planning and control address decisions on the acquisition, utilization and allocation of production resources to satisfy customer requirements in the most efficient and effective way. Typical decisions include Workforce level, production lot sizes, assignment of overtime and sequencing of production runs. Optimization models are widely applicable for providing decision support in this context.

We focus on optimization models for production planning for discrete-parts, batch manufacturing environments. We do not cover detailed scheduling or sequencing models, nor do we address production planning for continuous processes. We consider only discrete-time models, and do not include continuous-time models such as developed by Hackman and Leachman.

Our intent is to provide an overview of applicable optimization models; we present the most generic formulations and briefly describe how these models are solved. There is an enormous range of problem contexts and model formulations, as well as solution methods. We make no effort to be exhaustive in the treatment herein. Rather, we have made choices of what to include based on personal Judgement and preferences. We have organized the substance into four major parts. In the first part we present a framework for the decisions, issues and tradeoffs involved in implementing an optimization model for discrete-part production planning. The remaining three parts present and discuss three distinct types of models. In the second part we discuss linear programming models for production planning, in which we have linear costs.

This category is of great practical interest, as many important problem features can be captured with these models and powerful solution methods for linear programmes are readily available. In the third part, we present a production-planning model for a single aggregate product with quadratic costs; this model is of historical significance as it represents one of the earliest applications of optimization to manufacturing planning. In the final part we introduce the multi-item capacitated lot-size problem, which is modeled as a mixed integer linear programme. This is an important model as it introduces economies of scale in production, due to the presence of production setups.

FRAMEWORK

There are a variety of considerations that go into the development and implementation of an optimization model for manufacturing planning and control. In this part we highlight and comment upon a number of key issues and questions that should be addressed. Excellent general references on production planning are Thomas and McClain, Shapiro and Silver et al..

Any planning problem starts with a specification of customer demand that is to be met by the production plan. In most contexts, future demand is at best only partially known, and often is not known at all. Consequently, one relies on a forecast for the future demand. To the extent that any forecast is inevitably inaccurate, one must decide how to account for or react to this demand uncertainty. The optimization models described in this substance treat demand as being known; as such they must be periodically revised and rerun to account for forecast updates.

A key choice is what planning decisions to include in the model. By definition, production-planning models include decisions on production and inventory quantities. But in addition, there might be resource acquisition and allocation decision, such as adding to the Workforce and upgrading the training of the current Workforce. In many planning contexts, an important construct is to set a planning hierarchy. Namely, one structures the planning process in a hierarchical way by ordering the decisions according to their relative importance.

Hax and Meal introduced the notion of hierarchical production planning and provide a specific framework for this, whereby there is an optimization model with each level of the hierarchy. Each optimization model imposes a constraint on the model at the next level of the hierarchy. Bitran and Tirupati provide a comprehensive survey of hierarchical planning methods and models. The identification of the relevant costs is also an important issue. For production planning, one typically needs to determine the variable production costs, including setuprelated costs, inventory holding costs, and any relevant resource acquisition costs. There might also be costs associated with imperfect customer service, such as when demand is backordered.

A planning problem exists because there are limited production resources that cannot be stored from period to period. Choices must be made as to which resources to include and how to model their capacity and behaviour, and their costs. Also, there may be uncertainty associated with the production function, such as uncertain yields or lead times. One might only include the most critical or limiting resource in the planning problem, e. g., a bottleneck. Alternatively, when there is not a dominant resource, then one must model the resources that could limit production. We describe in this substance two types of production functions.

The first assumes a linear relationship between the production quantity and the resource consumption. The second assumes that there is a required fixed charge or setup to initiate production and then a linear relationship between the production quantity and resource usage. Related to these choices is the selection of the time period and planning horizon. The planning literature distinguishes between "big bucket" and "small bucket" time periods. A time period is a big bucket if multiple items are typically produced within a time period; a small bucket is such that at most one item would be produced in the time period. For big bucket models, one has to worry about how to schedule or sequence the production runs assigned to any time period. The choice of planning horizon is dictated by the lead times to enact production and resource-related decisions, as well as the quality of knowledge about future demand.

Planning is typically done in a rolling horizon fashion. A plan is created for the planning horizon, but only the decisions in the first few periods are implemented before a revised plan is issued. Indeed the plan must be periodically revised due to the uncertainties in the demand forecasts and production. For instance a firm might plan for the next 26 weeks, but then revise this once a month to incorporate new information on demand and production.Production planning is usually done at an aggregate level, for both products and resources. Distinct but similar products are combined into aggregate product families that can be planned together so as to reduce planning complexity. Similarly production resources, such as distinct machines or labour pools, are aggregated into an aggregate machine or labour resource. Care is required when specifying these aggregates to assure that the resulting aggregate plan can be reasonably disaggregated into feasible production schedules. Finally for complex products, one must decide the level and extent of the product structure to include in the planning process. For instance, in some contexts it is sufficient to just plan the production of end items; the production plan for components and subassemblies is subservient to the master production schedule for end items.

In other contexts, planning just the end items is sub-optimal, as there are critical resource constraints applicable to multiple levels of the product structure. In this instance, a multistage planning model allows for the simultaneous planning of end items and components or subassemblies. Of course, this produces a much larger model.

FUNCTION OF CONTROL MANAGEMENT

Control is one of the managerial functions like planning, organizing, staffing and directing. It is an important function because it helps to check the errors and to take the corrective action so that deviation from standards are minimized and stated goals of the organization are achieved in desired manner. Modern concepts, control is a foreseeing action whereas earlier concept of control was used only when errors were detected. Control in management means setting standards, measuring actual performance and taking corrective action. Thus, control comprises these three main activities.

CHARACTERISTICS OF CONTROL

- Control is a continuous process
- Control is a management process
- Control is embedded in each level of organizational hierarchy
- Control is forward looking
- Control is closely linked with planning
- Control is a tool for achieving organizational activities

Elements of Control

The four basic elements in a control system:

1. The characteristic or condition to be controlled,
2. The sensor,
3. The comparator, and
4. *The activator*: Occur in the same sequence and maintain a consistent relationship to each other in every system.

The first element is the characteristic or condition of the operating system which is to be measured. We select a specific characteristic because a correlation exists between it and how the system is performing. The characteristic may be the output of the system during any stage of processing or it may be a condition that has resulted from the output of the system. For example, it may be the heat energy produced by the furnace or the temperature in the room which has changed because of the heat generated by the furnace. In an elementary school system, the hours a teacher works or the gain in knowledge demonstrated by the students on a national examination are examples of characteristics that may be selected for measurement, or control. The second element of control, the sensor, is a means for measuring the characteristic or condition. The control subsystem must be designed to include a sensory device or method of measurement. In a home heating system this device would be the thermostat, and in a quality-control system this measurement might be performed by a visual inspection of the product.

The third element of control, the comparator, determines the need for correction by comparing what is occurring with what has been planned. Some deviation from plan is usual and expected, but when variations are beyond those considered acceptable, corrective action is required. It is often possible to identify trends in performance and to take action before an unacceptable variation from the norm occurs. This sort of preventative action indicates that good control is being achieved.

The fourth element of control, the activator, is the corrective action taken to return the system to expected output. The actual person, device, or method used to direct corrective inputs into the operating system may take a variety of forms. It may be a hydraulic controller positioned by a solenoid or electric motor in response to an electronic error signal, an employee directed to rework the parts that failed to pass quality inspection, or a school principal who decides to buy additional books to provide for an increased number of students. As long as a plan is performed within allowable limits, corrective action is not necessary; this seldom occurs in practice, however. Information is the medium of control, because the flow of sensory data and later the flow of corrective information allow a characteristic or condition of the system to be controlled. To illustrate how information flow facilitates control, let us review the elements of control in the context of information.

Relationship between the Elements of Control and Information

Controlled Characteristic or. Condition The primary requirement of a control system is that it maintain the level and kind of output necessary to achieve the system's objectives. It is usually impractical to control every feature and condition associated with the system's output. Therefore, the choice of the controlled item is extremely important. There should be a direct correlation between the controlled item and the system's operation. In other words, control of the selected characteristic should have a direct relationship to the goal or objective of the system.

Sensor

After the characteristic is sensed, or measured, information pertinent to control is fed back. Exactly what information needs to be transmitted and also the language that will best facilitate the communication process and reduce the possibility of distortion in transmission must be carefully considered. Information that is to be compared with the standard, or plan, should be expressed in the same terms or language as in the original plan to facilitate decision making. Using machine methods may require extensive translation of the information.

Since optimal languages for computation and for human review are not always the same, the relative ease of translation may be a significant factor in selecting the units of measurement or the language unit in the sensing element. In many instances, the measurement may be sampled rather than providing a complete and continuous feedback of information about the operation. A sampling procedure suggests measuring some segment or portion of the operation that will represent the total.

Comparison with Standard

In a social system, the norms of acceptable behaviour become the standard against which so-called deviant behaviour may be judged. Regulations and laws provide a more formal collection of information for society. Social norms change, but very slowly. In contrast, the standards outlined by a formal law can be changed from one day to the next through revision, discontinuation, or replacement by another.

Information about deviant behaviour becomes the basis for controlling social activity. Output information is compared with the standard or norm and significant deviations are noted. In an industrial example, frequency distribution may be used to show the average quality, the spread, and the comparison of output with a standard.

If there is a significant and uncorrectable difference between output and plan, the system is "out of control." This means that the objectives of the system are not feasible in relation to the capabilities of the present design. Either the objectives must be reevaluated or the system redesigned to add new capacity or capability.

For example, the traffic in drugs has been increasing in some cities at an alarming rate. The citizens must decide whether to revise the police system so as to regain control, or whether to modify the law to reflect a different norm of acceptable behaviour.

Implimentor

The activator unit responds to the information received from the comparator and initiates corrective action. If the system is a machine-to-machine system, the corrective inputs are designed into the network.

When the control relates to a man-to-machine or man-to-man system, however, the individual(s) in charge must evaluate:

- The accuracy of the feedback information,
- The significance of the variation, and
- What corrective inputs will restore the system to a reasonable degree of stability. Once the decision has been made to direct new inputs into the system, the actual process may be relatively easy. A small amount of energy can change the operation of jet airplanes, automatic steel mills, and hydroelectric power plants. The pilot presses a button, and the landing gear of the airplane goes up or down; the operator of a steel mill pushes a lever, and a ribbon of white-hot steel races through the plant; a worker at a control board directs the flow of electrical energy throughout a regional network of stations and substations. It takes but a small amount of control energy to release or stop large quantities of input.

The comparator may be located far from the operating system, although at least some of the elements must be in close proximity to operations. For example, the measurement is usually at the point of operations. The measurement information can be transmitted to a distant point for comparison with the standard and when deviations occur, the correcting input can be released from the distant point. However, the input will be located at the operating system. This ability to control from afar means that aircraft can be flown by remote control, dangerous manufacturing processes can be operated from a safe distance, and national organizations can be directed from centralized headquarters.

Process of Controlling

- Setting performance standards.
- Measurement of actual performance.
- Comparing actual performance with standards.
- Analysing deviations.
- Correcting deviations.

Kinds of Control

Control may be grouped according to three general classifications:

1. The nature of the information flow designed into the system,
2. The kind of components included in the design, and
3. The relationship of control to the decision process.

Open- and Closed-Loop Control

A street-lighting system controlled by a timing device is an example of an open-loop system. At a certain time each evening, a mechanical device closes the circuit and energy flows through the electric lines to light the lamps. Note, however, that the timing mechanism is an independent unit and is not measuring the objective function of the lighting system. If the lights should be needed on a dark, stormy day the timing device would not recognize this need and therefore would not activate energy inputs. Corrective properties may sometimes be built into the controller but this would not close the loop. In another instance, the sensing, comparison, or adjustment may be made through action taken by an individual who is not part of the system. For example, the lights may be turned on by someone who happens to pass by and recognizes the need for additional light. If control is exercised as a result of the operation rather than because of outside or predetermined arrangements, it is a closed-loop system. The home thermostat is the classic example of a control device in a closed-loop system. When the room temperature drops below the desired point, the control mechanism closes the circuit to start the furnace and the temperature rises. The furnace-activating circuit is turned off as the temperature reaches the preselected level. The significant difference between this type of system and an open-loop system is that the control device is an element of the system it serves and measures the performance of the system. In other words, all four control elements are integral to the specific system.

An essential part of a closed-loop system is feedback; that is, the output of the system is measured continually through the item controlled, and the input is modified to reduce any difference or error Towards zero. Many of the patterns of information flow in organizations are found to have the nature of closed loops, which use feedback. The reason for such a condition is apparent when one recognizes that any system, if it is to achieve a predetermined goal, must have available to it at all times an indication of its degree of attainment. In general, every goal-seeking system employs feedback.

Man and Machine Control

The elements of control are easy to identify in machine systems. For example, the characteristic to be controlled might be some variable like speed or temperature, and the sensing device could be a speedometer or a thermometer. An expectation of precision exists because the characteristic is quantifiable and the standard and the normal variation to be expected can be described in exact terms. In automatic machine systems, inputs of information are used in a process of continual adjustment to achieve output specifications. When even a small variation from the standard occurs, the correction process begins. The automatic system is highly structured, designed to accept certain kinds of input and produce specific output, and programmed to regulate the transformation of inputs within a narrow range of variation.For an illustration of mechanical control, as the load on a steam engine increases and the engine starts to slow down, the regulator reacts by opening a valve that releases additional inputs of steam energy. This new input returns the engine to the desired number of revolutions per minute.

This type of mechanical control is crude in comparison to the more sophisticated electronic control systems in everyday use. Consider the complex missile-guidance systems that measure the actual course according to predetermined mathematical calculations and make almost instantaneous corrections to direct the missile to its target.Machine systems can be complex because of the sophisticated technology, whereas control of people is complex because the elements of control are difficult to determine. In human control systems, the relationship between objectives and associated characteristics is often vague; the measurement of the characteristic may be extremely subjective; the expected standard is difficult to define; and the amount of new inputs required is impossible to quantify. To illustrate, let us refer once more to a formalized social system in which deviant behaviour is controlled through a process of observed violation of the existing law, court hearings and trials, incarceration when the accused is found guilty and release from custody after rehabilitation of the prisoner has occurred.

The speed limit established for freeway driving is one standard of performance that is quantifiable, but even in this instance, the degree of permissible variation and the amount of the actual variation are often a subject of disagreement between the patrolman and the suspected violator. The complexity of our society is reflected in many of our laws and regulations, which establish the general standards for economic, political, and social operations. A citizen may not know or understand the law and consequently would not know whether or not he was guilty of a violation.Most organized systems are some combination of man and machine; some elements of control may be performed by machine whereas others are accomplished by man. In addition, some standards may be precisely structured whereas others may be little more than general guidelines with wide variations expected in output. Man must performanceas the controller when measurement is subjective and Judgement is required. Machines such as computers are incapable of making exceptions from the specified control criteria regardless of how much a particular case might warrant special consideration. A pilot acts in conjunction with computers and automatic pilots to fly large jets. In the event of unexpected weather changes, or possible collision with another plane, he must intercede and assume direct control.

ORGANIZATIONAL AND OPERATIONAL CONTROL MANAGEMENT

The concept of organizational control is implicit in the bureaucratic theory of Max Weber. Associated with this theory are such concepts as "span of control", "closeness of supervision", and "hierarchical authority". Weber's view tends to include all levels or types of organizational control as being the same. More recently, writers have tended to differentiate the control process between that which emphasizes the nature of the organizational or systems design and that which deals with daily operations.

To illustrate the difference, we "evaluate" the performance of a system to see how effective and efficient the design proved to be or to discover why it failed. In contrast, we operate and "control" the system with respect to the daily inputs of material, information, and energy. In both instances, the elements of feedback are present, but organizational control tends to review and evaluate the nature and arrangement of components in the system, whereas operational control tends to adjust the daily inputs. The direction for organizational control comes from the goals and strategic plans of the organization. General plans are translated into specific performance measures such as share of the market, earnings, return on investment, and budgets.

The process of organizational control is to review and evaluate the performance of the system against these established norms. Rewards for meeting or exceeding standards may range from special recognition to salary increases or promotions. On the other hand, a failure to meet expectations may signal the need to reorganize or redesign. In organizational control, the approach used in the programme of review and evaluation depends on the reason for the evaluation — that is, is it because the system is not effective (accomplishing its objectives)? Is the system failing to achieve an expected standard of efficiency? Is the evaluation being conducted because of a breakdown or failure in operations? Is it merely a periodic audit-and-review process?

When a system has failed or is in great difficulty, special diagnostic techniques may be required to isolate the trouble areas and to identify the causes of the difficulty. It is appropriate to investigate areas that have been troublesome before or areas where some measure of performance can be quickly identified. For example, if an organization's output backlog builds rapidly, it is logical to check first to see if the problem is due to such readily obtainable measures as increased demand or to a drop in available man hours. When a more detailed analysis is necessary, a systematic procedure should be followed.

In contrast to organizational control, operational control serves to regulate the day-to-day output relative to schedules, specifications, and costs. Is the output of product or service the proper quality and is it available as scheduled? Are inventories of raw materials, goods-in-process, and finished products being purchased and produced in the desired quantities? Are the costs associated with the transformation process in line with cost estimates? Is the information needed in the transformation process available in the right form and at the right time? Is the energy resource being utilized efficiently?

The most difficult task of management concerns monitoring the behaviour of individuals, comparing performance to some standard, and providing rewards or punishment as indicated. Sometimes this control over people relates entirely to their output. For example, a manager might not be concerned with the behaviour of a salesman as long as sales were as high as expected. In other instances, close supervision of the salesman might be appropriate if achieving customer satisfaction were one of the sales organization's main objectives.

The larger the unit, the more likely that the control characteristic will be related to some output goal. It also follows that if it is difficult or impossible to identify the actual output of individuals, it is better to measure the performance of the entire group. This means that individuals' levels of motivation and the measurement of their performance become subjective judgments made by the supervisor. Controlling output also suggests the difficulty of controlling individuals' performance and relating this to the total system's objectives.

PROBLEMS OF CONTROL

The perfect plan could be outlined if every possible variation of input could be anticipated and if the system would operate as predicted. This kind of planning is neither realistic, economical, nor feasible for most business systems. If it were feasible, planning requirements would be so complex that the system would be out of date before it could be operated. Therefore, we design control into systems.

This requires more thought in the systems design but allows more flexibility of operations and makes it possible to operate a system using unpredictable components and undetermined input. Still, the design and effective operation of control are not without problems. The objective of the system is to perform some specified function. The purpose of organizational control is to see that the specified function is achieved; the objective of operational control is to ensure that variations in daily output are maintained within prescribed limits. It is one thing to design a system that contains all of the elements of control, and quite another to make it operate true to the best objectives of design. Operating "in control" or "with plan" does not guarantee optimum performance. For example, the plan may not make the best use of the inputs of materials, energy, or information — in other words, the system may not be designed to operate efficiently. Some of the more typical problems relating to control include the difficulty of measurement, the problem of timing information flow, and the setting of proper standards.

Measurement of Output

When objectives are not limited to quantitative output, the measurement of system effectiveness is difficult to make and subsequently perplexing to evaluate. Many of the characteristics pertaining to output do not lend themselves to quantitative measurement. This is true particularly when inputs of human energy cannot be related directly to output. The same situation applies to machines and other equipment associated with human involvement, when output is not in specific units.

In evaluating man-machine or human-oriented systems, psychological and sociological factors obviously do not easily translate into quantifiable terms. For example, how does mental fatigue affect the quality or quantity of output? And, if it does, is mental fatigue a function of the lack of a challenging assignment or the fear of a potential injury? Subjective inputs may be transferred into numerical data, but there is always the danger of an incorrect appraisal and transfer, and the danger that the analyst may assume undue confidence in such data after they have been quantified. Let us suppose, for example, that the decisions made by an executive are rated from 1 to 10, 10 being the perfect decision. After determining the ranking for each decision, adding these, and dividing by the total number of decisions made, the average ranking would indicate a particular executive's score in his decision-making role. On the basis of this score, judgments — which could be quite erroneous — might be made about his decision-making effectiveness. One executive with a ranking of 6.75 might be considered more effective than another who had a ranking of 6.25, and yet the two managers may have made decisions under different circumstances and conditions. External factors over which neither executive had any control may have influenced the difference in "effectiveness".

Quantifying human behaviour, despite its extreme difficulty, subjectivity, and imprecision in relation to measuring physical characteristics is the most prevalent and important measurement made in large systems. The behaviour of individuals ultimately dictates the success or failure of every man-made system.

Information Flow

Another problem of control relates to the improper timing of information introduced into the feedback channel. Improper timing can occur in both computerized and human control systems, either by mistakes in measurement or in Judgement. The more rapid the system's response to an error signal, the more likely it is that the system could overadjust; yet the need for prompt action is important because any delay in providing corrective input could also be crucial. A system generating feedback inconsistent with current need will tend to fluctuate and will not adjust in the desired manner.

The most serious problem in information flow arises when the delay in feedback is exactly one-half cycle, for then the corrective action is superimposed on a variation from norm which, at that moment, is in the same direction as that of the correction. This causes the system to overcorrect, and then if the reverse adjustment is made out of cycle, to correct too much in the other direction, and so on until the system fluctuates out of control. If, at Point A, the trend below standard is recognized and new inputs are added, but not until Point B, the system will overreact and go beyond the allowable limits. Again, if this is recognized at Point C, but inputs are not withdrawn until Point D, it will cause the system to drop below the lower limit of allowable variation.

One solution to this problem rests in anticipation, which involves measuring not only the change but also the rate of change. The correction is outlined as a factor of the type and rate of the error. The difficulty also might be overcome by reducing the time lag between the measurement of the output and the adjustment to input.

If a trend can be indicated, a time lead can be introduced to compensate for the time lag, bringing about consistency between the need for correction and the type and magnitude of the indicated action. It is usually more effective for an organization to maintain continuous measurement of its performance and to make small adjustments in operations constantly. Information feedback, consequently, should be timely and correct to be effective. That is, the information should provide an accurate indication of the status of the system.

Setting Standards

Setting the proper standards or control limits is a problem in many systems. Parents are confronted with this dilemma in expressing what they expect of their children, and business managers face the same issue in establishing standards that will be acceptable to employees. Some theorists have proposed that workers be allowed to set their own standards, on the assumption that when people establish their own goals, they are more apt to accept and achieve them.

Standards should be as precise as possible and communicated to all persons concerned. Moreover, communication alone is not sufficient; understanding is necessary. In human systems, standards tend to be poorly defined and the allowable range of deviation from standard also indefinite. For example, how many hours each day should a professor be expected to be available for student consultation? Or, what kind of behaviour should be expected by students in the classroom? Discretion and personal Judgement play a large part in such systems, to determine whether corrective action should be taken. Perhaps the most difficult problem in human systems is the unresponsiveness of individuals to indicated correction. This may take the form of opposition and subversion to control, or it may be related to the lack of defined responsibility or authority to take action. Leadership and positive motivation then become vital ingredients in achieving the proper response to input requirements.

Most control problems relate to design; thus the solution to these problems must start at that point. Automatic control systems, provided that human intervention is possible to handle exceptions, offer the greatest promise. There is a danger, however, that we may measure characteristics that do not represent effective performance or that improper information may be communicated.

8

Functions of Production Engineering and Management Technology

INTRODUCTION

The functions of Production Management depend upon the size of the firm. In small firms the production Manager may have to look after production planning and control along with Personnel, Marketing, Finance and Purchase functions. In medium sized firms, there may be separate managers for Personnel, marketing and Finance functions.

But the production planning and control and Purchase and stores may be under the control of Production management department. In large sized firms the activities of Production Management is confined to the management of production activities only.

As such, there are no hard and fast rule or guidelines to specify the function of Production Management, but in the academic interest we can mention some of the functions, which are looked after by the Production Management department.

They are:

- *Materials*: The selection of materials for the product. Production manager must have sound Knowledge of materials and their properties, so that he can select appropriate materials for his product. Research on materials is necessary to find alternatives to satisfy the changing needs of the design in the product and availability of material resumes.
- *Methods*: Finding the best method for the process, to search for the methods to suit the available resources, identifying the sequence of process are some of the activities of Production Management.
- *Machines and Equipment*: Selection of suitable machinery for the process desired, designing the maintenance policy and design of layout of machines are taken care of by the Production Management department.
- *Estimating*: To fix up the Production targets and delivery dates and

to keep the production costs at minimum, production management department does a thorough estimation of Production times and production costs. In competitive situation this will help the management to decide what should be done in arresting the costs at desired level.

- *Loading and Scheduling*: The Production Management department has to draw the time table for various production activities, specifying when to start and when to finish the process required. It also has to draw the timings of materials movement and plan the activities of manpower. The scheduling is to be done keeping in mind the loads on hand and capacities of facilities available.
- *Routing*: This is the most important function of Production Management department. The Routing consists of fixing the flow lines for various raw materials, components etc., from the stores to the packing of finished product, so that all concerned knows what exactly is happening on the shop floor.
- *Despatching*: The Production Management department has to prepare various documents such as Job Cards, Route sheets, Move Cards, Inspection Cards for each and every component of the product. These are prepared in a set of five copies. These documents are to be released from Production Management department to give green signal for starting the production. The activities of the shop floor will follow the instructions given in these documents. Activity of releasing the document is known as dispatching.
- *Expediting or Follow up*: Once the documents are dispatched, the management wants to know whether the activities are being carried out as per the plans or not. Expediting engineers go round the production floor along with the plans, compare the actual with the plan and feed back the progress of the work to the management. This will help the management to evaluate the plans.
- *Inspection*: Here inspection is generally concerned with the inspection activities during production, but a separate quality control department does the quality inspection, which is not under the control of Production Management. This is true because, if the quality inspection is given to production Management, then there is a chance of qualifying the defective products also. For example Teaching and examining of students is given to the same person, then there is a possibility of passing all the students in the first grade. To avoid this situation an external person does correction of answer scripts, so that the quality of answers are correctly judged.
- *Evaluation*: The Production department must evaluate itself and its contribution in fulfilling the corporate objectives and the departmental

objectives. This is necessary for setting up the standards for future. What ever may be the size of the firm; Production management department alone must do Routing, Scheduling, Loading, Dispatching and expediting.

This is because this department knows very well regarding materials, Methods, and available resources etc. If the firms are small, all the functions (i to x) are to be carried out by Production Management Department. In medium sized firms in addition to Routing, Scheduling and Loading, Dispatching and expediting, some more functions like Methods, Machines may be under the control of Production Management Department.

In large firms, there will be Separate departments for Methods, Machines, Materials and others but routing, loading and scheduling are the sole functions of Production Management. All the ten functions are categorized in three stage, that is Preplanning, Planning and control stages as shown in figure.

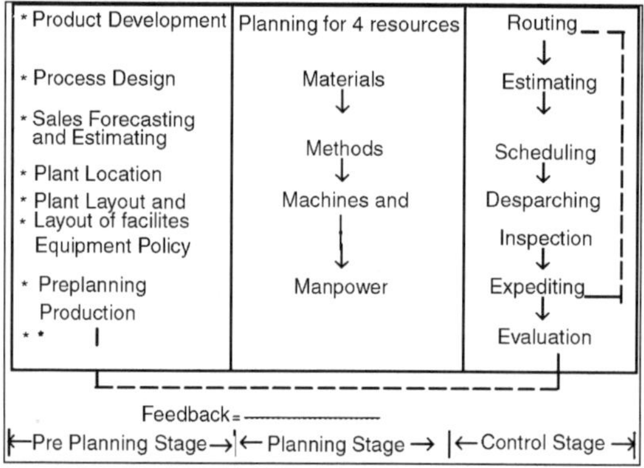

Fig. Production Fuction

PRODUCT DECISIONS

Marketing starts with the product since it is what an organization has to offer its target market. As we've stressed many times in this tutorial, organizations attempt to provide solutions to a target market's problems. These solutions include tangible or intangible (or both) product offerings marketed by an organization. In addition to satisfying the target market's needs, the product is important because it is how organizations generate revenue. It is the "thing" that for-profit companies sell in order to realise profits and satisfy stakeholders and what non-profit organizations use to generate funds needed to sustain itself. Without a well-developed product strategy that includes input from the target market, a marketing organization will not have long-term success.

PRODUCT

In marketing, the term "product" is often used as a catch-all word to identify solutions a marketer provides to its target market. We will follow this approach and permit the term "product" to cover offerings that fall into one of the following categories:

- *Goods*: Something is considered a good if it is a tangible item. That is, it is something that is felt, tasted, heard, smelled or seen. For example, bicycles, cell phones, and donuts are all examples of tangible goods. In some cases there is a fine line between items that affect the senses and whether these are considered tangible or intangible. We often see this with digital goods accessed via the Internet, such as listening to music online or visiting an information Web site. In these cases there does not appear to be anything that is tangible or real since it is essentially computer code that is proving the solution. However, for our purposes, we distinguish these as goods since these products are built (albeit using computer code), are stored (*e.g.*, on a computer hard drive), and generally offer the same benefits each time (*e.g.*, quality of the download song is always the same).
- *Services:* Something is considered a service if it is an offering a customer obtains through the work or labour of someone else. Services can result in the creation of tangible goods (*e.g.*, a publisher of business magazines hires a freelance writer to write an article) but the main solution being purchased is the service. Unlike goods, services are not stored, they are only available at the time of use (*e.g.*, hair salon) and the consistency of the benefit offered can vary from one purchaser to another (*e.g.*, not exactly the same hair styling each time).
- *Ideas:* Something falls into the category of an idea if the marketer attempts to convince the customer to alter their behaviour or their perception in some way. Marketing ideas is often a solution put forth by non-profit groups or governments in order to get targeted groups to avoid or change certain behaviour. This is seen with public service announcements directed Towards such activity as youth smoking, automobile safety, and illegal drug use.

While in some cases a marketer offers solutions that provide both tangible and intangible attributes, for most organizations their primary offering — the thing that is the main focus of the marketing effort — is concentrated in one area. So while a manufacturer may offer intangible services or a service firm provides certain tangible equipment, these are often used as add-ons that augment the organization's main product.

CATEGORIES OF CONSUMER PRODUCTS

In addition to categorizing by type of offering, most products intended for consumer use can be further categorized by how frequently and where they are purchased.

- *Convenience Products:* These are products that appeal to a very large market segment. They are generally consumed regularly and purchased frequently. Examples include most household items such as food, cleaning products, and personal care products. Because of the high purchase volume, pricing per item tends to be relatively low and consumers often see little value in shopping around since additional effort yields minimal savings. From the marketer's perspective the low price of convenience products means that profit per unit sold is very low. In order to make high profits marketers must sell in large volume. Consequently, marketers attempt to distribute these products in mass through as many retail outlets as possible.
- *Shopping Products:* These are products consumers purchase and consume on a less frequent schedule compared to convenience products. Consumers are willing to spend more time locating these products since they are relatively more expensive than convenience products and because these may possess additional psychological benefits for the purchaser, such as raising their perceived status level within their social group. Examples include many clothing products, personal services, electronic products, and household furnishings. Because consumers are purchasing less frequently and are willing to shop to locate these products, the target market is much smaller than that of convenience goods. Consequently, marketers often are more selective when choosing distribution outlets to sell their products.
- *Specialty Products:* These are products that tend to carry a high price tag relative to convenience and shopping products. Consumption may occur at about the same rate as shopping products but consumers are much more selective. In fact, in many cases consumers know in advance which product they prefer and will not shop to compare products. But they may shop at retailers that provide the best value. Examples include high-end luxury automobiles, expensive champagne, and celebrity hair care experts. The target markets are generally very small and outlets selling the products are very limited to the point of being exclusive.

In addition to the three main categories above, products are classified in at least two additional ways:

- *Emergency Products*: These are products a customer seeks due to sudden events and for which pre-purchase planning is not considered. Often the decision is one of convenience (*e.g.*, whatever works to fix a problem) or personal fulfillment (*e.g.*, perceived to improve purchaser's image).
- *Unsought Products:* These are products whose purchase is unplanned by the consumer but occur as a result of marketer's actions. Such

purchase decisions are made when the customer is exposed to promotional activity, such as a salesperson's persuasion or purchase incentives like special discounts offered to certain online shoppers. These promotional activities often lead customers to engage in Impulse Purchasing.

CATEGORIES OF BUSINESS PRODUCTS

The amount spent on business purchasing far exceeds consumer purchasing. Products sold within the b-to-b market fall into one of the following categories:

- *Raw Materials:* These are products obtained through mining, harvesting, fishing, etc., that are key ingredients in the production of higher-order products.
- *Processed Materials:* These are products created through the processing of basic raw materials. In some cases the processing refines original raw materials while in other cases the process combines different raw materials to create something new. For instance, several crops including corn and sugar cane can be processed to create ethanol which has many uses including as a fuel to power car and truck engines.
- *Equipment:* These are products used to help with production or operations activities. Examples range from conveyor belts used on an assembly line to large buildings used to house the headquarters staff of a multi-national company.
- *Basic Components:* These are products used within more advanced components. These are often built with raw material or processed material. Electrical wire is an example.
- *Advanced Components:* These are products that use basic components to produce products that offer a significant function needed within a larger product. Yet by itself an advanced component does not stand alone as a final product. In computers the motherboard would be an example since it contains many basic components but without the inclusion of other products (*e.g.*, memory chips, microprocessor, etc.) would have little value.
- *Product Component*: These are products used in the assembly of a final product though these could also function as stand alone products. Dice included as part of a children's board game would be an example.
- *MRO (Maintenance, Repair and Operating) Products*: These are products used to assist with the operation of the organization but are not directly used in producing goods or services. Office supplies, parts for a truck fleet and natural gas to heat a factory would fall into this category.

COMPONENTS OF A PRODUCT

On the surface it seems a product is simply a marketing offering, whether tangible or intangible, that someone wants to purchase and consume. In which case one might believe product decisions are focused exclusively on designing and building the consumable elements of goods, services or ideas.

For instance, one might think the key product decision for a manufacturer of floor cleaners is to focus on creating a formula that cleans more effectively. In actuality, while decisions related to the consumable parts of the product are extremely important, the Total Product consists of more than what is consumed. The total product offering and the decisions facing the marketer can be broken down into three key parts:

- Core Benefits
- Actual Product
- Augmented Product

CORE BENEFITS

Consider what we have talked about many times in this tutorial; people make buying decisions that satisfy their needs. While many needs are addressed by the consumption of a product or service, some needs are not. For instance, customers may need to be perceived highly by other members of their group or need a product that is easy to use or need a risk-free purchase. In each of these cases, and many more, the core product itself is the benefit the customer receives from using the product. In some cases these core benefits are offered by the product itself (*e.g.*, floor cleaner) while in other cases the benefit is offered by other aspects of the product (*e.g.*, the can containing the floor cleaner that makes it easier to spread the product). Consequently, at the very heart of all product decisions is determining the key or core benefits a product will provide. From this decision, the rest of the product offering can be developed.

ACTUAL PRODUCT

The core benefits are offered through the components that make up the actual product the customer purchases. For instance, when a consumer returns home from shopping at the grocery store and takes a purchased item out of her shopping bag, the actual product is the item she holds in her hand. Within the actual product is the consumable product, which can be viewed as the main good, service or idea the customer is buying.For instance, while toothpaste may come in a package that makes dispensing it easy, the Consumable Product is the paste that is placed on a toothbrush. But marketers must understand that while the consumable product is, in most cases, the most critical of all product decisions, the actual product includes many separate product decisions including product features, branding, packaging, labeling, and more. Full coverage of several of these important areas is provided later in this tutorial.

AUGMENTED PRODUCT

Marketers often surround their actual products with goods and services that provide additional value to the customer's purchase. While these factors may not be key reasons leading customers to purchase (*i.e.*, not core benefits), for some the inclusion of these items strengthens the purchase decision while for others failure to include these may cause the customer not to buy. Items considered part of the augmented product include:

- *Guarantee:* This provides a level of assurance that the product will perform up to expectations and if not the company marketing the product will support the customer's decision to replace, have it repaired or return for a refund.
- *Warranty*: This offers customers a level of protection that often extends past the guarantee period to cover repair or replacement of certain product components.
- *Customer Service*: This consists of additional services that support the customer's needs including offering training and assistance via telephone or online.
- *Complementary Products* : The value of some product purchases can be enhanced with add-on products, such as items that make the main product easier to use (*e.g.*, laptop carrybag), enhance styling (*e.g.*, cellphone face plates) or extend functionality (*e.g.*, portable keyboard for PDAs).
- *Accessibility:* How customers obtain the product can affect its perceived value depending on such considerations as how easy it is to obtain (*e.g.*, stocked at nearby store, delivered directly to office), the speed at which it can be obtained, and the likelihood it will be available when needed.

KEY PRODUCT DECISIONS

The actual product is designed to provide the core benefits sought by the target market. The marketer offers these benefits through a combination of factors that make up the actual product. Below we discuss in detail four key factors that together help shape the actual product. These factors include:

- Consumable Product Features
- Branding
- Packaging
- Labeling

CONSUMABLE PRODUCT FEATURES

Features are characteristics of a product that offer benefits to the customer. In most cases, the most important features are those associated with the consumable product since they are the main reason a customer makes a purchase. For this tutorial we separate the benefits of consumable product features into two groups: functional and psychological.

FUNCTIONAL BENEFITS

Are benefits derived from features that are part the consumable product. For instance, a plasma television includes such features and benefits as:

Feature	Functional Benefit
Screen size	Offers greater detail and allows for more distant viewing
Screen resolution	Viewing provides clear, more realistic picture
Surround sound	Immerses all senses in the viewing experience
Remote control	Allows for greater comfort while viewing

These features are called functional because they result in a benefit the user directly associates with the consumable product. For marketers functional benefits are often the result of materials, design and production decisions. How the product is built can lead to benefits such as effectiveness, durability, speed, ease-of-use, and cost savings to name just few.

PSYCHOLOGICAL BENEFITS

Are benefits the customer perceives to receive when using the product though these may be difficult to measure and may vary by customer. These benefits address needs such as status within a group, risk reduction, sense of independence, and happiness. Such benefits are developed through promotional efforts that target customer's internal makeup (see discussion in Part 4: Consumer Buying Behaviour).

In addition to determining the type of features to include in a product, the marketer faces several other decisions related to features:

- *Quantity and Quality vs. Cost:* For the marketers an important decision focuses on the quantity and quality of features to include in a product. In most cases the more features included or the higher the quality level for a particular feature, the more expensive the product is to produce and market.
- *Is More Better?:* Even if added cost is not a major concern, the marketer must determine if more features help or hurt the target market's perception of the product. A product with too many features could be viewed as too difficult to use. This was often the case when video cassette recorders (VCR) were the principle device for taping television Programmes and watching rented movies. Many of the higher-level features introduced in the 1990s as the product matured, such as advanced television recording, proved too difficult for the average consumer to master.
- *Who Should Choose the Features*?: Historically marketers determined what features to include in a product. However, technology, and especially the Internet, offer customers the opportunity to choose

their own features to custom build a product. For instance, companies offering Web site hosting services allow Web site owners to choose from a list of service options that best suits their needs. Also, for traditional products, such as clothing, companies allow customers to stylize their purchases with logos and other personalized options.

BRANDING MANAGEMENT

Branding involves decisions that establish an identity for a product with the goal of distinguishing it from competitors' offerings. In markets where competition is fierce and where customers may select from among many competitive products, creating an identity through branding is essential. It is particularly important in helping position the product (see discussion of product position) in the minds of the product's target market. While consumer products companies have long recognized the value of branding, it has only been within the last 10-15 years that organizations selling component products in the business-to-business market have begun to focus on brand building strategies. The most well-known company to brand components is Intel with its now famous "Intel Inside" slogan. Intel's success has led many other b-to-b companies and even non-profits to incorporate branding within their overall marketing strategy.

BRAND NAMES AND BRAND MARKS

At a very basic level branding is achieved through the use of unique brand names and brand marks. The brand name, which may be either the individual product name or a name applied to a group or family of products, is important for many reasons including suggesting what the product is or does (*e.g.*, Mop-and-Glow). The name is also what we utter when we discuss the product (*i.e.*, word-of-mouth marketing). The brand mark is a design element, such as a symbol (*e.g.*, Nike swoosh), logo (*e.g.*, Yahoo! graphic), a character (*e.g.*, Keebler elves) or even a sound (*e.g.*, Intel inside sound), that provides visual or auditory recognition for the product.

ADVANTAGES OF BRANDS

A strong brand offers many advantages for marketers including:

- Brands provide multiple sensory stimuli to enhance customer recognition. For example, a brand can be visually recognizable from its packaging, logo, shape, etc. It can also be recognizable via sound, such as hearing the name on a radio advertisement or talking with someone who mentions the product.
- Customers who are frequent and enthusiastic purchasers of a particular brand are likely to become Brand Loyal. Cultivating brand loyalty among customers is the ultimate reward for successful

marketers since these customers are far less likely to be enticed to switch to other brands compared to non-loyal customers.

- Well-developed and promoted brands make product positioning efforts more effective. The result is that upon exposure to a brand (*e.g.*, hearing it, seeing it) customers conjure up mental images or feelings of the benefits they receive from using that brand. The reverse is even better. When customers associate benefits with a particular brand, the brand may have attained a significant competitive advantage. In these situations the customer who recognizes he needs a solution to a problem (*e.g.*, needs to bleach clothes) may automatically think of one brand that offers the solution to the problem (*e.g.*, Clorox). This "benefit = brand" association provides a significant advantage for the brand that the customer associates with the benefit sought.
- Firms that establish a successful brand can extend the brand by adding new products under the same "family" brand. Such branding may allow companies to introduce new products more easily since the brand is already recognized within the market.
- Strong brands can lead to financial advantages through the concept of Brand Equity in which the brand itself becomes valuable. Such gains can be realized through the out-right sale of a brand or through licensing arrangements. For example, Company A may have a well-recognized brand (Brand X) within a market but for some reason they are looking to concentrate their efforts in other markets. Company B is looking to enter the same market as Brand X.

If circumstances are right Company A could sell to Company B the rights to use the Brand X name without selling any other part of the company. That is, Company A simply sells the legal rights to the Brand X name but retains all other parts of Brand X, such as the production facilities and employees. In cases of well developed brands such a transaction may carry a very large price tag. Thus, through strong branding efforts Company A achieves a large financial gain by simply signing over the rights to the name. But why would Company B seek to purchase a brand for such a high price tag? Because by buying the brand Company B has already achieved an important marketing goal – building awareness within the target market. The fact the market is already be familiar with the brand allows the Company B to concentrate on other marketing decisions.

Packaging

Nearly all tangible products (*i.e.*, goods) are sold to customers within a container or package that, as we will discuss, serves many purposes including protecting the product during shipment. In a few cases, such as with certain produce items, the final customer may purchase the product without a package but the produce marketer still faces packaging decisions when it comes to shipping to the store. Thus, for many products there are two packaging decisions – final customer and distribution.

FINAL CUSTOMER PACKAGING

This relates to the package the final customer receives in exchange for their payment. When the final customer makes a purchase he or she is initially exposed to the Primary Package – the outermost container that is seen and touched by the final customer. This primary package can be further divided into the following:

- *First-Level Package* : This is packaging that holds the actual product (*e.g.*, Tylenol Bottle). In some cases this packaging is minimal since it only serves to protect the product. For instance, certain frozen food products are sold to consumers in a cardboard box with the product itself contained in a plastic bag found inside the box. This plastic bag represents the first-level package. In other cases frozen food products are sold in the plastic bag that contains the product. In these cases the plastic bag is both first-level package and the primary package for convey product information.
- *Second-Level Package:* In some cases the first-level package is surrounded by one or more outer packages (*e.g.*, box holding the Tylenol Bottle). This second-level package may act as the primary package for the product.
- *Package Inserts*: Marketers use a variety of other methods to communicate with customers after they open the product package. These methods are often inserted within, or sometimes on, the product's package. Insertions include information such as instruction manuals and warranty cards, promotional incentives such as coupons, and items that add value such as recipes and software.

DISTRIBUTION PACKAGING

This packaging is used to transport the customer package through the supply chain. It generally holds multiple customer packages and also offers a higher level of damage protection than that of customer packaging.

Factors to Consider When Making Packaging Decision

Packaging decisions are important for several reasons including:

- *Protection:* Packaging is used to protect the product from damage during shipping and handling, and to lessen spoilage if the protect is exposed to air or other elements.
- *Visibility*: Packaging design is used to capture customers' attention

as they are shopping or glancing through a catalog or Web site. This is particularly important for customers who are not familiar with the product and in situations, such as those found in grocery stores, where a product must stand out among thousands of other products. Packaging designs that standout are more likely to be remembered on future shopping trips.

- *Added Value:* Packaging design and structure can add value to a product. For instance, benefits can be obtained from package structures that make the product easier to use while stylistic designs can make the product more attractive to display in the customer's home.
- *Distributor Acceptance:* Packaging decisions must not only be accepted by the final customer, they may also have to be accepted by distributors who sell the product for the supplier. For instance, a retailer may not accept packages unless they conform to requirements they have for storing products on their shelves.
- *Cost:* Packaging can represent a significant portion of a product's selling price. For example, it is estimated that in the cosmetics industry the packaging cost of some products may be as high as 40% of a product's selling price. Smart packaging decisions can help reduce costs and possibly lead to higher profits.
- *Expensive to Create* : Developing new packaging can be extremely expensive. The costs involved in creating new packaging include: graphic and structural design, production, customer testing, possible destruction of leftover old packaging, and possible advertising to inform customer of the new packaging.
- *Long Term Decision:* When companies create a new package it is most often with the intention of having the design on the market for an extended period of time. In fact, changing a product's packaging too frequently can have negative effects since customers become conditioned to locate the product based on its package and may be confused if the design is altered.
- *Environmental or Legal Issues:* Packaging decisions must also include an assessment of its environmental impact especially for products with packages that are frequently discarded. Packages that are not easily bio-degradable could draw customer and possibly governmental concern. Also, caution must be exercised in order to create packages that do not infringe on intellectual property, such as copyrights, trademarks or patents, held by others.

Labeling

Most packages, whether final customer packaging or distribution packaging, are imprinted with information intended to assist the customer. For consumer products, labeling decisions are extremely important for the following reasons.

- Labels serve to capture the attention of shoppers. The use of catchy words may cause strolling customers to stop and evaluate the product.
- The label is likely to be the first thing a new customer sees and thus offers their first impression of the product.
- The label provides customers with product information to aid their purchase decision or help improve the customer's experience when using the product (*e.g.*, recipes).
- Labels generally include a universal product codes (UPC) and, in some cases, radio frequency identification (RFID) tags, that make it easy for resellers, such as retailers, to checkout customers and manage inventory.
- For companies serving international markets or diverse cultures within a single country, bilingual or multilingual labels may be needed.
- In some countries many products, including food and pharmaceuticals, are required by law to contain certain labels such as listing ingredients, providing nutritional information or including usage warning information.

MANAGING PRODUCTS

Marketers are confronted with many issues when building the product component of their marketing strategy. While product decisions represent just one aspect of marketer's overall activities, these decisions are often the most important because they lead directly to the reasons (*i.e.*, benefits offered, solutions to problems) for why the customer decides to choose the organization's goods, services or ideas.The coverage of product decisions by exploring additional product issues facing the marketer. In particular, we examine four important areas. First, we categorize the roles played by those involved in product management and show how the scope of a manager's responsibilities changes as these roles take on greater importance.

Second, we return to a discussion of branding by focusing on overall branding strategies that may be adopted by the marketing organization.

Third, we spend a large part of this tutorial covering the importance of ew product development including an analysis of the steps firms may follow to bring new products to market. Finally, we will see that once new products have been established in the market numerous factors force the marketer to continually adjust their product decisions.

PRODUCT MANAGEMENT RESPONSIBILITIES

While this tutorial touches on basic concepts and strategies applicable to a large percentage of marketing situations, the reader should understand that no two marketing situations are the same. Yet while some concepts and strategies important to one marketer may not hold the same weight with another, in general, the basic principles of marketing (*e.g.*, satisfying target markets, support decisions using research, etc.) hold no matter the type of industry, type of company or type of product being sold.

What is often different between two marketing situations is the level of complication and challenge that arises as a marketer's scope of responsibility increases. For our purposes a marketer's level of responsibility is measured in terms of:

- The number and variety of tasks that must be performed (*i.e.*, what has to be done)
- The value these tasks represent to the organization (*i.e.*, how important marketing is perceived within the company)
- The overall financial stake the marketing position holds (*i.e.*, total sales volume and profit generation).

As responsibilities change so to do the marketer's tasks. For instance, with regard to product decisions, as a marketer's responsibilities become greater her or his day-to-day job shifts from being involved in specific product issues (*e.g.*, finding a graphics design company to create a new label) to decisions concerning many products and focusing on setting the future marketing direction of the company (*e.g.*, developing marketing plans for numerous products). We can see this in greater detail by examining the responsibilities associated with four different marketing management levels:

- *Product Item Level:* At this level responsibilities are associated with marketing a single product or brand. By "single" we are limiting the marketer's responsibility to one item. For instance, a startup software development company may initially market just one product. In some organizations the person in charge has the title Product Manager, though in smaller companies this person may simply be the Marketing Manager.
- *Brand Product Line Level:* At this level responsibilities are associated with managing two or more similar product items. By "similar" we are referring to products carrying the same brand name that fit within the same product category and offer similar solutions to customers' needs. Procter and Gamble, one of the largest consumer products companies in the world, markets Tide laundry detergent in several different packaging sizes (*e.g.*, 50oz., 100oz., 200oz.), in different forms (*e.g.*, powder, liquid) and with different added features (*e.g.*, softener, bleach). Tide's product line consists of over 100 different versions of the product. Differences in the product offerings indicate these are targeted to different segments within the larger market (*e.g.*, those

preferring liquid vs. those preferring powder), however, it may also represent a choice for the same target market who may seek variety. A product line is often measured by its depth, relative to competitors, with deep product lines offering extensive product items. Brand product lines are often managed by a Brand or Product Line Manager.

- *Category Product Line Level*: At this level responsibilities are associated with managing two or more brand product lines within the same product category. In this situation the marketer may manage products that offer similar basic benefits (*e.g.*, clean clothes) but target their offerings to slightly different needs (*e.g.*, product for tough to clean clothing vs. product to clean delicate clothing). Multiple brand product lines allow the marketer to cover the needs of more segments and, consequently, increase their chance to generate sales. Often in larger companies category product lines are the responsibility of the Product Category or Divisional Marketing Manager who may have Brand Product Managers reporting to him/her.
- *Product Mix Level:* At this level responsibilities include two or more category product lines that are directed to different product categories. In some cases the category product lines may yield similar general solutions (*e.g.*, cleaning) but are aimed at entirely different target markets (*e.g.*, cleaning dishes vs. cleaning automobiles). In large companies, the product lines are very diverse and offer different solutions. For example, BIC sells writing instruments, shaving products, and lighters. This diversification strategy cushions against an "all-eggs-in-one-basket" risk that may come if a company directs all resources to one product category. A product mix can be classified based on its width (how many different category product lines) and its depth (how many different brand product lines within a category product line). Generally responsibility for this level belongs to a company's Vice President for Marketing.

BRANDING STRATEGY

Branding is an important decision designed to enhance the identity of the product through the use of unique brand names, symbols and other distinctive measures. With competition growing more intense in almost all industries, establishing a strong brand allows an organization's products to stand out and avoid potential pitfalls, such as price wars, that have befallen many products. Therefore, a clear understanding of branding strategy is essential in order to build solid products and product lines. In particular, marketers should be aware of various branding approaches that can be pursued.

By branding approach we are referring to different product identification strategies that can be deployed to establish a product within the market. As we will see, the purpose of these approaches is to build a brand that will exist for the long term. Making smart decisions up front is crucial since a company may have to live with the decision for a long time.

Branding approaches include the following:

- *Individual Product Branding*: Under this branding approach new products are assigned new names with no obvious connection to existing brands offered by the company. Under individual product branding the marketing organization must work hard to establish the brand in the market since it cannot ride the coattails of previously introduced brands. The chief advantage of this approach is it allows brands to stand on their own thus lessening threats that may occur to other brands marketed by the company. For instance, if another company brand receives negative publicity this news is less likely to rub off on the company's other brands that carry their own unique names. Brands can create financial gains through the concept known as brand equity. Under an individual branding approach, each brand builds its own separate equity which allows the company, if they choose, to sell off individual brands without impacting other brands owned by the company. The most famous marketing organization to follow this strategy is Procter and Gamble, which has historically introduced new brands without any link to other brands or even to the company name.
- *Family Branding:* Under this branding approach new products are placed under the umbrella of an existing brand. The principle advantage of this approach is that it enables the organization to rapidly build market awareness and acceptance since the brand is already established and known to the market. But the potential disadvantage is that the market has already established certain perceptions of the brand. For instance, a company that sells low-end, lower priced products may have a brand that is viewed as an economy brand. This brand image may create customer confusion and hinder the company if they attempt to introduce higher-end, higher priced products using the same brand name. Additionally, with family branding any negative publicity that may occur for one product within a brand could spread to all other products that share the same name.
- *Co-Branding:* This approach takes the idea of individual and family branding a step further. With co-branding a marketer seeks to partner with another firm, which has an established brand, in hopes synergy of two brands on a product is even more powerful than a single brand. The partnership often has both firms sharing costs but also sharing the gains. For instance, major credit card companies, such as Visa and MasterCard, offer co-branding options to companies and

organizations. The cards carry the name of a co-branded organization (*e.g.*, University name) along with the name of the issuing bank (*e.g.*, Citibank) and the name of the credit card company. Besides tapping into awareness for multiple brands, the co-branding strategy is also designed to appeal to a larger target market, especially if each brand, when viewed separately, does not have extensive overlapping target markets with the other brand. Thus, co-branding allows both firms to tap into market segments where they did not previously have a strong position.

- *Private or Store Branding:* Some suppliers are in the business of producing products for other companies including placing another company's brand name on the product. This is most often seen in the retail industry where stores or online sellers contract with suppliers to manufacture the retailer's own branded products. In some cases the supplier not only produces product for the retailer's brand but also markets their own brand so that store shelves will contain both brands.
- *No-Name or Generic Branding:* Certain suppliers supply products that are intentionally "brandless." These products are mostly basic commodity-type products that consumer or business customers purchase as low price alternatives to branded products. Basic household products such as paper products, over-the-counter medicines such as ibuprofen, and even dog food are available in a generic form.
- *Brand Licensing:* Under brand licensing a contractual arrangement is created in which a company owning a brand name allows others to produce and supply products carrying the brand name. This is often seen when a brand is not directly connected with a product category. For instance, several famous children's characters, such as Sesame Street's Elmo, have been licensed to toy and food manufacturers who market products using the branded character's name and image.

MANUFACTURING MATERIALS INVENTORY

A canned food manufacturer's materials inventory includes the ingredients to form the foods to be canned, empty cans and their lids (or coils of steel or aluminum for constructing those components), labels, and anything else (solder, glue...) that will form part of a finished can. The firm's work in process includes those materials from the time of release to the work floor until they become complete and ready for sale to wholesale or retail customers.

This may be vats of prepared food, filled cans not yet labelled or sub-assemblies of food components. It may also include finished cans that are not yet packaged into cartons or pallets.

Its finished good inventory consists of all the filled and labelled cans of food in its warehouse that it has manufactured and wishes to sell to food distributors (wholesalers), to grocery stores (retailers), and even perhaps to consumers through arrangements like factory stores and outlet centres.

Examples of case studies are very revealing, and consistently show that the improvement of inventory management has two parts: the capability of the organisation to manage inventory, and the way in which it chooses to do so. For example, a company may wish to install a complex inventory system, but unless there is a good understanding of the role of inventory and its perameters, and an effective business process to support that, the system cannot bring the necessary benefits to the organisation in isolation.

Typical Inventory Management techniques include Pareto Curve ABC Classification and Economic Order Quantity Management. A more sophisticated method takes these two techniques further, combining certain aspects of each to createThe K Curve Methodology. A case study of k-curve benefits to one company shows a successful implementation.

Unnecessary inventory adds enormously to the working capital tied up in the business as well as the complexity of the supply chain. Reduction and elimination of these inventory 'wait' states is a key concept in Lean.

Too big an inventory reduction too quickly can cause a business to be anorexic. There are well proven processes and techniques to assist in inventory planning and strategy, both at business overview and part number level. Many of the big MRP/and ERP systems do not offer the necessary inventory planning tools within their integrated planning applications.

PRINCIPLE OF INVENTORY PROPORTIONALITY

PURPOSE

Inventory proportionality is the goal of demand driven inventory management. The primary optimal outcome is to have the same number of days (or hours, etc.) worth of inventory on hand across all products so that the time of runout of all products would be simultaneous. In such a case, there is no"excess inventory", that is, inventory that would be left over of another product when the first product runs out. Excess inventory is sub-optimal because the money spent to obtain it could have been deployed better elsewhere, *i.e.* to the product that just ran out.

The secondary goal of inventory proportionality is inventory minimization. By integrating accurate demand forecasting with inventory management, replenishment inventories can be scheduled to arrive just in time to replenish the product destined to run out first, while at the same time balancing out the inventory supply of all products to make their inventories more proportional, and thereby closer to achieving the primary goal.

Accurate demand forecasting also allows the desired inventory proportions to be dynamic by determining expected sales out into the future; this allows for inventory to be in proportion to expected short term sales or consumption rather than to past averages, a much more accurate and optimal outcome.

Integrating demand forecasting with inventory management in this way also allows for the prediction of the"can fit" point when inventory storage is limited on a per product basis.

APPLICATIONS

The technique of inventory proportionality is most appropriate for inventories that remain unseen by the consumer. As opposed to "keep full" systems where a retail consumer would like to see full shelves of the product they are buying so as not to think they are buying something old, unwanted, or stale; and differentiated from the "trigger point" systems where product is reordered when it hits a certain level; inventory proportionality is used effectively by just-in-time manufacturing processes and retail applications where the product is hidden from view.

One early example of inventory proportionality used in a retail application in the United States is for motor fuel. Motor fuel (*e.g.* gasoline) is generally stored in underground storage tanks. The motorists do not know whether they are buying gasoline off the top or bottom of the tank, nor need they care. Additionally, these storage tanks have a maximum capacity and cannot be overfilled.Finally, the product is expensive. Inventory proportionality is used to balance the inventories of the different grades of motor fuel, each stored in dedicated tanks, in proportion to the sales of each grade. Excess inventory is not seen or valued by the consumer, so it is simply cash sunk (literally) into the ground. Inventory proportionality minimizes the amount of excess inventory carried in underground storage tanks. This application for motor fuel was first developed and implemented by Petrolsoft Corporation in 1990 for Chevron Products Company. Most major oil companies use such systems today.

ROOTS

The use of Inventory Proportionality in the United States is thought to have been inspired by Japanese just-in-time (business) parts inventory management made famous by Toyota Motors in the 1980s.

PLANNING (DRP) AND MATERIAL

REQUIREMENTS PLANNING (MRP) SYSTEMS

The time period used is usually weeks or months, and as time passes the schedule rolls to the left. When time period 1 becomes the present time period, appropriate action is taken, such as placing an order. The forecast or gross requirements line is used to display the demand requirements by time period (note the variability in demand).This line includes both forecast and known sales. The scheduled receipts line is used when an order has been placed with a vendor but has not yet been received. The ordered quantity is placed in the appropriate time period. The planned order receipt is used to calculate the planned order size and its timing. When the projected available balance is below the safety stock level, a planned order should arrive in that time period. The actual quantity ordered depends on the lotsizing technique used.

Projected available balance is defined as beginning balance plus receipts minus requirements. Balance is shown as of the end of the period.For period 1, ten items were on hand initially. Scheduled receipts are 40; forecast demand is 20. Ending balance (projected available) is 10 40 - 20 = 30. Fifteen more are used during period 2, leaving 15 available.Ten units are forecast to be used during period 3, leaving 5. Since a projected available balance of 5 is below the safety stock of 10, 5 units must be ordered. The order policy is to order 2 periods' worth whenever an order is placed, so 30 more units covering periods 4 and 5 are ordered. The total order is 35. In period 6 an order of size 90 is needed to cover periods 6 and 7.

The appropriate lot-sizing technique for TPOP includes examining the forecast or gross requirements line, instead of working with averages and annual demand. The planned order release line is used to determine when the order should be placed by backward scheduling from the planned receipt time period for the item lead time. In the example provided, orders of 35 and 90 should arrive in time periods 3 and 6, respectively, to prevent inventory stockouts.

These orders should be placed in time periods 1 and 4, respectively, based upon the two-period lead time. As time passes the time schedule is rolled to the left until a time period becomes the "action' period (present) and an order is placed.Micro-computers offer the potential for significant savings in several areas of small businesses. In this chapter three inventory control systems have been presented which are well-suited for implementation by small businesses on micro- or mini-computers. Two of these systems (the Periodic Review and Mixed Models) can be implemented without maintaining a perpetual inventory record.

The most commonly discussed model, Reorder Point/Economic Order Quantity, requires that a perpetual inventory be kept. For companies which do maintain a perpetual inventory, the Time Phased Order Point Technique (TPOP) offers an attractive alternative to ROP/EOQ and overcomes many of the shortcomings of this technique.

TPOP works well in seasonal or lumpy demand patterns, allows immediate updating, keeps track of released orders and their expected arrivals, and allows combining demand from several sources. However, use of TPOP almost certainly requires the use of a computer to maintain changes in demand over time.

THE BASIS OF INVENTORY ACCOUNTING

Inventory needs to be accounted where it is held across accounting period boundaries since generally expenses should be matched against the results of that expense within the same period. When processes were simple and short then inventories were small but with more complex processes then inventories became larger and significant valued items on the balance sheet.This need to value unsold and incomplete goods has driven many new behaviours into management practise. Perhaps most significant of these are the complexities of fixed cost recovery, transfer pricing, and the separation of direct from indirect costs.

This, supposedly, precluded "anticipating income" or "declaring dividends out of capital". It is one of the intangible benefits of Lean and the TPS that process times shorten and stock levels decline to the point where the importance of this activity is hugely reduced and therefore effort, especially managerial, to achieve it can be minimised.

ACCOUNTING FOR INVENTORY

Each country has its own rules about accounting for inventory that fit with their financial reporting rules. So for example, organizations in the U.S. define inventory to suit their needs within US Generally Accepted Accounting Practices (GAAP), the rules defined by the Financial Accounting Standards Board (FASB) (and others) and enforced by the U.S. Securities and Exchange Commission (SEC) and other federal and state agencies. Other countries often have similar arrangements but with their own GAAP and national agencies instead.

It is intentional that financial accounting uses standards that allow the public to compare firms' performance, cost accounting functions internally to an organization and potentially with much greater flexibility. A discussion of inventory from standard and Theory of Constraints-based (throughput) cost accounting perspective follows some examples and a discussion of inventory from a financial accounting perspective.

The internal costing/valuation of inventory can be complex. Whereas in the past most enterprises ran simple one process factories, this is quite probably in the minority in the 21st century. Where 'one process' factories exist then there is a market for the goods created which establishes an independent market value for the good.

Today with multi-stage process companies there is much inventory that would once have been finished goods which is now held as 'work-in-process' (WIP). This needs to be valued in the accounts but the valuation is a management decision since there is no market for the partially finished product. This somewhat arbitrary 'valuation' of WIP combined with the allocation of overheads to it has led to some unintended and undesirable results.

FINANCIAL ACCOUNTING

An organization's inventory can appear a mixed blessing, since it counts as an asset on the balance sheet, but it also ties up money that could serve for other purposes and requires additional expense for its protection. Inventory may also cause significant tax expenses, depending on particular countries' laws regarding depreciation of inventory, as in Thor Power Tool Company v. Commissioner.

Inventory appears as a current asset on an organization's balance sheet because the organization can, in principle, turn it into cash by selling it. Some organizations hold larger inventories than their operations require in order to inflate their apparent asset value and their perceived profitability.

In addition to the money tied up by acquiring inventory, inventory also brings associated costs for warehouse space, for utilities, and for insurance to cover staff to handle and protect it, fire and other disasters, obsolescence, shrinkage (theft and errors), and others. Such holding costs can mount up: between a third and a half of its acquisition value per year.

Businesses that stock too little inventory cannot take advantage of large orders from customers if they cannot deliver. The conflicting objectives of cost control and customer service often pit an organization's financial and operating managers against its sales and marketing departments.

Sales people, in particular, often receive sales commission payments, so unavailable goods may reduce their potential personal income. This conflict can be minimised by reducing production time to being near or less than customer expected delivery time. This effort, known as "Lean production" will significantly reduce working capital tied up in inventory and reduce manufacturing costs.

INVENTORY ACCOUNTING

By helping the organization to make better decisions, the accountants can help the public sector to change in a very positive way that delivers increased value for the taxpayer's investment.

It can also help to incentivise progress and to ensure that reforms are sustainable and effective in the long term, by ensuring that success is appropriately recognized in both the formal and informal reward systems of the organization.

To say that they have a key role to play is an understatement. Finance is connected to most, if not all, of the key business processes within the organization. It should be steering the stewardship and accountability systems that ensure that the organization is conducting its business in an appropriate, ethical manner. It is critical that these foundations are firmly laid. So often they are the litmus test by which public confidence in the institution is either won or lost.

Finance should also be providing the information, analysis and advice to enable the organizations' service managers to operate effectively. This goes beyond the traditional preoccupation with budgets – how much have we spent so far, how much have we left to spend? It is about helping the organization to better understand its own performance.

That means making the connections and understanding the relationships between given inputs – the resources brought to bear – and the outputs and outcomes that they achieve. It is also about understanding and actively managing risks within the organization and its activities.

FIFO VS. LIFO ACCOUNTING

When a merchant buys goods from inventory, the value of the inventory account is reduced by the cost of goods sold (CoG sold). This is simple where the CoG has not varied across those held in stock; but where it has, then an agreed method must be derived to evaluate it.

For commodity items that one cannot track individually, accountants must choose a method that fits the nature of the sale. Two popular methods which normally exist are: FIFO and LIFO accounting (first in - first out, last in - first out). FIFO regards the first unit that arrived in inventory as the first one sold. LIFO considers the last unit arriving in inventory as the first one sold.

Which method an accountant selects can have a significant effect on net income and book value and, in turn, on taxation. Using LIFO accounting for inventory, a company generally reports lower net income and lower book value, due to the effects of inflation. This generally results in lower taxation. Due to LIFO's potential to skew inventory value, UK GAAP and IAS have effectively banned LIFO inventory accounting.

STANDARD COST ACCOUNTING

Standard cost accounting uses ratios called efficiencies that compare the labour and materials actually used to produce a good with those that the same goods would have required under "standard" conditions. As long as similar actual and standard conditions obtain, few problems arise. Unfortunately, standard cost accounting methods developed about 100 years ago, when labour comprised the most important cost in manufactured goods. Standard methods continue to emphasize labour efficiency even though that resource now constitutes a (very) small part of cost in most cases. Standard cost accounting can hurt managers, workers, and firms in several ways. For example, a policy decision to increase inventory can harm a manufacturing managers' performance evaluation. Increasing inventory requires increased production, which means that processes must operate at higher rates. When (not if) something goes wrong, the process takes longer and uses more than the standard labour time. The manager appears responsible for the excess, even though s/he has no control over the production requirement or the problem.In adverse economic times, firms use the same efficiencies to downsize, rightsize, or otherwise reduce their labour force. Workers laid off under those circumstances have even less control over excess inventory and cost efficiencies than their managers.

Many financial and cost accountants have agreed for many years on the desirability of replacing standard cost accounting. They have not, however, found a successor.

THEORY OF CONSTRAINTS COST ACCOUNTING

Eliyahu M. Goldratt developed the Theory of Constraints in part to address the cost-accounting problems in what he calls the "cost world". He offers a substitute, called throughput accounting, that uses throughput (money for goods sold to customers) in place of output (goods produced that may sell or may boost inventory) and considers labour as a fixed rather than as a variable cost.

He defines inventory simply as everything the organization owns that it plans to sell, including buildings, machinery, and many other things in addition to the categories listed here. Throughput accounting recognizes only one class of variable costs: the trully variable costs like materials and components that vary directly with the quantity produced.

Finished goods inventories remain balance-sheet assets, but labour efficiency ratios no longer evaluate managers and workers. Instead of an incentive to reduce labour cost, throughput accounting focuses attention on the relationships between throughput (revenue or income) on one hand and controllable operating expenses and changes in inventory on the other.

Those relationships direct attention to the constraints or bottlenecks that prevent the system from producing more throughput, rather than to people - who have little or no control over their situations.

NATIONAL ACCOUNTS

Inventories also play an important role in national accounts and the analysis of the business cycle. Some short-term macroeconomic fluctuations are attributed to the inventory cycle.

DISTRESSED INVENTORY

Also known as distressed or expired stock, distressed inventory is inventory whose potential to be sold at a normal cost has or will soon pass. In certain industries it could also mean that the stock is or will soon be impossible to sell.

Examples of distressed inventory include products that have reached its expiry date, or has reached a date in advance of expiry at which the planned market will no longer purchase it (*e.g.* 3 months left to expiry), clothing that is defective or out of fashion, and old newspapers or magazines. It also includes computer or consumer-electronic equipment that is obsolescent or discontinued and whose manufacturer is unable to support it. One current example of distressed inventory is the VHS format.

PERSPECTIVE OF MATERIALS AND LOGISTICS MANAGEMENT

This chapter proposes an integrated model of the consumer household's materials and logistics management system. It reviews a recognized organizational logistics framework and then compares it to the proposed consumer inventory ownership cycle and materials management system. Specific stages are defined and explained, and their general relevance is discussed. Examples describing behavioral activities at each stage are provided to illustrate definitions.

This also explore preliminary evidence that consumers may consider factors from preceding or following stages throughout the materials management cycle. Finally, relevant suggestions for marketers, researchers, and policy makers, as to usefulness of this conceptual framework, form the conclusions section.

In 1976, Nicosia and Mayer noted the need to broaden the study of buyer behaviour beyond pre-acquisition and acquisition to include consumption and disposal activities. Reviewing the state-of-the-art of buyer behaviour research, Jacoby reiterated this need. Jacoby with Berning and Dietvorst, in fact, was one of the first to explore "disposition" (disposal).

Some researchers have begun to pay more attention to Non-traditional modes of acquisition, experiential aspects of usage, and occasion of usage.

Also, disposition has received attention because of environmental issues such as waste stream reduction. However, these efforts generally have been non-integrative; that is, the stages of ownership have been treated more or less separately. The following discussion introduces a framework for such integration. The authors have termed this framework the Inventory Ownership Cycle (IOC).

To introduce the concept of consumer materials management, an organizational materials and logistics management model is presented as a starting perspective. This brief description is followed by a presentation of a model of the Inventory Ownership Cycle. The former provides a well researched and understood parallel to the latter.

INDUSTRIAL MATERIALS AND LOGISTICS MANAGEMENT (MLM) MODEL

In this system, an industrial manufacturer receives raw/processed materials from a source of supply and manages those materials through a process that adds value. The goods are then "disposed of" through a system of-physical distribution.

The main difference between an industrial manufacturer and a household seems to be that the manufacturer is more likely to process and combine raw materials or components into output that has "... exchange value with transactions characterized by formal money or in-kind exchange".

Whereas a manufacturer buys and stores materials which are then assembled to make a finished product of greater value than the sum of the inputs, a household usually "processes" goods or adds value for the purpose of meeting family goals or increasing well-being. There are, however, many examples of how consumer goods as inputs can also involve added value for transmission to parties outside the household (*e.g.*, craft materials turned into gift items or eggs for a cake baked for a friend or a bake sale). While experts have addressed household production and the valuation of household production activity, the general intent of most purchasing by most households is consumption, even if items are internally processed into products or services. Conversely, organizations process raw materials into products with the intention of moving them to end users outside of the organization.

Through adaptation of and expansion on the above industrial model, the consumer ownership/inventory management system model emerged. Both models clearly show products moving into and out of ownership and/or possession.

Although the logistics model for organizations tends to focus on entering goods that will be incorporated into products for sale, conceptually it could apply equally to operating supplies that are consumed, capital equipment that could be disposed of eventually, and/or waste stream materials that leave the operation regularly.

The consumer adaptation is thus quite similar, with some products staying in the individual's possession longer and others being incorporated, consumed, or disposed of more quickly.

To maintain consistency with the industrial model, it seems appropriate to describe consumer goods in terminology parallel to that of industrial goods.

ENTERING GOODS

In industrial terms, these are parts and materials (raw, processed, or partially assembled) incorporated into value-added products that are then sold to customers. Although most entering goods for consumers are used by themselves or combined for internal use (*e.g.*, food products as components of meals, fabric for a dress), others may be combined to create gifts (*e.g.*, crafts materials to make dolls, dried floral arrangements, handmade furniture).

The important similarity from an inventory perspective is that entering goods are materials usually stored at the "operation" to use in the production of something else related to household goals or values, although the holding period may be extremely brief, as with just-in-time inventories.

In the industrial setting, these are capital improvements that are built into the facility, for example, an elevator or conveyor belt assembly. Consumers, likewise, build in bookshelves and install wallpaper and alarm systems. Generally, in either setting, "disposal" of such goods usually occurs when the entire physical facility is sold, although replacement or upgrade is common in both settings. Decisions about acquiring installations, in both cases, involve considerations about the relative benefits of long-term ownership. The physical facility, while not part of the model, provides the context for activities described in the model.

Accessory equipment is defined as items that are not consumable but are not physically attached to the facility. For the industrial buyer, such items may include fax machines, fork lifts, and office furniture.

Similarly, consumers buy furniture, appliances, lawn mowers, etc. Space for storage, use, and maintenance are some of the considerations in accessory equipment purchases. Consumer accessories can be functional, entertaining, value expressive, or have investment value.

FACILITATING GOODS

These are usually referred to as maintenance, repair, and operating (MRO) "supply" items in the industrial context. Repair, cleaning, and maintenance consumables (*e.g.*, nails, soaps, lubricants, respectively) as well as operating items (*e.g.*, stationery, paper clips) are often strikingly similar to those held in inventory by consumers.

Consumer supplies, of course, also include health and beauty aids and pet supplies. They are not held for long periods of time but create routine expenses associated with running the operation or household.

PROPOSED INVENTORY OWNERSHIP CYCLE (IOC)

In simple terms, the IOC depicts a model of stages in consumers' management of physical goods and materials, similar to the key material management stages in a business-to-business logistics system. The consumer gathers information and makes decisions about acquiring products within categories and selects brands or suppliers (Pre-acquisition Decision Making). Some form of commitment occurs by ordering, purchasing, or otherwise agreeing to accept goods (Acquisition/Purchase). Goods must then be moved from the supplia's location to the consumer's household (Transportation-Inbound External Movement). The consumer may use the product immediately or store it for use/reuse (Possession and Ownership).

The item may move within the household from one area to another or in and out of storage (Transportation-Internal Movement). If the item is no longer needed, it is transported for "disposal" (Disposition) to another person or organization. Even "trashed" items are transferred to a disposal company for removal (Transportation-Outbound External Movement) and final permanent storage in a landfill or incineration at a waste-to-energy plant.Exploring the consumer cycle of inventory ownership from start to finish, an attempt was made to identify issues within and among the goods management constructs. Internal and external movement flows are indicated by arrows.

Although the uses to which materials are put in these stages may differ widely between the two systems, both have some goods which are incorporated (entering goods), some consumable facilitating supplies, accessory goods which are used and/or stored, and permanent installations. However, consumers, in fact, increasingly also sell some goods (*e.g.*, at garage sales, by consignment, etc.). Thus, each system disposes of some waste and "disposes" of some goods for use by others.

9

Managing Product Movement

In addition to enlisting the assistance of retailers and wholesalers to make products available to customers, marketers also face additional concerns when trying to meet their distribution objectives. In this section we examine the tasks that must be carried out in order to physically move products to customers. In some cases the marketer will take on the responsibility of carrying out some functions, while other tasks may be assigned to distribution service providers. Whether handled by the marketer or contracted to others, these functions are crucial to having a cost-effective and efficient distribution system.We explore the movement of product by first examining how physical distribution decisions often involve analyzing the trade-off between the service level the marketer offers to customers versus the costs associated with providing these services.

Next we provide an in-depth examination of three major tasks that the marketer or distribution service providers may need to carryout in order to ship products to customers. These tasks include:

- Ordering and Inventory Management
- Product Storage
- Transportation

It is worth noting that while most physical distribution is concerned with moving tangible products, some of the issues covered here are also applicable to intangible products, such as services and to digital products.

TRADE-OFF ANALYSIS: SERVICE-LEVEL VS. COST

The distribution activities we discuss in this part of the Principles of Marketing tutorial are important elements in the marketer's overall customer service package. Marketers strive to deliver an optimal level of service to their customers. However, "optimal" does not always translate into providing the "best" service options to customers. The service-level marketers' offer for their distribution activities, like the service-level offered by other company-related activities that impact customers (*e.g.*, customer help desk), is determined using trade-off analysis. With service-level trade-off analysis, the marketer compares the number and quality of distribution features (*e.g.*, speed of delivery, ease of placing orders, order tracking, etc.) they would like to offer versus the cost of providing the features. For instance, when it comes to transportation options (*e.g.*, truck, railroad, air, etc.), trade-off analysis may show that choosing the fastest method for delivery may not make economic sense since options for fast delivery often are very expensive compared to slower methods. While the customer may appreciate having their order arrive quickly, the marketer may find fast delivery to be an expensive proposition that significantly reduces their profit margin.

Since most distribution activities are non-revenue producing (*i.e.*, are used to support the selling of a product but do not actually create a sale) and, thus, represent a cost to the marketer, it should be understood that the marketer's distribution system choice may not be the overall best available in terms of getting the product into customer's hand as fast as possible. Rather, the marketer's choice for what is optimal will be determined by analyzing distribution features and costs and evaluating how these fit within the marketer's overall objectives (*e.g.*, financial objectives, product positioning, etc.).

ORDERING AND INVENTORY MANAGEMENT

Having products available when customers want to make purchases may seem like a relatively straightforward process. All a seller needs to do is make sure there is product (*i.e.*, inventory) in their possession and ready for the customer to purchase. Unfortunately, being prepared for customer purchasing is not always easy.

Having the right product available when the customer is ready to buy requires a highly coordinated effort involving order entry and processing systems, forecasting techniques, customer knowledge, strong channel relationships and efficiency at physically handling products.

Order Entry and Processing System

The marketer must have a system allowing customers to easily place orders. This system can be as simple as a consumer walking to the counter of small food stand to purchase a few vegetables or as complicated as automated computer systems where an electronic order is triggered from a retailer to a manufacturer each time a consumer purchases a product at the retailer's store. In either case, the order processing system must be able to meet the purchasing needs of the customer. In some cases, an efficient ordering system can be turned into a competitive advantage. Firms such as Amazon.com, turned their order handing system into a product feature with the patented "1-click" ordering option that streamlines online ordering by reducing the number of clicks needed to make purchases.

Forecasting

Inventory management is often an exercise in predicting how customers will respond in the future. By predicting purchase behaviour the marketer can respond by making sure the right amount of product is available. For most large-scale resellers effective inventory forecasting requires the use of sophisticated statistical tools that look at many variables, such as past purchase history, amount of promotional effort that triggers an increase in customer ordering, and other market criteria to determine how much of the product will be needed to meet customer demand.

Customer Knowledge

Inventory management can be fine-tuned to respond to customer's needs. As a marketer learns more about a customer they begin to observe trends in how and when purchases are made. Combining customer knowledge with forecasting techniques allows the marketer to better estimate product demand and inventory requirements. The key to understanding customers is to have in place a customer relationship management (CRM) system that tracks all customer activity and allows for data mining activities that analyse customer information in order to identify patterns in customer activity.

Channel Relationships

While the marketer who uses channel members to sell consumer products has access to information for their immediate customers (*e.g.*, resellers) they often do not have access to sales and customer behaviour information controlled by the party selling to the final consumer (*e.g.*, retailer). Knowing the demand patterns at the final consumer level can give marketers good insight into how the reseller may order.

Developing strong relationships with the holder of consumer information can result in the reseller sharing this information with the marketer. In fact, some retailers allow marketers direct access to real-time, store-level inventory information so the marketer can monitor how products are selling in stores and be in a position to respond quickly if inventory needs change.

Physical Product Handling

An often overlooked area of inventory management involves the actions and skills needed to prepare a product to move from one point to another. Some products require special attention be given to ensure the product is not damaged during shipment. Such efforts must be carefully balanced against increased costs that arise (*e.g.*, stronger packaging) in order to provide greater protection to products. Because of this, many marketers will accept the fact that some small level of damage to occur during the distribution process.

PRODUCT STORAGE

The second important element in physical distribution concerns storing products for future delivery. Marketers of tangible products, and even digital products, may have storage concerns. Storage facilities, such as warehouses, play an important role in the distribution process for a number of reasons including:

- *Hold Wide Assortment:* Many resellers allow their customers to purchase small quantities of many different products. Yet to obtain the best prices from suppliers, resellers must purchase in large quantities. The need, thus, exists for storage facilities that not only hold a large volume of product, but also can hold a wide-variety of resellers' inventory. Additionally, these facilities must be organized in a way that permits resellers to easily fill orders for their customers.
- *Meet Unanticipated Demand:* Holding products in storage offers a safeguard in cases of unexpected increases in demand for products.
- *Needed for Large Shipping Quantities:* As we noted in our discussion of transportation, manufacturers generally prefer to ship in large product quantities in order to more effectively spread transportation costs. This often means manufacturers must create storage areas in which the manufactured goods can build up in the quantities needed for such shipments to occur.
- *Offer Faster Response:* Additional storage facilities, strategically located in different geographical areas, allows a marketing organization to respond quickly to customers' needs. The ability to respond with quick delivery can be a major value-added feature since it reduces the buyer's need to maintain large inventory at their own locations.
- *Security and Backup:* For digital products, additional storage facilities are not only needed to offer customers faster access to products (*e.g.*, online content and software) but are also needed to protect against technical glitches and security threats.

Types of Warehouses

The warehouse is the most common type of storage though other forms do exist (*e.g.*, storage tanks, computer server farms). Some warehouses are massive structures that simultaneously support the unloading of numerous inbound trucks and railroad cars containing suppliers' products while at the same time loading multiple trucks for shipment to customers.

Below we discuss five types of warehouses:

- *Private Warehouse:* This type of warehouse is owned and operated by channel suppliers and resellers and used in their own distribution activity. For instance, a major retail chain may have several regional warehouses supplying their stores or a wholesaler will operate a warehouse at which it receives and distributes products.
- *Public Warehouse:* The public warehouse is essentially space that can

be leased to solve short-term distribution needs. Retailers that operate their own private warehouses may occasionally seek additional storage space if their facilities have reached capacity or if they are making a special, large purchase of products. For example, retailers may order extra merchandise to prepare for in-store sales or order a large volume of a product that is offered at a low promotional price by a supplier.

- *Automated Warehouse:* With advances in computer and robotics technology many warehouses now have automated capabilities. The level of automation ranges from a small conveyor belt transporting products in a small area all the way up to a fully automated facility where only a few people are needed to handle storage activity for thousands of pounds/kilograms of product. In fact, many warehouses use machines to handle nearly all physical distribution activities such as moving product-filled pallets (*i.e.*, platforms that hold large amounts of product) around buildings that may be several stories tall and the length of two or more football fields.
- *Climate-Controlled Warehouse:* Warehouses handle storage of many types of products including those that need special handling conditions such as freezers for storing frozen products, humidity-controlled environments for delicate products, such as produce or flowers, and dirt-free facilities for handling highly sensitive computer products.
- *Distribution Centre:* There are some warehouses where product storage is considered a very temporary activity. These warehouses serve as points in the distribution system at which products are received from many suppliers and quickly shipped out to many customers. In some cases, such as with distribution centers handling perishable food (*e.g.*, produce), most of the product enters in the early morning and is distributed by the end of the day.

TRANSPORTATION FEATURES AND MODES

A key objective of product distribution is to get products into customers' hands in a timely manner. While delivery of digital products can be handled in a fairly smooth way by allowing customers to access their purchase over the Internet (*e.g.*, download software, gain access to subscription material), tangible products require a more careful analysis of delivery options in order to provide an optimal level of customer service. But as we noted earlier, "optimal" does not always translate into fastest.

In terms of delivering products to customers, there are six distinct modes of transportation: air, digital, pipeline, rail, truck, and water. However, not all modes are an option for all marketers. Each mode offers advantages and disadvantages on key transportation features that include:

- *Product Options:* This feature is concerned with the number of different products that can realistically be shipped using a certain mode. Some modes, such as pipeline, are very limited in the type of products that can be shipped while others, such as truck, can handle a wide-range of products.
- *Speed of Delivery:* This refers to how quickly it takes products to move from the shipper's location to the buyer's location.
- *Accessibility:* This transportation feature refers to whether the use of a mode can allow final delivery to occur at the buyer's desired location or whether the mode requires delivery to be off-loaded onto other modes before arriving at the buyer's destination. For example, most deliveries made via air must be loaded onto other transportation modes, often trucks, before they can be delivered to the final customer.
- *Cost:* The cost of shipment is evaluated in terms of the cost per item to cover some distance (*e.g.*, mile, kilometre). Often for large shipments of tangible products cost is measured in terms of tons-per-mile or metric-tons-per-kilometre.
- *Capacity:* Refers to the amount of product that can be shipped at one time within one transportation unit. The higher the capacity the more likely transportation cost can be spread over more individual products leading to lower transportation cost per-item shipped.
- *Intermodal Capable:* Intermodal shipping occurs when two or more modes can be combined in order to gain advantages offered by each mode. For instance, in an intermodal method called piggybacking truck trailers are loaded onto railroad cars without the need to unload the trailer. When the railroad car has reached a certain destination the truck trailers are off-loaded onto trucks for delivery to the customer's location.

Modes of Transportation Comparison

In the chart below the six main modes of transporting products are compared for each of the key transportation features. Also shown are the estimated percentages of product movement (*i.e.*, freight traffic) that occurs within the United States for the five modes that handle tangible products. These percentages are taken from the 2006 Statistical Abstracts of the United States and reflect estimates as of 2001.

PRODUCT DIFFERENTIATION AND COMPETITIVE ADVANTAGE

Having established the *V*alue of product differentiation, we next consider the *R*areness and *I*mitability of product differentiation. The answer to the question of rareness can safely be assumed to be affirmative at this point in the analysis. The assumption is that the focal firm has established a differentiated product, which implies that the product is rare. We therefore turn our attention to the question of imitability. If a product differentiation strategy is costly to imitate, the focal firm can reasonably expect to enjoy a competitive advantage.

Easy to Duplicate

Product Features:

- Are easy for competitors to observe
- Unless there is a patent, competitors face little cost in imitation
- May lead to temporary competitive advantage until competitors are able to imitate
- *Example*: Wrinkle-free, 100% cotton in shirts, blouses, and pants is a product feature that has been rapidly duplicated. This innovation meant that customers could enjoy the feel of 100% cotton without having to iron or professionally launder their clothing. Nordstrom was an early adopter with its SmartCare line. Most other department stores now have their own line of all cotton clothing that is wrinkle-free.

DIFFUSION (BUSINESS)

Diffusion is the process by which a new idea or new product is accepted by the market. The rate of diffusion is the speed that the new idea spreads from one consumer to the next. Adoption is similar to diffusion except that it deals with the psychological processes an individual goes through, rather than an aggregate market process. In economics it is more often named "technological change".

THEORIES

There are several theories that purport to explain the mechanics of diffusion:

- *The two-step hypothesis*: Information and acceptance flows, via the media, first to opinion leaders, then to the general population
- *The trickle-down effect*: Products tend to be expensive at first, and therefore only accessible to the wealthy social strata - in time they become less expensive and are diffussed to lower and lower strata
- *The Everett Rogers Diffusion of innovations theory*: For any given product category, there are five categories of product adopters:
  - *Innovators*: Venturesome, educated, multiple info sources;
  - *Early adopters*: Social leaders, popular, educated;
  - *Early majority*: Deliberate, many informal social contacts;
  - *Late majority*: Skeptical, traditional, lower socio-economic status;
  - *Laggards*: Neighbours and friends are main info sources, fear of debt.

- *Crossing the Chasm model developed by Geoffrey Moore*: This is basically a modification of Everett Rogers' theory applied to technology markets and with a chasm added. Moorc, the marketer should focus on one group of customers at a time, using each group as a base for marketing to the next group. The most difficult step is making the transition between visionaries and pragmatists. This is the chasm that he refers to. If successful, a firm can create a bandwagon effect in which the momentum builds and the product becomes a de facto standard.
- *Technology driven models*: These are particularly relevant to software diffusion. The rate of acceptance of technology is determined by factors such as ease of use and usefulness.

RATE

Everett M. Rogers, the rate of diffusion is influenced by:

- The product's perceived advantage or benefit.
- Riskiness of purchase.
- Ease of product use - complexity of the product.
- Immediacy of benefits.
- Observability.
- Trialability.
- Price.
- Extent of behavioural changes required.
- Return on investment in the case of industrial products.

Models

There are several types of diffusion rate models:

- *Penetration models*: Use test market data to develop acceptance equations of expected sales volume as a function of time. Three examples of penetration models are:
  - Bass trial only model
  - Bass declining trial model
  - Fourt and Woodlock model
- *Trial/Repeat models*: Number of repeat buyers is a function of the number of trial buyers.
- *Deterministic models*: Assess number of buyers at various states of acceptance - later states are determined from calculations to previous states.
- *Stochastic models*: Recognize that many elements of the diffusion process are unknown but explicitly incorporate probabilistic terms.

PRODUCT DECISIONS

Marketers think of a product as a bundle of physical, service, and symbolic characteristics expected to yield benefits to the consumer. Products may range from goods to services, although most products will have some degree of both characteristics.

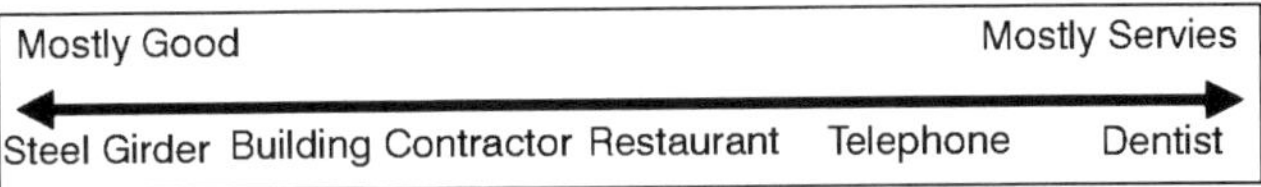

A product item is a specific version of a product that has a unique designation in the seller's list of products. A product line is a series of related product items. A product mix is the company's total assortment of product items.

The product mix may be described by three characteristics:

- Width: the number of product lines
- Depth: the average number of items per line
- *Consistency*: how closely related the product lines are

American Brands, for example, has five major product lines: tobacco products, distilled spirits, office products, home improvement and hardware, and golf and leisure. The tobacco line itself consists of several lines: cigarettes, cigars, pipe tobacco, and roll-your-own supplies. The home improvement and hardware line includes Master Lock and Moen products. A particular style of kitchen faucet would be a product item within the Moen line.There are several ways to classify products. A popular way is to think of four categories based on the amount of effort a consumer might be expected to expend on obtaining the product: convenience, shopping, specialty, and unsought. In general, a person will expend little effort to obtain a convenience product, so marketers will focus on maximizing product availability via distribution and will try to build brand identity and competitive prices. Shopping products are items people do not buy as frequently, expending a moderate amount of effort to obtain the item and/or compare different alternatives. Distribution can be more selective, and marketers will attempt to build brand differentiation through promotion and the type of outlet carrying the merchandise. If consumers do not believe there really are brand differences, then price will be very important.

Specialty products are not bought very often and will usually be more expensive items. Consumers will expend maximum effort to obtain what they want. Marketers want to build an image of exclusiveness through promotion and distribution; only exclusive outlets will carry the merchandise. Unsought goods are generally those that consumers will expend no effort to obtain and are bought only after extensive promotion by the marketer. Life insurance might be an example of an unsought good.

There are thousands of "new" products introduced every year. It has been estimated that only about 10 per cent of these are new in the sense that they did not exist before. More than half of "new" products are really product modifications or product improvement. *Consumers tend to perceive "newness" based on the amount of behaviour change necessary to use the product*:

- Discontinuous innovation: pioneering products so new that no previous product performed an equivalent function; necessitate new consumption or usage patterns
- Dynamically continuous innovation: changes and improvements that do not strikingly change buying and usage patterns; these occupy the middle range on the continuum of newness
- Continuous innovations: ongoing, commonplace changes, such as minor product alterations or imitative products

Although definitions of success and failure vary, there is no doubt that the majority of new products are not successes.

Common reasons for failure include:

- Inadequate product superiority or uniqueness, as when a "me too" product does not offer a relative advantage
- Inadequate or inferior planning, such as failing to do proper marketing research to understand consumers' needs or failure to develop realistic estimates of demand
- Poor execution, which may occur when management believes the product is so good it will succeed without resources to support it
- Technical problems, as when a product fails because of design or production problems
- Poor timing, as when a company enters a market too early or too late in the product life cycle or when the marketing environment changes

The typical process for developing new products looks like this:

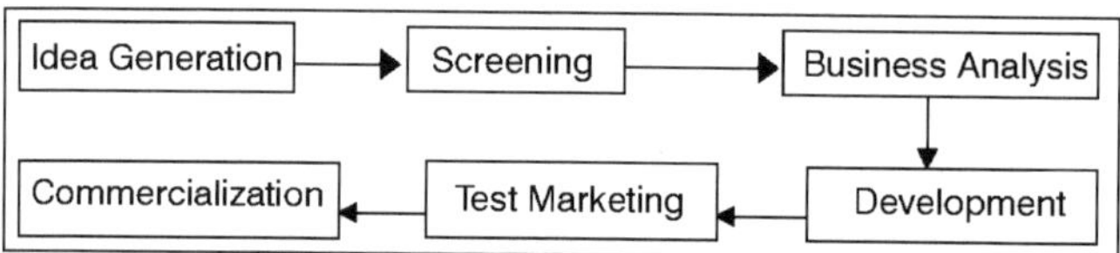

Step 1: *Idea Generation*: Perfom a continuous, systematic search for new ideas. Sources of ideas include scientists, consumers, salespeople, top management, and competitors.

Step 2: *Screening*: Delete from further consideration those ideas that are not consistent with company objectives and resources or with the market needs that the company tries to serve. Common tools include screening checklists and concept testing.

Step 3: *Business Analysis*: Do financial and marketing analyses to see whether the product idea appears to be profitable and what type of marketing efforts it will require.

Step 4: *(Product) Development*: See if the idea can actually be realised. Is it technically and commercially feasible? This stage often involves a host of other decisions, such as package design, brand name selection, trademark registration, etc.

Step 5: *Test Marketing*: Put the product on the market in limited areas to gauge market reaction. The amount of test marketing needed varies by product. Generally little or no test marketing is done when development costs are low, management is very confident, the innovation is a minor product modification or is an imitative product, and/or the product is a high-ticket item.

Step 6: *Commercialization*: Introduce and market the new product. Decisions include when, where, to whom, and how. Once a product is launched, it enters a product life cycle. The PLC describes how a typical new product category follows a set of four stages, the important thing being the marketing implications that accompany each stage.

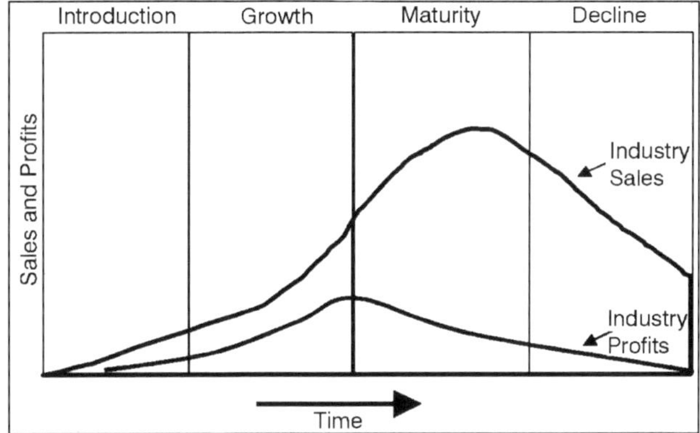

In the introduction stage, the firm faces little if any direct competition for its new product. The objective is to gain awareness and acceptance in the market both by consumers and by middlemen who might carry the product. Price is typically set high, both to take advantage of the fact that the earliest buyers of a new product are often willing to pay premium prices for something new and to begin to regain some of the investment expenses incurred in developing the product.

Sometimes, especially if competition might be expected early, a low price is used to discourage competition from entering. Promotion is designed to inform and educate the market about the new product. Distribution is limited to those few middlemen who might be willing to accept a new product. In the growth stage, competitors enter the market with their own versions of the product, and competition often is based on real product differences. The strategic focus now becomes building market share and establishing product differentiation. Price tends to remain high but will fall Towards the end of the stage as it becomes more of a competitive tool. Distribution will expand considerably, and the tone of promotion shifts to being more persuasive, stressing product differences.

The maturity stage is marked by stable sales and high total industry profits. Many competitors dominate the market, although many more marginal ones that entered during the growth stage have left. The objective now is maintaining the market built in the growth stage. Although firms will have full product lines with many variations, real product differences are fewer. Price tends to fall, being used more competitively. Distribution will be at its maximum. Promotion is of a "reminder" nature.

In the decline stage, sales are falling, as are profits. Firms begin to exit the industry, and the objective now becomes one of trying to pull as much profit as possible from the product in its waning days. The product lines are pruned, with only the few best versions remaining. Both promotion and distribution are reduced as much as possible to help pare back costs. Because the maturity stage is the most profitable, firms will derive strategies for prolonging it as much as possible through either product or market modifications.

Product modifications may include the following:

- *Quality improvements*: Quality is defined by *consumers* and measures how well a product does what it is supposed to do. Marketers need to
  - Provide the desired level of quality,
  - Work constantly to improve quality, and
  - Accurately communicate quality to market.
- *Design improvements*: Styling, aesthetics, and/or function of a product is altered to offer more convenience, safety, efficiency, or versatility.
- *Style improvements*: The aesthetic appeal of the product is increased, especially with an eye Towards creating a unique look.

The Product Life Cycle results from a diffusion process that is the the sequence of acceptance of new products by the members of a community or social system.

Five groups are visible in the diffusion process, based on the speed with which they adopt an innovation:

- Innovators initially purchase a new product. They are motivated by novelty and tend to be younger, more affluent, better educated, and confident about their decision-making ability.
- Early Adopters are similar to innovators. They are motivated more by improvement than novelty and are generally considered the most important group because of their opinion leadership qualities—others will follow them.
- Early Majority members are aware of and willing to accept change. They tend to be average in age, affluence, and education.
- Late Majority members are less aware of and less willing to accept change. They may be of an older average age and a little below average in affluence and education; they tend to be conservative and traditional.
- Laggards are the last group to adopt a product. They are generally the oldest, most conservative group.

Part of the "product decision area" involves branding, packaging, and labeling. Both consumers and marketers rely on branding. Think how much easier it is to buy products based on your familiarity with the brand—it certainly makes the search and evaluation stages much simpler than when buying a brand you aren't familiar with. For consumers, benefits include quality assurance, a reduced search/selection time, a known quantity, and prestige. For marketers, benefits include differentiation of their product from competitors', improved brand identity, and more effective marketing communications.

There are several terms to be familiar with:

- *Brand*: A name, term, sign, symbol, design, or combination thereof used to identify and differentiate a company's products from competitors'
- *Brand name*: The element of the brand that can be vocalized
- *Brand mark*: The element of the brand that cannot be vocalized
- *Trademark*: A brand or part of a brand that is registered with the U.S. Patent and Trademark office. This provides the owner of the brand with legal protection for excluding competitors from use of the same or very similar name or logo.
- *Service mark*: the "trademark" for services

Marketers must choose from several brand strategies. One choice involves the sponsor of the brand. A national brand is owned by a manufacturer who then bears the cost of marketing the brand. A distributor or private brand is owned by a retailer or wholesaler, although the product generally is made by a well-known manufacturer. The retailer or wholesaler is responsible for any marketing of the brand. A generic brand has no visible brand name—ownership cannot be determined, and usually no marketing outside of distribution is done.

Another decision is "family vs. individual" branding. In a family, one name is used for a set of products, such as the Craftsman name on a variety of tools. A variation on this is licensing, where the owner of a trademark permits others to use it on various products. In multibranding, each product has its own name, such as with Procter and Gamble's Tide, Cheer, and Ivory Snow laundry detergents. In a combination strategy, combined family and individual brands are used, such as with Kellogg's Frosted Flakes and Kellogg's Corn Flakes. As with other marketing decisions, there is no one best way; each strategy carries certain advantages and drawbacks. Ideally, marketers try to build "brand equity," which reflects the value a brand has beyond its basic functional value. Brand equity has a financial dimension to it that results from having a large enough part of the market desiring that brand above others.

Typically, brand equity results from a long-term strategy that leads a market to that point in a series of stages:

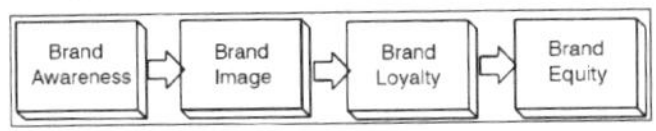

First, the market must realise that the brand exists in the marketplace. Next, the marketer builds strong, positive associations with the brand. From that comes preference, where the ideal is for the consumer to buy that brand exclusively. From long-term use comes consumer identification with the brand. The importance of packaging and labeling differs by product. Packaging may serve various functions. For many consumer products, especially those typically bought in self-serve environments, promotion is a critical element in helping the consumer identify the product and in increasing the product's visibility in a retail setting.

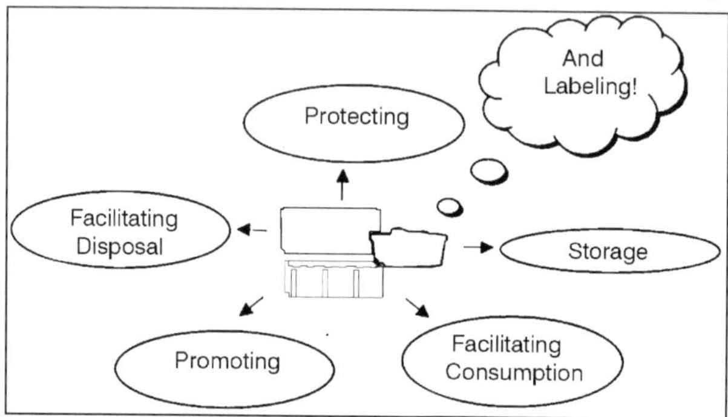

Services differ from goods in several distinct ways.
The diagram shows these key differences:

Goods are tangible; services are intangible. Although some goods have very short lifespans, they can be stored for at least a while before consumption; if services are not used when available, they are unrecoverable. Goods can be separated from their makers, but services cannot be separated from the provider.Goods may be made just as to a standard procedure that makes consistency of output; service delivery is difficult to standardize, so delivery is always, to some degree, inconsistent. Finally, goods may be bought from someone other than the actual producer; with services, the buyer is directly involved with the process: the dental hygienist cannot clean your teeth without you being there.

Because of these differences, the marketing mix elements must be modified for services:

- *Product*: Can be classified like goods. Same marketing mix ideas would then apply. Things like packaging and labeling are of minimal or no importance.

- *Pricing*: Harder to determine because cost of "production" is often more difficult to determine. Price negotiation may be more prevalent for services.
- *Place*: Channels are usually short. Storage, transportation, and inventory are of minimal or no concern.
- *Promotion*: Can be "tangibilized" by linking service to a specific benefit. Creation of a favourable image is critical. Desire for "personal relationship" with provider increases importance of personal selling.

The intangibility of services makes it very difficult for consumers to judge the quality of the service.

Hence, consumers rely on a variety of indicators to suggest quality:

- *Reliability*: Is the service likely to be delivered as expected?
- *Tangibles*: What are the physical characteristics of the place of delivery?
- *Responsiveness*: How willing is the provider to deliver the service?
- *Empathy*: How willing is the provider to take time to determine the exact nature of the service desired?
- *Assurance*: How confident does the consumer feel that the service will be provided as expected?

PRODUCT MIX

Product mix is a combination of products manufactured or traded by the same business house to reinforce their presence in the market, increase market share and increase the turnover for more profitability.Normally the product mix is within the synergy of other products for a medium size organization. However large groups of Industries may have diversified products within core competency.Larsen and Toubro Ltd, Godrej, Reliance in India are some of the examples. One of the realities of business is that most firms deal with multi-products.This helps a firm diffuse its risk across different product groups/Also it enables the firm to appeal to a much larger group of customers or to different needs of the same customer group.

So when Videocon chose to diversify into other consumer durables like music systems,washing machines and refrigerators,it sought to satisfy the needs of the middle and upper middle income group of consumers. Likewise, Bajaj Electricals.a household name in India, has almost ninety products in i8ts portfolio ranging from low value items like bulbs to high priced consumer durables like mixers and luminaires and lighting projects.The number of products carried by a firm at a given point of time is called its product mix. This product mix contains product lines and product items.In other words it's a composite of products offered for sale by a firm.

PRODUCT MIX DECISIONS

Often firms take decisions to change their product mix. These decisions are dictated by the factors and also by the changes occurring in the market place. Like the changing life-styles of Indian consumers led BPL-Sanyo to launch an entire range of white goods like refrigerators, washing machines, and microwave ovens.It also motivate the firm to launch other entertainment electronics.

Rahejas, a well-known builders firm in Bombay, took a major decision to convert one of its theatre buildings in the western suburbs of Bombay into a large garments and accessories store for men,women and children, perhaps the first of its kind in India to have almost all products required by these customer groups Competition from low priced washing powders forced Hindustan Levers to launch different brands of detergent powder at different price levels positioned at different market segments.Customer preferences for herbs, mainly shikakai motivated Lever to launch black Sunsilk Shampoo,which has shikakai.Also,low purchasing power. and cultural bias against shampoo market made Hindustan Lever consider smaller packaging mainly sachets, for single use.So, it is the changes or anticipated changes in the market place that motivates a firm to consider changes in its product mix.

PLANNED OBSOLESCENCE

Planned obsolescence or built-in obsolescence is the process of a product becoming obsolete or non-functional after a certain period or amount of use in a way that is planned or designed by the manufacturer. Also known as "Designed to Fail".

Planned obsolescence has potential benefits for a producer because the product fails and the consumer is under pressure to purchase again, whether from the same manufacturer or from a competitor which might also rely on planned obsolescence. The purpose of planned obsolescence is to hide the real cost per use from the consumer, and charge a higher price than they would otherwise be willing to pay.

For an industry, planned obsolescence stimulates demand by encouraging purchasers to buy sooner if they still want a functioning product. Built-in obsolescence is in many different products, from vehicles to light bulbs, from buildings to proprietary software.

There is, however, the potential backlash of consumers who learn that the manufacturer invested money to make the product obsolete faster; such consumers might turn to a producer that offers a more durable alternative.

Planned obsolescence was first developed in the 1920s and 1930s when mass production had opened every minute aspect of the production process to exacting analysis.

Estimates of planned obsolescence can influence a company's decisions about product engineering. Therefore the company can use the least expensive components that satisfy product lifetime projections. Such decisions are part of a broader discipline known as value engineering.The use of planned obsolescence is not always easy to pinpoint, and it is complicated by related problems, such as competing technologies or creeping featurism which expands functionality in newer product versions.

PRODUCT LINING

Product lining is the marketing strategy of offering for sale several related products. Unlike product bundling, where several products are combined into one, lining involves offering several related products individually. A line can comprise related products of various sizes, types, colours, qualities, or prices. Line depth refers to the number of product variants in a line. Line consistency refers to how closely related the products that make up the line are. Line vulnerability refers to the percentage of sales or profits that are derived from only a few products in the line.

The number of different product lines sold by a company is referred to as width of product mix. The total number of products sold in all lines is referred to as length of product mix. If a line of products is sold with the same brand name, this is referred to as family branding. When you add a new product to a line, it is referred to as a line extension. When you add a line extension that is of better quality than the other products in the line, this is referred to as trading up or brand leveraging. When you add a line extension that is of lower quality than the other products of the line, this is referred to as trading down. When you trade down, you will likely reduce your brand equity. You are gaining short-term sales at the expense of long term sales.

Image anchors are highly promoted products within a line that define the image of the whole line. Image anchors are usually from the higher end of the line's range. When you add a new product within the current range of an incomplete line, this is referred to as line filling.

Price lining is the use of a limited number of prices for all your product offerings. This is a tradition started in the old five and dime stores in which everything cost either 5 or 10 cents. Its underlying rationale is that these amounts are seen as suitable price points for a whole range of products by prospective customers. It has the advantage of ease of administering, but the disadvantage of inflexibility, particularly in times of inflation or unstable prices.

There are many important decisions about product and service development and marketing. In the process of product development and marketing we should focus on strategic decisions about product attributes, product branding, product packaging, product labeling and product support services. But product strategy also calls for building a product line.

PROJECT PORTFOLIO MANAGEMENT

Project Portfolio Management is about more than running multiple projects.

Each portfolio of projects needs to be assessed in terms of its business value and adherence to strategy. The portfolio should be designed to achieve a defined business objective or benefit. Project management guru Bob Buttrick summarised it when he said; "Directing the individual project correctly will ensure it is done right. Directing 'all the projects' successfully will ensure we are doing the right projects."

While at individual project level it is important to know how each project is performing, the impact of each project on the portfolio is just as important.

The following questions should be asked:

- Does each project contribute to the overall achievement of the portfolio?
- How well is each project performing?
- Will any project have a negative impact on other projects to come?
- What projects in the portfolio are dependent on others?
- Will the successful delivery of all projects deliver the desired objective or benefit?

Working at portfolio level is about working with summary or key data. It is important to avoid information overload. The detail of each project should be kept at the project team level, administered by the individual project managers. Key information should be rolled up and presented at each level within the organisation as appropriate. At executive, VP level you are likely to be providing a summary of performance, progress, a measurement of estimates against actuals and costs.

Within almost all project portfolio management systems there is a project evaluation process. This process is used to evaluate the projects at various points during their lifecycle. At the beginning of each stage, often called a 'gate,' the responsible party evaluates the business case, asking whether it is still relevant and able to deliver the defined organisational objectives. If the answer is no, then the project should be stopped. This way the organisation can ensure that they stay focussed on delivering a strategy, goal or other defined benefit and that resources are deployed where they will offer the best return.

Project portfolio management asks the following questions:

- Are we doing the right things?
- Are we doing them the right way?
- Are we doing them well?
- Are we getting the benefits?

If the answer to any of these questions is no, immediate action is required to bring the portfolio back on track.

BCG GROWTH-SHARE MATRIX

The BCG Growth-Share Matrix is a portfolio planning model developed by Bruce Henderson of the Boston Consulting Group in the early 1970's.

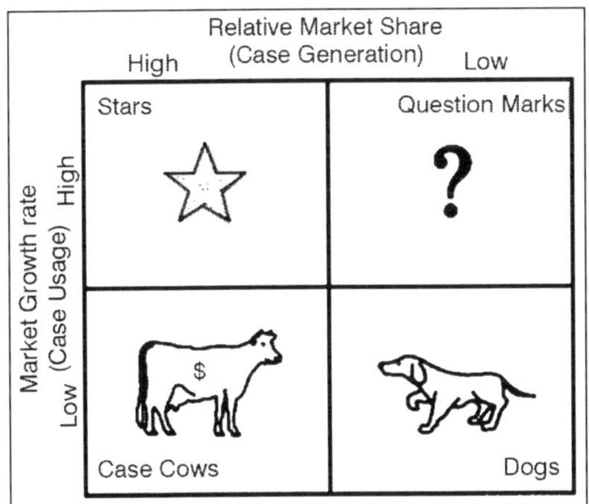

Fig. BCG Growth-Share Matrix

It is based on the observation that a company's business units can be classified into four categories based on combinations of market growth and market share relative to the largest competitor, hence the name "growth-share". Market growth serves as a proxy for industry attractiveness, and relative market share serves as a proxy for competitive advantage. The growth-share matrix thus maps the business unit positions within these two important determinants of profitability.

This framework assumes that an increase in relative market share will result in an increase in the generation of cash. This assumption often is true because of the experience curve; increased relative market share implies that the firm is moving forward on the experience curve relative to its competitors, thus developing a cost advantage. A second assumption is that a growing market requires investment in assets to increase capacity and therefore results in the consumption of cash. Thus the position of a business on the growth-share matrix provides an indication of its cash generation and its cash consumption.

Henderson reasoned that the cash required by rapidly growing business units could be obtained from the firm's other business units that were at a more mature stage and generating significant cash. By investing to become the market share leader in a rapidly growing market, the business unit could move along the experience curve and develop a cost advantage. From this reasoning, the BCG Growth-Share Matrix was born.

The four categories are:

- *Dogs*: Dogs have low market share and a low growth rate and thus neither generate nor consume a large amount of cash. However, dogs are cash traps because of the money tied up in a business that has little potential. Such businesses are candidates for divestiture.
- *Question marks*: Question marks are growing rapidly and thus consume large amounts of cash, but because they have low market

shares they do not generate much cash. The result is a large net cash comsumption. A question mark has the potential to gain market share and become a star, and eventually a cash cow when the market growth slows. If the question mark does not succeed in becoming the market leader, then after perhaps years of cash consumption it will degenerate into a dog when the market growth declines. Question marks must be analysed carefully in order to determine whether they are worth the investment required to grow market share.

- *Stars*: Stars generate large amounts of cash because of their strong relative market share, but also consume large amounts of cash because of their high growth rate; therefore the cash in each direction approximately nets out. If a star can maintain its large market share, it will become a cash cow when the market growth rate declines. The portfolio of a diversified company always should have stars that will become the next cash cows and ensure future cash generation.
- *Cash cows*: As leaders in a mature market and thus generate more cash than they consume. Such business units should be"milked", extracting the profits and investing as little cash as possible. Cash cows provide the cash required to turn question marks into market leaders, to cover the administrative costs of the company, to fund research and development, to service the corporate debt, and to pay dividends to shareholders. Because the cash cow generates a relatively stable cash flow, its value can be determined with reasonable accuracy by calculating the present value of its cash stream using a discounted cash flow analysis.

Under the growth-share matrix model, as an industry matures and its growth rate declines, a business unit will become either a cash cow or a dog, determined soley by whether it had become the market leader during the period of high growth.

While originally developed as a model for resource allocation among the various business units in a corporation, the growth-share matrix also can be used for resource allocation among products within a single business unit. Its simplicity is its strength.

LIMITATIONS

The growth-share matrix once was used widely, but has since faded from popularity as more comprehensive models have been developed.

Some of its weaknesses are:

- Market growth rate is only one factor in industry attractiveness, and relative market share is only one factor in competitive advantage. The growth-share matrix overlooks many other factors in these two important determinants of profitability.

- The framework assumes that each business unit is independent of the others. In some cases, a business unit that is a"dog" may be helping other business units gain a competitive advantage.
- The matrix depends heavily upon the breadth of the definition of the market. A business unit may dominate its small niche, but have very low market share in the overall industry. In such a case, the definition of the market can make the difference between a dog and a cash cow.

While its importance has diminished, the BCG matrix still can serve as a simple tool for viewing a corporation's business portfolio at a glance, and may serve as a starting point for discussing resource allocation among strategic business units.

PRODUCT BUNDLING

Product bundling is the process of securing two or more necessary goods or services from a single vendor. This strategy usually provides several advantages, including saving a great deal of money. Long a practice among businesses, the concept of product bundling has expanded to include residential customers over the last twenty years, especially in regard to various types of communication services.

The basic nature of product bundling involves the willingness of a supplier or vendor to provide two or more services to a customer for basic rate. This rate normally provides significant savings over purchasing the products individually. For example, a communications company may choose to offer a cable TV bundle that allows the subscriber to enjoy cable television, local telephone service, and Internet access as a single product offering, rather than having to purchase three different services at a cumulative higher rate.Along with saving money, product bundling also provides other benefits for the customer. One has to do with sheer convenience. Rather than having to deal with multiple vendors in order to have access to multiple products, the customer has one central vendor for all his or her needs. This concept of one-stop shopping means the client spends less time keeping up with payments to various vendors, and has one central pipeline when there is a need for customer support or if there is a question about one of the services.

Vendors also benefit from providing various types of bundled packages to their clients. In many cases, the cost and convenience created by product bundling go a long way Towards promoting customer loyalty. This makes the client less likely to switch to another vendor for any of the services, especially if the price for the bundle is competitive. Product bundling also simplifies the billing process for the vendor, since all services and products are usually billed on one monthly invoice, rather than several different ones.Product bundling is also a common strategy with software products. For example, office suites offered by different manufacturers will normally include a data processing prigramme, a spreadsheet prigramme, an e-mail client, and presentation creation software, all in one package. This makes it much easier for customers, since they can purchase all these software options as part of one package, rather than paying for them individually. Depending on which software manufacturer is involved, the savings can be substantial.

The idea of product bundling is also used in other ways. For example, a local business that mows lawns as its main service many offer customers a bundled package that also includes shrub trimming and basic landscaping, for a small additional fee. Often, this is less expensive to the customer than purchasing the different services separately. Even businesses like delicatessens can use this basic approach of product bundling, such as offering an entrée along with two or three sides for a single price that is lower than buying the items separately.

Bibliography

A Jayakumar: *Food Security Management : A Comparative Study*, Anmol Publication, Delhi, 2007.

A. Brand, J.P.T.M. Noordhuizen and Y.H. Schukken: *Herd Health and Production Management in Dairy Practice*, IBDCO Publication, Delhi, 2003.

A.R. Prasad: *A Study on the Theory of Production*, Reliance Publications, Delhi, 2005.

Ajoy Gangopadhyay: *Assessment of Improved Crop Production Technologies*, Gene Tech Books, 2007.

Anil Bhat and Jyoti Kachroo: *Economics of Production and Marketing of Citrus*, Daya Publications, Delhi, 2012.

Anubhav Dwivedi: *A Fragrance from Food Production World*, Axis Publications, Delhi, 2010.

Bhagaban Swain: *Adoption of New Technology : Production Efficiency and Agrarian Relations*, Kalpaz, 2002.

C. Gangaiah: *Area Production and Productivity of Horticulture Crops*, Serials Publications, 2011.

C. Venkatesan and D. Namasivayam: *Agricultural Production in India*, Global Research Pub, 2011.

C.P. Malik: *Genetic Engineering: A New Hope for Crop Production and Improvement*, Aavishkar Publications, Delhi, 2010.

D N Singh and S P Singh: *Production Management of Underutilized Vegetables*, Agrihortica Pub, 2007.

D.V. Kamath: *Vegetable and Crop Production*, Oxford Book Company, Jaipur, 2007.

Dave Ingram:*Applied Practices And Principles For Production-Ready Software Development:Design-Build-Run*, Wiley.

David Ludden: *Agricultural Production and South Asian History*, Oxford University Press, Jaipur, 2005.

Jagjit Kaur: *Global Climate Change and Agriculture Production*, Oxford Book Company, Jaipur, 2007.

Jaya Banerjee: *Production Management: Modern Methods and Techniques*, Shree Niwas Publications, Delhi, 2011.

K K Singh: *Natural Resource Conservation and Management*, MD Publication, Delhi, 2008.

K. Shridhara Bhat: *Production and Operations Management*, Himalaya Publishing House, Delhi, 2011.

L.L. Somani and S.C. Bhandari: *Organic Recycling and Bioinoculants: For Sustainable Crop Production*, Agrotech Publications, Jaipur, 2007.

M.A. Shewan: *Production Management*, Sonali Publications, Delhi, 2008.

M.K. Rana: *Fundamentals of Vegetable Production*, New India Publishing Agency, Delhi, 2011.

Martin k.starr: *Production and Operations Management (Biztantra)*, Dreamtech Press, Delhi, 1999.

Mudit Bhojwan: *Food Service Management : Principles and Practices*, Rajat Publication, Delhi, 2007.

N.N Sarkar: *Art and Print Production*, Oxford University Press, 2008.

Nirmal Sengupta: *A New Institutional Theory of Production : An Application*, Sage, 2001.

Nursadh Ali: *Natural Resource Management and Sustainable Development in North-East India*, Mittal Publication, Delhi, 2007.

R K Arora: *Food Service and Catering Management*, APH Publication, Delhi, 2007.

R.B. Khanna: *Production and Operations Management*, PHI Learning, Delhi, 2003.

S. Anil Kumar and N. Suresh: *Production and Operations Management*, New Age International, Delhi, 2009.

S. Solomon, H.N. Shahi, A.P. Gupta, G.P. Rao and B.L. Srivastava: *Cane Sugar Production Management*, IBDCO Publication, Delhi, 2000.

S. Suresh Babu: *Coconut Production and Marketing*, Abhijeet Publications, Delhi, 2010.

S.C. Bhatia: *Global Climate Change and Cultivated Production*, Agrotech Press, Jaipur, 2013.

Sangeeta Shree and Rajeev Kumar: *Handbook of Fruit Production*, Enkay Publishing House, Delhi, 2012.

T. Telsang Mertand: *Industrial Engineering and Production Management*, S. Chand Publisher, Delhi, 2002.

V P Gupta and Ila Sinha: *Operations Management*, Researchco Book Centre, 2007.

V.L. Sharma: *Production Management*, ABD Publications, Delhi, 2001.

Index

Y.B. Rajeshwari, Mahadevappa D. Gouri and T.M. Prabhu: *Handbook on Rabbit Production and Management*, New India Publishing Agency, Delhi, 2011.